FIFTY
MIGHTY MEN

FIFTY MIGHTY MEN

GRANT MacEWAN

GREYSTONE BOOKS
Douglas & McIntyre
Vancouver / Toronto

Copyright © 1975 by Grant MacEwan

First softcover edition 1975
First Greystone edition 1995

95 96 97 98 99   7 6 5 4 3

This book was published originally by Western Producer Prairie Books, a
publishing venture owned by Saskatchewan Wheat Pool.

Greystone Books
A division of Douglas & McIntyre Ltd.
1615 Venables Street
Vancouver, British Columbia
V5L 2H1

Canadian Cataloguing in Publication Data

MacEwan, Grant, 1902–
    Fifty mighty men

        (Grant MacEwan classics)
        "Greystone Books."
        ISBN 1-55054-415-2

        1. Men — Canada, Western — Biography. 2. Canada,
Western — Biography. I. Title. II. Series: MacEwan, Grant, 1902
— Grant MacEwan classics.
FC3208.M32 1995   971.2'092'2   C95-910056-3
F1060.3.M32 1995

Cover design by Jim Skipp
Cover illustration by Michael J. Downs
Book illustrations by William W. Perehudoff
Printed and bound in Canada by Best Book Manufacturers Inc.
Printed on acid-free paper ∞

CONTENTS

FOREWORD

Western Canada may well be proud of the achievements — wheat, cattle, oil, highways, factories and other symbols of progress — in an area where trapping was the sole industry a century ago. It is a striking record but for many of us, the most inspiring part of the story concerns the distinctive people in the vanguard. Their performance, characterized by vigor, courage and resourcefulness, holds priceless messages for today. It would be tragic misfortune if the records became lost or if the trials, triumphs and humor of those early years of our section of Canada were ignored.

And so, the author hastens to express thanks to those who direct policy at The Western Producer and Modern Press for the opportunity of giving added permanency to these sketches. The series, under general title of Fifty Mighty Men, was carried in the Magazine Section of The Western Producer from May 9, 1957, to April 24, 1958. Public interest was most encouraging.

Now that the complete series is being published in book form, special thanks should be directed to Executive Editor R.H. Macdonald and T.R. Melville-Ness for their generous interest and co-operation; also to Bill Perehudoff for his imaginative work in providing illustrations.

GRANT MacEWAN
(1975)

CHAPTER I

FRONTIER HERO WITH A CRUCIFIX

NOT all the heroes in Canadian story wore military uniforms and carried guns—not by any means. One of the sterling men of the early West walked the most dangerous paths, armed with nothing more than a crucifix. He was father Albert Lacombe who spent his life dispensing Christian service.

Well may his admirers dream about those qualities of courage displayed when, as guest of the Chief, Father Lacombe was staying at a Blackfoot encampment in 1865. Out of the night came the fiendish whoops of Cree killers. Clearly, the Blackfeet were outnumbered and unprepared. Massacre seemed inevitable.

Bullets pierced the night air and the shrieks of dying could be heard above the gunfire. Instead of seeking protection for himself, the black-robed priest moved fearlessly among his red-skinned people, bringing relief to the wounded and baptism to the dying.

1

With the light of morning, Blackfoot reinforcements arrived but Lacombe called upon the strengthened defenders to cease firing. As they yielded to his bidding, they saw the priest, crucifix aloft in one hand and Red Cross flag in the other, walking directly into enemy fire. With all the voice he could master, he called: "My children, you Crees, fire no more. Stop this bloodshed."

A bullet grazed his shoulder and forehead; blood covered his face and he fell. But instantly the direction of battle reversed. The Blackfeet were infuriated. Chief Crowfoot leaped forward in rage, calling: "You dogs, you have shot Good Heart. You have killed the Man of Prayer."

Recognizing the man who fell and sensing their mistake, the Crees stopped their fire and with guilt on their faces, tried to disappear. Anyway, it was the end of the battle.

* * *

But it was not the only time Father Lacombe faced flying bullets. At Fort Edmonton, when Indians attacked a small group of whites, the little priest repeated that act of courage. It was bravery of the highest order.

Nobody understood the Indians better or loved them more. Of course, there was Indian blood in his own veins and it may have sharpened his devotion.

Away back about the year 1695, Algonquin Indians carried a white girl from her home farm in Lower Canada. Parents and friends searched ceaselessly but no trace was discovered until five years later, an uncle, travelling with traders to Sault Ste. Marie, heard about a young white woman, able to speak French and living with the Indians.

He arranged to meet her, ostensibly that she might interpret for him. They recognized each other but neither betrayed emotion. That night, however, the woman gathered her two babies in her arms, slipped away from the tent of of the Indian who had claimed her as his wife, and joined the uncle's canoe. It was a happy day when she arrived back at her parents' farm and one of the children became a forebear of Albert Lacombe.

It was on the same farm at St. Suplice, Quebec, from which the girl was kidnapped, that the boy Albert was born in 1827. His father and mother were of habitant stock, earnest folk and thrifty.

As a boy on the home farm, Albert worked hard, in the bush, in the fields and in the stables. Very early in life, however, he set his heart upon being a missionary to the Indians.

The parish priest gave encouragement, helped pay for education, and after several years spent at L'Assomption college, and ordination, Albert Lacombe hied away to the back country where Indians divided their time between the warpath and the buffalo hunt.

For two years the young priest labored in a settlement near Pembina, south of Fort Garry. There he was getting the feel of things; he went with the local people on their hunts; he slept on a buffalo robe on the ground; he learned to make and eat pemmican and, altogether, to live like an Indian.

Bishop Tache from Fort Garry came that way and Father Lacombe volunteered for service farther west.

"Willing to go to Fort Edmonton?" the bishop asked, and the young priest said, "Yes."

* * *

In 1852, Father Lacombe made the thousand-mile journey and wintered within the walls of Fort Edmonton where a small building was assigned to him for a church. With the spring, he went to Lac Ste. Anne, some 50 miles farther northwest, and there settled down to ministering to the native people. There he faced blizzards, hunted buffalo, ate when food was available, tended the sick and won his way to Cree hearts.

His occasional excursions into Blackfoot country were less encouraging. These Blackfeet wore a thick crust of independence and rejected missionary advances. Here were stoical people, emotionless, cruel.

But in 1857 there was an outbreak of scarlet fever among the Blackfeet and when Medicine Men proved helpless, the savages of the south sent for the man who had a reputation for helping Indians. Together, Father Lacombe and his faithful servant, Alexis Cardinal, went south and

3

reached the Blackfoot camp while a snowstorm was doing all possible to impede their travel.

The priest toiled incessantly and even contracted the disease, but his generous devotion made an impression upon the Blackfeet. It was then that they called him "Good Heart."

When a Blackfoot girl was stolen by Crees and Father Lacombe was able to recover her and return her to her family the act further dissolved resistance to his teachings. Gradually he made his way into Blackfeet teepees and in 1881, he went to live with Chief Crowfoot's people.

* * *

When Bishop Tache was visiting the northwest in 1861, a site was chosen for a new mission north of Fort Edmonton. The mission at St. Albert was the result and, having completed the building and established himself there, Father Lacombe decided the Sturgeon river nearby needed a bridge.

Indians were not engineers in any sense and a bridge proved to be an almost unbelievable novelty. For a time it was the only bridge west of Red river. When the good Father called for helpers to build the bridge, he suggested that only those who helped to build it could expect permission to use it.

Red men turned out in numbers and when it was completed, they were fascinated. Not only did they cross and recross but some insisted upon camping on it and one of their numbers built his campfire on it and nearly burned it down.

To the little priest, the fields were "white and ready for harvest." He travelled extensively, often amid extreme hardship. He and Servant Alexis knew what it was to take refuge in a river to escape death-dealing flames of prairie fire and on winter trips they were sometimes near starvation.

On one of those winter journeys, they started with ample provisions but met starving Indians and shared what they had until their own rations were scant. Then Father Lacombe did the only thing that offered relief; he cooked some moccasins and some buffalo robes together, lunched on the stew and continued on. Had privation continued, it would have been necessary to kill the priest's horse but with better fortune the two travellers met friendly and well-provisioned Indians and the famine ended.

* * *

In the early 70s, when small pox was taking terrible toll among the Crees, Father Lacombe was in the middle of things. About a year earlier, the disease broke out on a river boat on the Mississippi and, after spreading westward across the plains of the United States, it was carried north by a Cree war party which had ravished a camp of dead. Father Lacombe estimated 2500 deaths among the Crees and nearly as many in the Blackfeet during the single season.

That Indian confidence which the priest gained over the years, paid handsomely when the Canadian Pacific Railway was being built and when Riel and his followers were inviting a general Indian uprising in 1885.

Indians took a dim view of the railroad. Locomotives would bring settlers to the country and Indians would be pushed back. There was threat of violence. Tracks laid in the daytime were pulled up at night.

Lacombe was asked to come to the scene of trouble. He brought tea, tobacco and food and after the Indians had eaten and the priest had talked to them, they quietly left the right-of-way to the builders. They might disbelieve the government but with Father Lacombe, they trusted him.

Canadian Pacific officials were grateful for what the "black-robed plainsman" had done to smooth the way for the surveyors and construction gangs as they worked through the Indian reservations. They wished to acknowledge their gratitude.

On August 10, 1883, when one of the first trains arrived at Calgary, carrying George Stephen, the railroad president, also Donald A. Smith, R. B. Angus, William Van Horne and Count Hermann von Hohenlohe, an invitation went to Father Lacombe, then in charge of the parish of St. Mary in Calgary to lunch with the group in the president's private car.

Lunch was about to begin when President George Stephen, later Lord Mount Stephen, announced his resignation for one hour. On a well planned motion of

Director R. B. Angus, Father Lacombe was elected to the presidency of the CPR for that period.

The priest accepted the high office but, in doing so, nominated George Stephen to a one-hour term as Rector of the Parish of St. Mary. As Stephen pictured himself in the new role, he gazed through the car window and muttered: "Poor souls of Calgary; I pity you." But the "poor souls" didn't fare badly from the events of that day because a gift of $10,000 for the promotion of Father Lacombe's work came from one of the members of the party.

* * *

As for Lacombe's part in checking Indian uprisings in 1885, a good deal has been written. If the Blackfeet had risen, bloodshed would have been terrible. Calgary people were filled with fear and called upon Father Lacombe to intercede. Yes, the good Father would talk to his old friend, Chief Crowfoot.

A special CPR locomotive went east to Blackfoot Crossing. It carried Father Lacombe who talked to Chief Crowfoot, assured him that the Metis at Duck Lake were making a foolish mistake and their cause would be lost. Crowfoot agreed and assured the Father that he would remain neutral and hold his braves in leash.

The trouble passed and Father Lacombe went to Ottawa to ask pardon for Chiefs Poundmaker and Big Bear. Again and again he stood in defence of his Indian friends who had understandable trouble in comprehending white man's laws. And when Crowfoot and other chiefs were invited by Sir John A. Macdonald to visit Ottawa, Father Lacombe went along.

In Eastern Canada, the Indian visitors were dined, toured and impressed with the might of the white man. It was a subtle reminder of the futility of Indian resistance and, with Father Lacombe present, the Indians accepted what was prepared for their visit without fear.

The CPR granted Father Lacombe a pass to travel where he chose and the priest used the privilege freely. He found many reasons for going to Ottawa on behalf of his mission and his Indians. When he was in Ottawa, the government knew it because the missionary believed in taking his problems directly to the Prime Minister or, at least, a member of the Cabinet.

A few years earlier, the priest made homestead entry on a quarter section within the limits of the present city of Calgary and later, in turning the land over to the church, a legal question arose. Lacombe went right to Ottawa and visited the minister in whose department the authority rested.

The minister listened to the missionary's complaint and in the best ministerial fashion promised to consider the matter and report later. But for Father Lacombe that was not good enough. He was a man of action and had no intention of leaving before getting the proper answer.

Smiling, he said he was disappointed at the prospect of delay but he reminded the minister of the Crown that he was accustomed to camping on the prairie when necessary and camping there on the handsome rug in the middle of the government office would be no hardship. He'd just squat there until the minister was ready to report.

It was perfectly clear that the little man from the West meant it. The wheels of government moved faster than usual and before the end of that hour, Father Lacombe had the answer he wanted.

* * *

He crossed the Atlantic to attend a great church assembly, had an audience with the Pope and presented His Holiness with a Cree Indian dictionary of his own making. Some folk said, "guess he'll never go back to the Indian lodges after this." But with neither hesitation nor delay, he went back to work among his Indian people who needed him.

Father Albert Lacombe for whom two Alberta towns were named, died on December 12, 1916, at the Lacombe Home which he founded and loved. He was 89 years of age. A special train carried his body northward to St. Albert but the heart of the great Westerner remained at his beloved Lacombe Home.

Those who knew him remembered him as one for whom neither frost, distance, bullets, hunger nor smallpox could stand in the way of duty.

CHAPTER II

PALLISER ON THE PRAIRIES

A S THIS IS being written, exactly one hundred years
after Captain John Palliser began his celebrated study
of the fur country known as Rupert's Land, the good
homes, factories, thousands of oil wells and a huge surplus
of unsold wheat should create at least academic interest in
the unenthusiastic but nonetheless important report he left
for posterity to enjoy.

For nearly 200 years the country held no attraction
for any except natives and the most daring of traders. Such
agriculture as existed was restricted to riverbank farms
close to the confluence of the Assiniboine and Red rivers
and, locally, there was practically no interest in cultivation
farther west where the soil was supposed to be poor and
the climate and Indians were cruel.

It might have been expected that the Hudson's Bay
Company, overlord of Rupert's Land, would invesigate the
possible opportunities for colonization and farming but "the
Honorable Company" achieved its eminence through the
fur trade—and settlement would be a threat to furs.

But in eastern Canada and overseas, where the full

force of local prejudices could not be felt, questions were being asked. Must that land remain forever as nothing more than fur country? Is it not possible that some better economy could be evolved? Why shouldn't governments seek unbiased reports from men with training in science?

And so, the Imperial government decided to act and appointed Captain John Palliser to examine that portion of British North America lying south of the North Saskatchewan river and between the Red river and the Rocky Mountains. The government's choice of leader for the exploration was a good one. Born in Ireland in the year 1807, Palliser was not a total stranger to the western section of the continent because, ten years before, he made a journey to the American prairies to shoot buffalo.

Palliser's instructions, though they may seem elementary, were quite specific; he was to observe the physical features of the country, the forest resources, coal and other minerals, the quality of the soil and the general suitability of the area for farming. The details were from Downing street in London and with them came caution about hidden dangers in Indian country and a well-worded reminder to observe economy in the spending of government money.

* * *

It was 1857, seventeen years before the North West Mounted Police carried the banner of law and order into the far West. Many of the Indians were unmistakably hostile —the more so when there was suggestion of farm settlement on their hunting ground. Hence this expedition which was to become an important link in the chain of agricultural development in the new West was not an outing for timid souls or men of faint heart.

Palliser had no difficulty, however, in securing qualified men to accompany him and the party as ultimately organized was well-equipped with scientists of various orders, astronomers, geographers, geologists, engineers, to say nothing of a staff of untrained men.

In what may have been an unguarded moment, the master classified his associates as: "Gentlemen, Scotch half-breeds, French half-breeds, Americans, Canadians and one colored man—Dan Williams."

Travelling over the fur traders' route from the east, the technical men in the party arrived at Fort Garry on July 11, 1857, where the reception showed curiosity more than sympathy or understanding. The day following being the Sabbath, Palliser and his men rode four miles to attend church, realizing, no doubt, that it was the last such opportunity for months.

On Monday, the Captain set about to hire more men, partly as a safeguard against the hazards ahead, especially in the vicinity of the South Saskatchewan river where gathering white scalps was the most popular local pastime. With all preliminary business completed, equipment for the expedition was loaded on two small "American wagons" and five Red River carts and the little calvalcade started south and westward.

* * *

At Fort Ellice, close to the confluence of Assiniboine and Qu'Appelle, the travellers were surprised to find an attempt at farming—a patch of ground growing potatoes and a few Hudson's Bay Company cattle thriving on native grass. As for the soil, Palliser was impressed and speculated about its suitability for wheat and barley as well as vegetables, realizing no doubt that he was being bold in suggesting such a thing.

Eight weeks after leaving Fort Garry the Palliser party was at Fort Qu'Appelle but it must be remembered that there were numerous side trips consuming much time. At this point Palliser conferred with Mr. Pratt, a Red river Cree working as a Church of England missionary.

Pratt reported growing wheat and corn in garden-sized plots close to the fort but it seems to have been the joy of horse trading that inspired Palliser's special enthusiam; unblushingly he recorded in his journal that: "Mr. Pratt gave us a very fine mare in exchange for two wretched horses, one of which is not likely to live long."

Evidently it was in the Captain's blood because four days later he was again trading horses, this time with a band of Crees between Moose Jaw Creek and the Elbow of the South Saskatchewan. On the latter exchange, however, there is no journalistic comment and one must conclude that the Indians got the better of him.

The party was now at the heart of the prairie region, traditional battleground of Cree and Blackfeet, "where none go to hunt for fear of meeting enemies."

Presumably Palliser was witnessing one of those dry years on the prairies. Not only was there drought but grasshoppers and only a little grass remained. To Palliser it was vegetation "characteristic of the great American desert."

Wild life, however, was present in abundance. Buffalo were now so numerous that at times "the whole region as far as the eye could reach was covered with buffalo, in bands varying from hundreds to thousands." Not far from the Elbow of the Saskatchewan a grizzly bear was encountered and writing on September 30, the Captain reported on shooting during "the last three days . . . elk, black tail deer, common deer and antelope."

In the same area, probably not far southwest of where Saskatoon now stands, the Indian guide, Nichiwa, shot a buffalo under circumstances that amused the captain.

Palliser told it this way: "Our Indian ran buffalo also that morning, killed a good cow but complained of having lost his ramrod, went back some distance to look for it. At length he abandoned his search and returned to cut up his animal, in the body of which he subsequently found the remains of his ramrod. He called to Mr. McKay and said 'I have been looking for my ramrod and see where it was all the time.' He had loaded with the ramrod and forgotten to withdraw it before firing."

* * *

While still at the Elbow, debating the wisdom or folly of penetrating more deeply into the southwest, Palliser sent some of his men to trace a tributary flowing from the east. To the astonishment of all, this was found to connect with the most western of the Qu'Appelle lakes and immediately there was speculation about an important "water communication between the South Saskatchewan and the Red river, and that a good sized boat, and even perhaps a small steamer might descend from the South Saskatchewan, ascend the West Qu'Appelle river, cross the Qu'Appelle lakes, and then descend the Qu'Appelle into Red river."

It was the same idea that brought the highest enthusiasm from another traveller, H. Y. Hind, who had visions of a dam on the South Saskatchewan where an irrigation dam has been proposed in recent years, with steamboats going all the way from Fort Garry into the area that is now southern Alberta.

Evidently the proposal to travel toward the country of the Blackfeet Indians at that time was not well received with Palliser's men and the Captain agreed to go on toward Fort Carlton which was to be winter quarters for most of them. On October 6, the men donned their best clothes, believing they were only an hour's walk from the fort and refusing to accept Palliser's estimate of 30 to 40 miles based on instrument calculation.

"How can you know when you have never been there?" the men asked Palliser and they laughed at his nerve in challenging the reliability of their experience.

But the wonders of mathematics were demonstrated and those who were going to walk to the fort before breakfast discovered to their embarrassment that they were still more than a day's journey from their destination.

At Fort Carlton, Palliser discharged a few men, saw the others settled for the winter, said farewell and left on a 2000-mile journey to Montreal. He'd be back in early spring, he promised. The journey to Fort Garry would be by horseback and the fact that he was there 21 days after leaving Fort Carlton shows the vigor and stamina of the man.

From Fort Garry he was on his way south to St. Paul but his horse was killed at Pembina and he was obliged to walk the next 450 miles. But difficulties notwithstanding he was at Montreal in good time to confer with George Simpson and make plans for the next season.

Dr. Hector, Palliser's able assistant, continued studies of the country about Fort Carlton through the winter and travelled as far as Fort Edmonton, "which is quite as large as Fort Garry . . . furnished with strong bastions and palisades . . . now the farm attached to the settlement, though the only one in the Saskatchewan, is of very small size, not exceeding 30 acres . . . nine-tenths of the little flour that is consumed in the Saskatchewan is brought either from Red river or all the way from England . . . the usual population within the fort is 150 souls. These are all fed on buffalo meat and if there happens to be a good crop they get a certain small allowance of potatoes. The consumption of meat is enormous, amounting to two buffaloes a day on the average."

* * *

Palliser was back at Fort Carlton on June 4, 1858, and the second season's work began 11 days later. The main area for study was between the North and South Saskatchewan in what is now within the province of Alberta, but sorties were made into the foothills and mountains because one of Palliser's charges was: "To ascertain whether one or more practicable passes exist over the Rocky Mountains within British Territory and south of that known to exist between Mount Brown and Mount Hooker."

Somebody was thinking about a transcontinental railway but Palliser was more concerned about a pass for horses and carts because he believed a railway through the mountains would be totally impractical.

Fort Edmonton provided winter quarters for the second winter and in the spring of the third season, the party worked its way southward to examine the Bow river country and eastward to Cypress Hills. This was the area associated with the greatest danger from Indians but Palliser led the way and was rewarded by what he found in the hills: "A perfect oasis in the desert we have travelled."

Late in the third and last season, Palliser's party divided with one group under the Captain going over the mountains to take ship for England and home. Thus, at the end of 1859, Western Canada's first technical survey was completed and the conclusions about the country's prospects were being prepared.

The conservative author of the now-famous Palliser Report recognized big variations in soil and climate and the need for thoughtful treatment. In this his judgment was

13

better than that of many who came later.

About the northern part or Park Belt, he was optimistic; it was his "fertile belt" and settlers could make homes and have some security there. But of the prairie section where he observed short grass and lack of wood and water, Palliser had nothing but most guarded comment. He may have seen it at its worst in dry years but it was "an extension of the Great American Desert," and offered but little in farming potential. "Wherever we struck out on the broad prairie," he wrote, "we generally found the soil worthless, except here and there . . ."

* * *

That pronouncement about prairie soil was probably Palliser's biggest mistake. The soil was dry, no doubt, but it was not worthless; most of it was actually very high in fertility but, having no experience with prairie soils, the man may have judged its quality by the vegetation. Anyway, when the dry land was delimited by lines on the map, the Palliser Triangle was created.

The base of the triangle was the International Boundary from longtitude 100° to 114° W., with apex at the 52nd parallel of latitude. Within the bounds of that triangle, the soil would not be fit for cropping, Palliser believed. It was an area which coincided closely with the drought area of some recent years but Palliser would have been surprised to learn how often the world's wheat championship would be won by samples grown in that area.

Settlement, he believed, would extend first on the fertile soil around Lakes Winnipeg and Manitoba, then along the Assiniboine, westward on the Saskatchewan and finally, perhaps, onto prairie land.

But with characteristic caution he added that, "The capabilities of this country and its climate" for growing cereals were still insufficiently tested. As for cattle, Palliser recognized some opportunities in the prairie grass, recognized that where quantity was low, grass quality was high. With pigs and sheep, however, there'd be the problem of "natural enemies—the wolves."

In assessing agricultural possibilities west of Red river, Palliser was the real pioneer. His mistakes seem plain enough

14

to people of a later generation but generally, his judgment was good, even to the handling of the Indians for whom he prescribed reservations, instruction in agriculture, rigid liquor laws and a force of mounted police.

On his return to England in 1859, Palliser was made a Fellow of the Royal Geographic Society and awarded a Society gold medal in recognition of his great work. Cautious to the last. he died in his native Ireland in 1887—still a bachelor.

CHAPTER III

POLICE SCOUT JERRY POTTS

I F Canadians want a counterpart to Davy Crockett, finding one should not be difficult. The nomination of Jerry Potts has much to commend it. The great little buckskin-clad frontiersman who guided the North West Mounted Police to the spot where Fort Macleod was built in 1874, would furnish hero material for Canadian boys and convincingly rival that of the highly publicized Mr. Crockett.

Jerry Potts wasn't what anybody would call handsome. He was small, pinched in features, round-shouldered, bow-legged, pigeon-toed and his stunted growth of whiskers was as untrimmed as native sagebrush. If he were to appear on a main street today, folk would whisper, "A suspicious-looking character in town!"

But however he appeared, Jerry Potts was one about whom westerners should not be allowed to forget. He possessed the courage of a bull-fighter and the stuff from which heroes are made. It may be that the movie people have missed an opportunity in failing to reconstruct a film story of that man who for 22 years served Canada's mounties so well.

* * *

Apart altogether from his long and effective association with the police, Jerry Potts has a strong claim to a place in Canadian history because he was one of the leaders in the last major Indian battle on the Canadian side of the boundary. Jerry, it must be understood, was a half-breed. His father, John Potts, was a Scot in charge of the American Fur Company at Fort Benton in Montana, and his mother was a Piegan squaw. Jerry was versatile, could be either Indian or white man as occasion demanded; and strangely enough, he succeeded in commanding the respect of both races.

Participation in that last Indian battle was rather by accident more than plan. Jerry was hunting with the Bloods and Piegans in the good buffalo country now called southern Alberta. Chief Piapot's Crees, 600 or 800 of them, made a sortie into that part, looking for enemy scalps. They attacked a small cluster of Blood and Blackfoot teepees on the Belly river and massacred many of the occupants, mostly old people and children.

The few defending warriors were far outnumbered but word was carried to the Piegans who were on the St. Mary river, above Fort Whoop-Up. The Piegans smeared themselves with war paint, commanded Jerry Potts to lead them and rode away to counter-attack.

It was bound to be a bitter fight because Crees and the tribesmen of the Blackfoot group hated each other at any time. The Crees from what would today be the province of Saskatchewan and the Blackfoot alliance defending Alberta soil, made the fray a forerunner of interprovincial contests—such as an Allen Cup play-off—but rougher and in no way handicapped by referees, rules and timekeepers.

* * *

One of the best accounts of the battle was discovered in an article appearing in The Lethbridge News of April 30, 1890, while at least a few people could remember something about it. Piegan scouts located the Crees resting beside the river, just across from the present city of Lethbridge.

Jerry and his Piegans came up quickly. They had the advantage of the more modern guns and when they attacked, the surprised Crees were forced to fall back. The retreating Indians drew toward the river and made their stand in a coulee within view of the Galt Hospital built about 20 years later.

For a time there was a stalemate, with Crees in one coulee and Piegans in another. Then Jerry Potts led his tribesmen in a frontal attack and made it a bad day for the Crees. The latter were forced back, obliged to plunge into the river and as many were shot in the water as were killed on land. According to Jerry's telling, the river was so full of fleeing Crees that all a pursuer had to do "to kill one was point his gun at the water and fire."

The Crees were almost wiped out. If, as has been told, Big Bear who took a prominent part in the skirmishes of the North West Rebellion, was with Chief Piapot's Indians that day, he was one of the few to escape.

In any case, Jerry Potts was the victor's hero, emerging with nothing he'd call a serious injury, just a head wound and a small lead gun-pellet embedded in the flesh below his left ear. The pellet he refused to have removed—having got it at the hour of his greatest success, it was his "good luck medicine."

*   *   *

Danger held no fear for Potts. Throughout his life he was close to it. While still in his teens, he tracked an Indian murderer for several hundred miles and gained the revenge he sought, right in the pursued man's own camp.

The Indian, it appears, shot and killed Jerry's father at Fort Benton. The bullet may have been intended for another but Jerry's father was the victim and the 17-year-old lad set out to settle with the killer, relying upon the only law of any use at that time; the "law" men carried in their holsters.

The Indian Jerry was trailing belonged to one of the Blackfoot bands on the Canadian side and after several days of flight, supposed he had gained the protection of his

18

tribal encampment. But home camp or no home camp, Jerry overtook the murderer and faced him with the challenge to fight it out.

It was a terrific fight and Jerry carried scars from it, but he settled the account in the manner considered appropriate in Indian society. One might have expected the killer's fellow-tribesmen would try to take Jerry's scalp but instead, they acknowledged his courage and let him depart homeward.

* * *

It was a fortunate day for the Mounted Police and their tasks in the buffalo country when Colonels French and Macleod met Jerry Potts at Fort Benton. To the Mounties, the country into which they were trekking was dangerously new and strange and their need for guidance was urgent. In bringing law and order to the country, their first purpose was to visit the notorious Fort Whoop-Up, but as they halted at Sweet Grass after weeks on the trail, they didn't know which way to turn in order to reach their goal.

The commissioner and his assistant made a side-trip to Fort Benton on the Missouri River and there they heard about the skill of Jerry Potts. No time was lost in making a deal with him and Colonel Macleod, in returning to the main body of the police, brought the new "hired man."

At first, the rank and file of constables and officers were not impressed by this bandy-legged, weasel-eyed and silent newcomer, but all that coolness toward him changed. Very soon they discovered that when they were in trouble, Jerry was the person who could help. When water was in short supply, Jerry could find a spring, and when food was needed urgently, he could always locate a fat buffalo.

One of his first acts was to guide the police in a direct course to Fort Whoop-Up at the junction of Belly and St. Mary rivers, where police anticipated a struggle but found an almost deserted post. Then on October 13, 1874, he brought them to the island in the Old Man river where they started to build their new home and headquarters to carry the name Fort Macleod.

* * *

One of the first blows at the whiskey traders from the

south, struck without delay, was at a Negro named Bond. Chief Three Bulls reported buying two gallons of bad liquor and paying with two good horses. With Jerry Potts as their guide, police set out to find the offender and after two days and 50 miles of travel northward, Bond, his 16 horses, two wagons loaded with whiskey and 116 buffalo robes taken in trade, were securely in police custody. The trader was convicted and sentenced to jail—a fair warning to others engaging in the foul business that was demoralizing Canadian Indians.

Potts was exactly what the police needed. He could converse in several Indian languages, was an expert hunter and was no less daring in the face of trouble than the police with whom he cast his lot.

He possessed the instincts of a homing pigeon, was never lost in either storm or darkness. Only once was there evidence of doubt; he was searching for a landmark in the form of a pile of stones and having some difficulty.

"What's the matter?" asked Col. Macleod, "are you lost?"

Irked that anyone would suggest such a thing, the little man replied sharply, "No! Stones lost."

Best of all, for police purposes, he was on good terms with the Indians, being one of those half-breeds willing to live more or less like a white man but retaining the instincts of and loyalty to the Indians.

Whatever the situation or however great the danger, Jerry Potts in his silent way, knew how to meet it—for example—that day in the Montana foothills when travelling with two prospectors. A big band of Sioux Indians charged out of a coulee, bent on slaughter.

Potts and his companions fled as fast as their horses could carry them and knowing there was a chance of being overtaken, they headed toward a deserted log cabin. Reaching it, they turned their horses loose and barricaded themselves inside with their guns and revolvers ready for action.

The Indians came on and were met by gunfire—gunfire directed with deadly accuracy. The prospectors loaded the guns and Jerry fired. Eight or ten Indians fell and the rest were shocked to discover how three men could fill the air with deadly bullets.

The survivors withdrew and held council. Jerry knew what they were planning—wait for nightfall, attack and burn the cabin and collect a trio of scalps. But, as darkness fell, Jerry, on his belly, crawled away through the tall grass, made a big circle and came upon the Indian camp from the rear.

Then, moving among them as one of themselves without creating suspicion, he untied three Indian horses, led them back the way he came and joined his friends at the cabin. The three men then mounted and rode away through the darkness to safety.

* * *

Any man capable of performing such feats and remaining loyal, would be indispensible to the police. During his 22 years as interpreter and guide, he was constantly making rescues of one kind or another. If there was trouble in an Indian encampment Jerry would ride along with the officers and if the evidence in a cattle stealing or whiskey trading case was inadequate Jerry knew how to augment it.

In unfamiliar territory, the officers had complete confidence if Jerry was their guide. There wouldn't be much conversation as they travelled—the police knew that. When a trail-weary constable searching the horizon for journey's end, asked, "Jerry, what's beyond that next hill?" he received a typical Potts reply, " 'Nother hill."

His body was tough and sinewy. He could miss a meal or several of them without complaining. He never admitted fatigue. But little Jerry had one physical weakness—his lungs. He had a chronic cough and lung trouble led to his death.

Early in 1896, the lead pellet from an Indian gun worked its way out of Jerry's neck-muscle and the little man was disturbed; he had lost the "good luck medicine" he carried for many moons. Late that year, he died and was buried with full military honors in the police plot at Fort Macleod, the customary volleys being fired across his grave.

* * *

"Jerry Potts is dead," wrote the old Macleod Gazette

of July 17, 1896. "Through the whole of the North West, in many parts of eastern Canada and in England, this announcement will excite sorrow. Jerry Potts was a type fast disappearing. . . . A half-breed, he had the proud distinction of being a very potent factor in the discovery and settlement of the western part of the North West Territories. When Colonels French and Macleod left their wearied and almost helpless columns at Sweet Grass in '74, after a march of 900 miles and a vain search for the much vaunted "Whoop-Up," it was the veriest accident of fortune that in Benton they found Jerry Potts, who as a modern Moses was to lead them out of the desert and bring them to the end of their difficulties.

"He took Macleod's column straight as a die to Whoop-Up; he brought it on to the present site of Macleod and for years afterward was the unfailing guide, the faithful interpreter and the true and loyal go-between that made it possible for a small and utterly insufficient force to occupy and gradually dominate what might so easily under other circumstances have been a hostile and difficult country. For years he stood between the police on one side and his natural friends the Indians on the other and his influence always made for peace."

And then the Macleod Gazette concluded its tribute to the quiet, weather-beaten man of the plains in these words: "Jerry Potts is dead but his name lives and will live. Faithful and true' is the character he leaves behind him— the best monument of a valuable life."

That was the editor's tribute and a good one. For western people it may be fascinating to speculate how the stream of development might have been changed had that great and loyal scout not been hired into the service of the Mounted Police.

CHAPTER IV

"CHIEF OF CHIEFS" CROWFOOT

ACROSS the stage which was the early West, there stalked the tall, lean, dignified and bronzed figure of an Indian chief known as Crowfoot, whose leadership and diplomacy must command for him an honored place in Canadian history.

That wise and noble Blackfoot was more than an ordinary chief—he was acclaimed "chief of Chiefs," monarch among his people. What he did to influence the destiny of this new and pleasant land was greater than most people realized.

It was he who led the Indians at the signing of Treaty Number Seven, and it was he who restrained the warriors of the Blackfoot Nation in the dark days of rebellion in 1885 when their rising might have led to cruel massacre and the wiping out of settlements at Gleichen, Calgary, Medicine Hat and other points.

Historians have done adequately by some of the great Indian chiefs but not by all. Tecumseh of the Shawnee Tribe, who came to the assistance of Sir Isaac Brock in 1812, will not be forgotten. Likewise, the educated Chief Joseph Brant of the Mohawks is secure in the records; he considered himself a king in his own right and when visiting abroad could see no reason for kissing the hand of England's king but neither pride nor principle prevented him from honoring the more kissable hand of the queen.

Then there was the Christian Chief Peguis of the Saulteaux tribe who was assured of a lasting place of honor in the story books when, at the forks of the Assiniboine and Red rivers in 1817, he made the first Indian treaty with Lord Selkirk.

Farther west, Poundmaker and Big Bear of the Crees gained recognition as the result of being involved in Riel's quarrel with marching civilization in 1885 and then going to jail. But Crowfoot, the mighty Blackfoot, deserved more honor than he has thus far been accorded.

* * *

The Prairie Indians had no interest in bookkeeping and preserved neither birth nor death records. The fact of a person being around was proof enough that he or she had been born and once an Indian died, the place and time didn't matter. Hence the exact date of Crowfoot's birth is uncertain but his friends believed he was 69 years old when he died in 1890. That, if correct, would fix his birth at the year 1821. As for the place of birth, it too was uncertain, beyond being "somewhere south of the Red Deer river."

In any case Crowfoot was the second son of a Blackfoot chief. The elder boy was given the name Sapo-makikow, meaning Crowfoot. But that boy met an early death; when he went to call upon Snake Indians, offering the pipe of peace, they ignored its deep and almost sacred meaning and killed the young Blackfoot.

The tribesmen in the Blackfoot camp were infuriated and with the murdered man's younger brother leading, they went on the warpath. A notable victory followed and immediately the new leader was given the dead brother's name —actually, Crow Big Foot. It may have been the North West Mounted Police interpreter, Jerry Potts, who shortened the name to Crowfoot.

An old Indian at Gleichen recalled recently that he was 12 years old when he first saw Crowfoot. It was at

Fort Whoop-Up, seven or eight miles south of the present site of Lethbridge. The impression lingered. Even at that time, the chief was recognized as a great warrior whose score was a hundred victories and a distinguished horseman who always rode a spotted horse. The man was tall and erect; his hair was long and unbraided and he ruled with a firm hand.

Bravery and horsemanship—that's the way he won the leadership. The Blackfeet were the first Indians of the northwest to have horses and they became superior horsemen. There was advantage in having good horses; two ordinary horses would buy a wife in Blackfoot country but one especially good specimen might satisfy the father of a young squaw and thus there was incentive to horse improvement.

The Blackfeet learned something about selective breeding from the Nez Perce Indians farther south but, as an indication of horsemanship, success in stealing was far ahead of any display of skill in breeding or feeding. Horse stealing was a pleasant pastime as well as a necessity. And nobody was more crafty and ingenious in whisking good horses from under the noses of neighboring tribesmen than the youthful Crowfoot. Thus he always rode the best horse and, in a run after buffalo, he rode the fastest.

*   *   *

Like a recent British Prime Minister, Crowfoot was an "umbrella man." The umbrella was one of the white man's luxuries for which the Blackfoot chief had passionate fondness. In rain or sunshine Crowfoot might be seen riding across the plains, his beloved umbrella open and held at a jaunty angle.

For the gift of the umbrella, Crowfoot no doubt asked Manitou to bless the white man but for the introduction of fire-arms and fire-water, he could only ask that the white man be forgiven. Drunkenness and lawlessness were increasing at an alarming rate when the North West Mounted Police arrived and began to build Fort Macleod in 1874. It was a gigantic assignment, that of restoring order, protecting the Indians and at the same time disciplining them.

25

At first the Indians misunderstood and were inclined to oppose the police. At times the situation was tense. When Sitting Bull and his war-crazed Sioux fled to Canada, they sent Crowfoot and his lesser chiefs a present of tobacco. It was an invitation to join with the Sioux against the whites but Crowfoot returned the tobacco and rejected the further promise of horses and white women who might be captured in the campaigns.

Rev. John McDougall, pioneer Methodist missionary, went to Crowfoot and explained the new order. Whiskey trading and horse stealing would have to stop. The Indians would have to co-operate.

The Blackfoot chief saw no sin in stealing horses, especially when the original owner had the chance to steal them back again, if he was smart enough. But Crowfoot favored anything which would halt the hellish work of whiskey traders. He was a prohibitionist, believed that no Indians should have whiskey, least of all his Blackfeet for whom traders cautiously diluted the trade rum, one part to six of water, instead of the usual one part to four where less ferocious tribes were concerned.

Said Crowfoot to Rev. John McDougall, "Your words make me glad. In the coming of the Big Knives with their firewater and quick shooting guns, we are weak. We want peace. When you tell us about this strong force which will govern with good laws and treat the Indians the same as white men, you make us rejoice. My brother, I believe you and am thankful."

It was one of those brief but forceful speeches for which the old chief should be remembered.

When the first young brave from his tribe was arrested by the Mounted Police, resentment spread through the camp. But when Crowfoot witnessed the trial he was ready to subscribe to police methods.

"This is good medicine," he said; "there is no forked tongue here. When my people do wrong, I will bring them here to be tried."

* * *

Blackfoot Treaty Number Seven, last of the major Indian treaties, was signed on September 22, 1877. It was an important date in the life of the young nation. Contemporary chiefs looked to Crowfoot as their mouthpiece and he spoke with appropriate authority.

When Fort Macleod was proposed as the place where Hon. David Laird, Lieutenant-Governor of the Territories, and Col. J. F. Macleod would meet the Indians, the dignified Crowfoot ruled otherwise.

"You can meet us on our campsite at Blackfoot Crossing on the Bow River," he said.

The site, four miles southeast of the present Cluny, was long a favorite Indian rendezvous.

To Blackfoot Crossing came the Indians, Blackfoot, Blood, Piegan, Stoney and Sarcee—four thousand of them—young ones, old ones, some in war paint and battle clothes and some with no clothes save for breach-cloth.

They arranged themselves on the ground, chiefs in front, head men next, then braves, and squaws and children in the rear. Among the leading chiefs were Eagle Tail of the Piegans, Bull's Head of the Sarcees, Weasle Calf and Old Sun of the Blackfeet, Rainy Chief of the Bloods, and ahead of all, Crowfoot. With the commissioners were about 80 Mounted Police who arrived some days before the signing.

Food rations were provided by the government but Crowfoot refused to accept anything for himself until the negotiations were under way and the terms drawn up. Nobody would be able to say that he had been influenced by gifts of tobacco and tea.

But after five days of meeting Crowfoot made a speech to the Queen's representatives: "I hope you will look upon the people of these tribes as your children now and that you will be charitable to them. . . ." He paid his tribute to the police "who have protected us as the feathers of the bird protect it from the frosts of winter." Then speaking of white people generally, he said: "I wish them all good and trust their hearts will increase in goodness. I am satisfied. I will sign the treaty."

The other chiefs agreed. Crowfoot was invited to sign first. "No," he replied, "I will be the last to sign; I will be the last to break the treaty."

The commissioners signed first and finally, Crowfoot

made his mark above his name. He and his people had "relinquished, surrendered and transferred their rights, title and interests to Her Majesty the Queen, her heirs and successors," for all the country between the boundary line and the Red Deer river "for as long as the sun shines and rivers run."

A salute of white men's guns marked the conclusion of the treaty and young braves set about to stage a sun dance.

* * *

The next few years witnessed the complete disappearance of buffalo and Indians were being forced to accept what must have seemed shocking changes in their way of living. Incoming whites seemed to be surrounding the reservations, restricting Indian freedom. Crowfoot might have been bitter but he saw the changes as inevitable and in the spirit of a philosopher resolved to make the best of the new order. His people must become cattlemen; it was their best chance.

Some things must have been especially difficult to accept, however. In 1883 the grade upon which that terrible, smoke-puffing, "iron horse" would run, was being constructed in the direction of Crowfoot's reserve. The approach of the rails happened to coincide with an illness that struck the chief.

The Indians were sure that smoke from the engines made Crowfoot sick and, moreover, that the offensive rails were contrary to treaty. They had not been consulted about a railroad on their land and they were ready to fight it out. New rails spiked down during the day were torn up at night. Robert Dixon, an undercover "special" agent with the police from 1883 to 1906, and better known as "Rattlesnake Pete," was there and confirmed that young braves were anxious to fight. But medicine to hasten the chief's recovery was sent to the reserve and Father Lacombe, known to the Indians as Good Heart, appealed to Crowfoot and the explosive problem confronting the Mounties was eased.

Indeed it was fortunate for the almost defenceless settlers across the prairie country that Crowfoot refused to join the Crees in 1885. His answer showed the quality of his reasoning: "To rise there must be an object. To rebel there must be a wrong done. To do either we should know how it would benefit us. Why should we kill? Let the government know we favor peace."

For his loyalty in that time of crisis, the Council of the North West Territories gave Crowfoot the munificent gift of fifty dollars. Nobody could accuse the government of extravagance. Sir William Van Horne of the Canadian Pacific Railway did better, presented the aging chief with a lifetime pass to travel on the company's lines. To Crowfoot, it was his "railroad key" and though he used it but little, he was very proud of it.

In the year following the North West Rebellion, Crowfoot and certain other chiefs were given a luxurious trip to eastern Canada where they saw the might of the new nation. Father Lacombe was with the "Chief of Chiefs" on that trip. It was an impressive experience for the old Indian and on his return he told his tribesmen to put revolt completely out of their minds.

"The white people," said he, "are as thick as flies in summer time." His advice was to think about cattle.

* * *

When Crowfoot, the sinewy chief, the brave warrior, thinker, man who loved umbrellas and beads and art, native with chiselled profile and piercing eyes, died, the Blackfoot Nation mourned. No smoke arose from the camps that day because no fires were kindled; nobody took food.

The constant beat of the tom-tom was for a dead hero. His best horse was shot and his saddle and rifle went to the grave. He would want a horse and saddle in the "Happy Hunting Ground."

The celebrated Will Rogers said he was sure there'd be a good horse and saddle waiting for him in Heaven. It's to be hoped that both men found their horses.

"A few days before his death," according to the Lethbridge News reporting on May 7, 1890, "a will was drawn up for Crowfoot. In this document he left his house and one of his medals to his favorite wife, the rest of his medals and his horses to his brother, Three Bulls, who is now chief of the tribe. . . . The Medicine Men received 15 horses as their fee."

29

Crowfoot's grave overlooks Blackfoot Crossing where Treaty Number Seven was negotiated and signed. It was where he wished to be buried. On the bronze cross which marked the place were the words: "Crowfoot, age 69, died April 25, 1890," and on the back of the cross: "Father of his people." There, on September 26, 1948, a stone cairn was unveiled to his memory.

He called himself a Canadian, which of course he was —a very great one.

CHAPTER V

THE GANDHI OF THE PRAIRIES

TWO THOUSAND years ago, skeptics were asking: "Can there any good thing come out of Nazareth?" and in comparatively recent times the same sort of doubters enquired if any good thing could come out of the Indian tribes occupying the Canadian prairies. "Primitive" and "savage" were terms used to describe those native people but in various respects they were misjudged, and to suppose that the teepees produced no great thinkers, is in itself an injustice.

The Indian way of life was different, strangely different, but it wasn't all inferior and what becomes increasingly clear, some members of the native race had minds of philosophers. Of such were Crowfoot of the Blackfoot nation, Red Crow of the Bloods, Piapot of the Crees and Peguis of the Saulteaux tribe. And that the buffalo country of a century ago produced a native who, in his life and death, had quite a lot in common with the great Asiatic Indian, Mohandas Gandhi, may be seen as the greatest surprise of all.

Maski-pitoon was the name of the Gandhi of the buffalo country, whose adherence to the principles of nonviolence upset many of the story-book theories about prairie Indians. Not only was he a thinker but one who had the courage of bold convictions. By his performance he earned

31

a place of highest honor in western story and, indeed, a monument set somewhere in that section of central Alberta which was traditionally a Blackfoot-Cree battleground.

Only a few whites knew Maski-pitoon and the student will be forced to conclude that they forgot him rather quickly after his death. The story was almost lost. From fragmentary bits of evidence gathered here and there, however, it has been possible to reconstruct the story of his life or, at least, an important part of it.

The pioneer missionary of the Methodist church, Rev. John McDougall, referred to Maski-pitoon in one of his books and the Regina Leader of December 10, 1885, referred to him as a "courteous, hospitable gentleman of nature." Best of all, some of the old Indians of recent years have been able to offer fragmentary information and Rev. Edward Ahenakew, Cree minister serving the Anglican church at Fort la Corne, Saskatchewan, and Augustus Steinhauer have furnished important help.

* * *

According to Rev. Ahenakew, grand nephew of Chief Big Bear, the name "Maski-pitoon" meant "One Whose Arm Was Broken." More important than that, however, Maski-pitoon, in his early years, displayed unusual courage. Without flinching, he faced the test of the Sun Dance —three days of feasting, dancing and torture, at which young men hoped to qualify as braves. An ambitious youth desiring to win the high distinction, cut slits in the flesh of his breast, placed skewers or thongs therein and from these tied himself to a central pole against which he strained and grinned at the pain until the flesh broke to release him.

Maski-pitoon passed all the tests of endurance and bravery; he could be savage and cruel; and in gathering scalps and stealing horses he displayed such commanding skill that he easily won the admiration of his people who were more impressed by horse thefts than by lofty ideas. More than that, this young man had an erect and muscular body and no doubt enjoyed the imperfectly hidden glances of all the Indian maidens.

It just seemed that this young man was born to be a chief and lead his people to victory against all enemies.

In due course, Maski-pitoon did become a chief and his tribesmen were proud of him. And why shouldn't they be? On the hunt his success was extraordinary and when he returned from battle no brave could show more of the bloody evidence of slaughter.

But with the passing years, Maski-pitoon saw many things in Indian society to disturb him. Although he had blindly accepted tribal customs, he now concluded that many of the inherited practices were wrong. Tribal customs should stand the test of reason. He was worried.

He made solitary journeys into the hills in order to think things through. More and more he was convinced that killing was wrong, that violence simply bred more violence and evil. It was terribly unorthodox for that time and place but he dared to ask himself why the tribes could not adopt a policy of good will and devote their energies to something more constructive than killing and stealing.

Any young Indian whose bravery was untried would not dare to express such thoughts because they would invite scorn and he would be sent to work with the women. Only a man whose courage and daring were proven could afford to be bold. The young chief shared his views with the Medicine Man but it was a waste of time. The wise man of the tribe could not imagine living without war and cruelty; it would be like an eagle living without feathers or a buffalo without horns. Maski-pitoon turned to his thoughtful old father and there he found encouragement.

* * *

Together, father and son withdrew into the hill country to be alone and commune with nature. There the truth was more likely to be seen without disguise; there the spirits hovered more closely to man. The days were calm and the nights clear—perfect for meditation. Finally, convictions confirmed, the father collected four black feathers and set them in a row in the ground, calling them Dishonesty, Hatred, Cruelty and War. Collecting four white feathers, the old Indian set them in another row, giving the names Honesty, Friendliness, Sympathy and Peace.

"Decide now, my son," said the elder: "will you choose

33

the way that leads to destruction and war or will you follow the way that can lead to peace and happiness?"

Maski-pitoon was ready for the important decision. He motioned toward the white feathers and asked his father to burn the black ones. The old Indian followed the instructions and after destroying the black feathers, he bound the white ones and handed them to the young chief with a father's advice to carry them always.

Thereafter, the way of Maski-pitoon was the way of peace. Though most of his people could not understand the change, at least he was able to hold their respect because of a record for bravery already made unquestionable. His devotion to the new and better way of life, however, was to be tested many times in the days ahead.

Blackfeet stole his horses and savage war-parties took Cree scalps but Maski-pitoon remained steadfast in his convictions that violent reprisals would achieve no good and only add to suffering. The Crees were astonished; this was beyond their understanding, especially when it came from a chief who won his high rank as a fighting man.

The supreme test came when a Blackfoot raiding party murdered Maski-pitoon's father. Now, thought the Crees, the young chief will renounce his strange theories and seek revenge. But there was no attempt at revenge. The young chief continued to wear the white feathers as a reminder of his pledge.

* * *

Months passed and, one day, Cree scouts brought word that a small party of Blackfeet was seen not far from Maski-pitoon's camp, close to where the city of Wetaskiwin stands today. Moreover, the Blackfoot who killed Maski-pitoon's father had been identified in that small and comparatively defenceless group.

Chief Maski-pitoon ordered that the Blackfoot killer be captured and brought to him. Instructions were carried out and the murderer stood before the Cree chief. Then, addressing the Blackfoot who had every reason to expect death as his punishment, Maski-pitoon said: "You killed my father; you killed a good man. Once I would have sought your life as revenge; but I have found a better way.

I will not kill you but I will ask you to think about the foolishness of Indians killing each other. Will you help foster a new feeling between our two tribes? Will you return to your Blackfeet and tell them that Indians can live in happiness without killing each other?"

Astonishment filled the Blackfoot slayer. Never did he suppose an Indian would miss such a fine chance to kill an enemy. But he seemed to catch the spirit of Maski-pitoon's words.

"Never have I heard such a thing," he said. "My people will ask, 'who is this young chief, so brave and yet so good. He stands alone'."

Then came another test, when the life of the young Apostle of Peace was threatened. The traditional hate between the tribes had scarcely lessened but Maski-pitoon knew that if his philosophy was to serve any purpose and survive, he must be bold about presenting it.

As it happened, he and a few followers were travelling south to invite a discussion of peace with the Blackfeet. Early on the journey, they encountered a Blackfoot war party and were hopelessly outnumbered. The Blackfeet were in no mood for peace talks and massacre might have seemed certain.

Maski-pitoon's followers deserted while still there was a chance of escaping. Blood-thirsty Blackfeet braves with guns cocked and knives ready, came on for the kill, but they found only the young Cree chief standing erect, motionless, unarmed and alone.

Blackfeet halted in their astonishment. What did this unusual performance mean? That it was part of a crafty trick to distract and destroy the attackers did not escape the Blackfoot leader's thoughts. Neither tribesmen in retreat nor tribesmen ready for battle would surprise the Indians from the south but, surely, a single and unarmed Cree would not challenge the warriors unless there was a subtle plot about it.

But before there was any violence, Blackfeet recognized the Cree as Maski-pitoon and they remembered what they heard about his courage and his new teachings. Their lust to kill temporarily forgotten, they approached in curiosity.

35

Maski-pitoon spoke quietly and his traditional enemies listened. The lone Cree invited them to send an envoy to discuss peace and promised safety for those who came.

* * *

About this time, Maski-pitoon met the Methodist missionary, Rev. John McDougall, and the meeting served to strengthen the Cree's convictions. McDougall was invited to be present when the Blackfoot representatives visited to discuss peace.

Indians on both sides saw this as a bold experiment and the atmosphere was charged with explosive danger. It was not a simple matter to hold young Crees in check when Blackfoot scalps were within reach. But Maski-pitoon was in command and the conference was a success; men of both tribes feasted, danced and smoked the Pipe of Peace. And Rev. John McDougall, sitting in the place of honor between Maski-pitoon and the Blackfoot leader, gave his approval. Indeed, the Maski-pitoon story might have been lost, had it not been for McDougall who set down enough information to make interested people want to search for more.

But peace treaties must be renewed and about the year 1865, Maski-pitoon invited the McDougalls, Rev. John and his father, Rev. George McDougall, to accompany him to the Blackfoot country. The McDougalls were glad to go and the party set out on the journey that brought these men to the Blackfoot camp, somewhere close to where the city of Red Deer is located today.

The arrival of foreign tribesmen was bound to create a stir and present moments of danger and this one was no exception until Maski-pitoon and the McDougalls were recognized. Alarm gave place to welcome. The visitors were escorted to the tent of Chief Three Bulls and the discussions which followed were cordial.

There was a feast and a dance and the most devoted friend Maski-pitoon had in the entire camp was the Blackfoot who led the charge that day when the Cree chief stood alone and unarmed. That Blackfoot, in pronouncing Maski-pitoon as "the bravest chief of all," was acknowledging that the unarmed man who stood firm for his ideals was displaying more courage than the fighting man loaded down with guns and knives. To be an Apostle of Peace called for courage of the highest order.

* * *

It was on such an excursion in the name of peace that Maski-pitoon met his end. As he resembled India's Gandhi in his adherence to the principles of non-violence, so his death at the hands of an assassin was similar. For the information about Maski-pitoon's death, all thanks go to Rev. Edward Ahenakew who obtained the story from Chief Thunderchild and jotted it down many years ago.

It was "the year before the small-pox," probably 1869, and Maski-pitoon was trying to arrange another truce between the rival tribes.

With six followers, he raised a Hudson's Bay Company flag and rode into the Blackfoot camp. Recognizing Maski-pitoon, the Blackfoot chief rode out to meet and greet him and the inter-tribal negotiations were about to get under way when, suddenly, "a foolish young Blackfoot arrives unnoticed and unsuspected; he rides around fast and shoots Broken Arm dead."

But Maski-pitoon's life was not wasted. The whites who lived in and about Fort Edmonton had a huge debt to that splendid Indian for the security they enjoyed. And in his thinking and manner of life, he was a fine example to both the natives and the newcomers to the country, a noble contradiction to the popular savage-race concept.

CHAPTER VI

FARMER FROM ST. VITAL—LOUIS RIEL

HISTORIANS make mistakes too. Louis David Riel who played such a big part in two insurrections in western Canada, was one who received less than justice from many of the early writers.

The story about this colorful native son cannot be detached from that of his people, the Metis, who were being crushed by the march of civilization. Nobody will condone all Riel's actions but impartial judges will acknowledge his brilliance, his intense loyalty to what he believed right and that there was more of rightness on his side than many people realized.

Born at St. Boniface in 1844, French and Indian blood flowed in his veins. It was a common blend in those years. When Manitoba's first census was taken, 9848 out of a total of 11,963 inhabitants were classified as half-breeds, one variety or another. They found it difficult to fit into either Indian or white society—became traders, freighters and voyageurs.

Louis Riel's father operated a flour mill on the Seine river, not far from where it entered the Red. A fighting man was this elder Riel, one who had taken a determined stand against Hudson's Bay Company monopoly in 1848.

Louis' mother was a daughter of distinguished French-Canadian parents, Jean Baptiste Lagimodiere who carried the message about dangers at Red river to Lord Selkirk in Montreal in 1816, and Marie Anne Lagimodiere who was the first white woman to make her home in the West. It was indeed robust stock from which Riel sprang.

The boy Louis attended school at St. Boniface, played lacrosse, went out on the buffalo hunts, fished when he should have been in school and was perfectly normal, perhaps a little more serious than those about him. With maturity he became deeply religious and with encouragement from Bishop Tache, he resolved to be a priest. To that end he went to Montreal to attend college but the elder Riel died and the young man returned to Red river before his course was completed.

For the next few years Louis Riel was an ox-driver in one of the famous Red river cart brigades which crawled north and south between St. Paul and Fort Garry. Perhaps it was while talking to the cart oxen that he acquired his skill in oratory. Shortly he took to farming on the east side of the Red river, in the district of St. Vital and had he not been swept into the treacherous current of local politics and conflicts, Louis Riel might have lived and died an inconspicuous but respected Red river farmer.

* * *

It was not to be, however. Riel's fellows of the mixed races were being squeezed between the old and the new; they were the forgotten people. Somebody had to take a stand.

After 200 years, the Hudson's Bay Company was retiring from active overlordship in Rupert's Land and the Canadian government was taking over—doing it awkwardly, without consulting the half-breeds or even the traders and settlers. Those native sons and daughters saw themselves with a moral claim to the land and yet immigration was coming at them like a steam roller.

The threat was not entirely new, a subdued hostility having existed from the time the Selkirk settlers arrived. Colonization was in direct conflict with the fur trade and to the only way of life known to the native people. The so-called massacre of Seven Oaks in 1816, when followers of half-breed Cuthbert Grant clashed with Governor Semple, was an expression of that deep-seated fear.

The year 1869 produced indignities which people with pride could not accept. The Hudson's Bay Company land on which most half-breeds lived was going to the Canadian government; laborers were being imported to build a road between Fort Garry and Lake of the Woods, and the Metis were being ignored.

Then, to cap it all, there arrived, unannounced, engineers who started to lay out the country in square sections and townships, totally foreign to those who had grown up on Peter Fidler's long, narrow and sensible river-lots with frontage on a water highway.

All western people had reason to be annoyed at the autocratic methods but they were the half-breeds who stood to suffer most in restraint of freedom and they were the most hostile. They needed a leader and turned to the young farmer at St. Vital. He was robust, a fine orator and already a member of the Metis council.

Hudson's Bay Company rule had ended and the province of Manitoba was not yet created. There was no constitutional government. On October 30, 1869, William McDougall who was to be the first lieutenant-governor in the new province, arrived at Pembina.

If the Metis were to register protest to the new order, they must act quickly. They did. Not waiting for McDougall's arrival, they went to meet him. Fingering their guns, they explained that any aspiring lieutenant-governor valuing his comfort and health should stay away. McDougall returned to Pembina.

Having taken a stand, Riel and his men felt they had to be firm. A few days later (Nov. 6), they seized Fort Garry and seized the newspaper, Nor-Wester; at once they printed a proclamation inviting the English section of the community to elect 12 councillors to meet with the Metis on November 16.

Even among the English speaking residents there was some sympathy for Riel's cause and the representatives were named and the meeting was held. Governor McTavish of the Hudson's Bay Company issued a perfunctory order for the group to disband but the order was ignored.

About where McTavish really stood in the matter, nobody was sure. W. B. O'Donohue who was associated with Riel, contended later that the insurrection had McTavish's hope for success, restrained as it had to appear. At the conclusion of the meeting, Riel announced that, since no government existed, it was his right and duty to set up a provisional government. He said he would not fight constituted authority but he would insist upon justice. The government was formed; Governor McTavish was placed under arrest and such others as Riel considered to be safer behind bars.

* * *

On most counts Riel's government acted sanely and progressively. Meeting on December 1, it passed the bill of rights with 15 points, none of them unreasonable. And, moreover, all 15 were ultimately accepted by the government at Ottawa.

McDougall who was fuming at Pembina, knew that Rupert's Land was supposed to pass to Canada on December 1, but communications were faulty and he did not learn about a postponement. Consequently, on that date he issued a proclamation authorizing Canadians in the area to take up arms against the enemies of the nation, meaning Riel and followers. A few did make an armed stand and were promptly taken prisoners.

Donald A. Smith arrived from the East to mediate. It was known that Sir John A. Macdonald considered Riel as cabinet material for the new Manitoba government and was anxious for an amicable settlement. Smith was invited to state his position to a meeting of a thousand people called by Riel on January 19, 1870.

Up at Portage la Prairie, there was indignation that Riel was holding prisoners and about a hundred men under Major Boulton began a march to Fort Garry to correct all wrongs. But Riel had 700 men under his command and was not worried. He did, however, release most of the captives and Boulton's men, anxious to take credit for the release, could not resist the urge to march past Fort Garry, as defiantly as you please.

By this time, Riel's men, also, had an urge and they simply marched out and took Boulton and his entire following as prisoners. Boulton was sentenced to death although it is doubtful if Riel ever intended carrying out the sentence. Instead, he invited Boulton to consider accepting a post in his cabinet, representing the English.

*　*　*

Riel's biggest mistake was in the execution of Thomas Scott. Had it not been for that incident, the Metis and Canadian government could have reconciled their differences without difficulty.

Scott had escaped from Riel's custody and was recaptured with the Portage la Prairie volunteers. He was a blustering fellow but whether the execution was carried out for the purpose of demonstrating authority or for some other reason, will never be known. But years later, when Riel was about to go to the scaffold, he volunteered to his priest, "I swear as I am about to appear before God that the shooting of Scott was not a crime. It was a political necessity. . . . I commanded the shooting, believing it necessary to save the lives of hundreds of others." It was a dying man's explanation.

Whatever may have been in Riel's thoughts, the shooting of Scott incensed the people of Ontario especially. There was an immediate demand for settlement by force and Colonel Garnet Wolseley with 400 men, travelling by Port Arthur, arrived at Fort Garry on August 24, 1870. As Wolseley appeared, Riel disappeared, leaving his breakfast on the table and friend Lepine's moustache oil beside it.

Still there was no evidence that Riel was not loyal to British North America. Time proved loyalty. Rather than support the Fenians, massing to attack the new order in Manitoba, Riel offered to protect the local people and did raise a company in St. Boniface when the threat seemed serious.

After leaving Fort Garry to Wolseley, Riel remained quietly with friends about St. Vital and with Father Richot at St. Norbert. He had lots of friends and in September, 1872, he was nominated to represent the federal constituency of Provencher. He declined, withdrawing in favor of Sir George Cartier. The latter died next year, however, and Riel was elected and re-elected in 1874.

But attempts to take seat in the House of Commons horrified Ontario. The result was expulsion on April 16, 1874, the vote being 123 to 68. But in September, he was again elected by the people back home who were determined to have him. A little later a warrant of outlawry was issued against him by the Court of Queen's Bench of Manitoba and Riel withdrew to the United States. He went to Montana, located at Sun River, taught school, married and became a citizen of the Republic.

* * *

As time went on, many of the Manitoba Metis sold the land they had been granted and pushed westward where they could follow the life they knew and loved, beyond the rim of settlement. Many halted on the long, narrow strips of land along the South Saskatchewan river, south of Prince Albert. But ere long the land-hungry immigrants caught up with them again and the problems of Red river were being repeated.

"Send for Louis," the Saskatchewan men said, and that's what they did. They found him teaching at Carrol, Montana, quite contented with his lot. But when the men from Saskatchewan pleaded for his leadership, he acquiesced. That was in June, 1884. In the months following, he was with the Canadian half-breeds.

Again there was a bill of rights, a seven point demand and again not unreasonable—creation of provinces in the North West Territories; half-breeds to receive grants and benefits similar to those granted in Manitoba; patents to be issued on land held; proceeds from the sale of half a million acres of land to be marked for hospitals; better provisions for the Indians, and so on.

But Ottawa's memory was short. The new bill of rights fell upon ears well trained to deafness. Again Riel proclaimed a provisional government and again eastern feeling mounted.

The shooting began when Major Crozier of the North West Mounted Police met half-breeds led by Gabriel Dumont, not far from Duck Lake, on March 26, 1885. Seventeen men were killed, 12 of them on Crozier's side. That officer abandoned Fort Carlton and Riel's men occupied it.

On April 2 there occurred that horrible massacre at Frog Lake—Big Bear's Indians out of control. Hell seemed to have broken loose across the West and the scattered settlers cringed with fear.

This time, the East responded very quickly with a military force and General Middleton's detachment reaching Winnipeg on March 27, went on to Qu'Appelle, from which point soldiers were to march overland to go against Riel and Dumont somewhere about Duck Lake. Col. Otter would travel north from Swift Current to keep Poundmaker in check and General Strange would proceed from Calgary to keep Big Bear occupied.

Middleton divided his men, sending one column across the Saskatchewan river. Both columns were to advance on Batoche. Middleton met the insurgents at Fish Creek on the east side of the river and routed them. After some days, the advance against Batoche began and Riel's defences collapsed. The rebellion was crushed. Dumont fled but the leader was captured.

Riel was taken to Regina where he was tried and sentenced to hang. Since, as shown in recent years, he was an American citizen, the charge of treason was misdirected. But after several delays, he was executed on November 16, 1885, and the body moved for burial beside the Cathedral at St. Boniface.

Strange fellow, this man Riel. He might touch off a rebellion and be hasty in ordering a shooting but, to the last, he was one with the strongest religious zeal, strong to the point of being fanatical and his sanity was questioned. Yet nobody could question the quality of his loyalty. Father d'Eschambault of St. Boniface told the writer that, just prior to the hanging, a guard asked for a souvenir and Riel replied: "I have nothing but my heart and I have given it long ago to my country."

Louis Riel . . . he made some mistakes, made a lot of history, and made the Canadian government attend to the plight of his unfortunate fellows.

CHAPTER VII

EDITOR EXTRAORDINARY—BOB EDWARDS

PRIOR to the outbreak of the First Great War, the newspaper with the widest circulation in all the country west of Winnipeg was the Calgary Eye Opener. Published "semi-occasionally," it was Canada's most fantastic journal and its editor, like the paper itself, was something of a curiosity. He was Robert Chambers Edwards, better known as Bob Edwards, and certainly the most controversial figure in his generation. Folk couldn't make up their minds if Bob Edwards was saint or sinner.

Most people enjoyed his humor but failed to understand the man who didn't try to be understood. They saw him as an unconventional fellow, refusing to accept either customs or teachings that would not stand against his reasoning. Hence, the Eye Opener readers who were not amused, were shocked.

With strong convictions about human behaviour, hypocrisy was the trait to draw his most caustic ire and in his humorous way, he made life miserable for public figures guilty of insincerity. Snobbishness in social circles showed human nature in its worst light and the humbug he recognized on the society pages of many orthodox newspapers led him to include his own satirical "Society Notes" in the Eye Opener. People who recognized themselves in Bob's social columns were horrified, of course, but other readers laughed and no society notes across Canada enjoyed more of reader interest.

It would be reported that: "The family of Mr. and Mrs. W. S. Stott, Eleventh Ave. West, all had the mumps last week. A swell time was had. Mr. Stott will not be able to deliver his address today at the Rotary convention, much to the relief of those who have heard him speak."

"Mrs. Alex. F. Muggsy, one of our most delightful West End Chatelaines, has notified her friends that her usual Friday Musicale is called off for this week. Her husband, old man Muggsy, has been entertaining his own friends with a boozical for a change and is in an ugly mood."

"Maud de Vere of Drumheller arrived in the city Wednesday afternoon and was run out of town Wednesday night. It is a pity Miss de Vere is not a race horse. She is very fast."

On the surface, the editor seemed as frivolous as he did contradictory. No wonder many people were confused. In politics he was supposed to be a Conservative but actually he was a robust reformer. He criticized church ministers but practiced the charity of which St. Paul preached. He was a heavy drinker and one who made constant fun about "booze" but when the prohibition fight was on in 1915, Bob Edwards was on the side of the "drys." He pestered the politicians, then went actively into politics.

Little wonder that opinions about the editor were so varied. An editor said of him, "Libeller . . . coward, liar, drunkard . . . and degenerate." But one better qualified to judge, said admiringly: "Such qualities of heart and mind we shall not see again."

And when a well-informed scholar from an American university was asked for his opinion of Bob Edwards, he said that if the man had lived longer, had more interest in acquiring personal fame and consumed less whiskey, he could have been another Mark Twain. What Edwards did with some of his fictitious characters like the remittance man, Albert Buzzard Cholomondeley, and the equally notorious editor and horse thief, Peter McGonigle, makes a reader wish that Edwards had given them a more permanent place in some slightly more refined frontier novels.

* * *

Bob Edwards arrived in Western Canada late in 1894. He was a Scot, born in Edinburgh. Parents died when he was very small and he and a brother were raised by an aunt and given a good education.

Bob was a gold medalist at Glasgow University and might have followed the family tradition for book publishing but he wanted to travel. The two boys were attracted by stories of life in the western ranching country and went to Wyoming. But before long, Bob was making his way into western Canada. Stopping at the village of Wetaskiwin in the North West Territories, the young fellow decided to start a local newspaper.

Wetaskiwin at that time, according to the editor, had a population of "287 souls and three total abstainers." The new paper, first to be published between Edmonton and Calgary, was to be called "The Wetaskiwin Bottling Works," because it was sure to be a "corker," but friends persuaded him to adopt a more conventional name and it ended up as The Wetaskiwin Free Lance.

But the Wetaskiwin publishing experience was brief and the editor moved to Leduc and then Strathcona. At the latter place, the name Bob selected for his paper was "The Strathcolic," because it would give "every reader a stomach ache," but again a more conventional name was finally chosen and the paper appeared as the Alberta Sun.

Bob was a rolling stone in those years. There was a stint of working with the Free Press at Winnipeg and then he landed at High River where, in 1902, the famous Eye Opener was born. If the High River people wanted a paper with a high moral tone, it would cost a dollar a year but if they wanted any other kind, they'd have to pay more for it—at least a dollar and a half.

At first it seemed that High River with its ranch-country atmosphere and Bob Edwards with his irregular habits would understand each other and be forgiving. But Bob's conduct was too unusual even for High River. Nobody could be quite sure when the paper would appear, nor who would get an editorial lambasting.

"Every man has his favorite bird," the editor wrote, explaining the paper's irregularity; "mine is the bat."

His final undoing at High River was the church episode of 1904. A salesman for church music on phonograph records came to town and interested the Methodist minister in his wares, a phonograph and well-selected collection of sacred music to replace the church choir; any minister who was having trouble with his choir leader or was worried because the young singers were not going straight home after choir practice, would find his problems solved. It was agreed that the salesman would demonstrate his mechanical choir at the Sunday evening service.

Everybody in the town turned out on Sunday evening to hear the "canned music" and when the minister announced the first hymn, "Hark, the Herald Angels Sing," the smug salesman took a record from his bag and set the machine in motion. The result was splendid and the salesman sat back with disgusting confidence.

The next hymn announced was "Nearer My God to Thee" and again the machine was wound up and started at the proper moment but this time, the strains that filled the church were not as expected but those of "Just Because She Made Them Goo-goo Eyes," and a righteous congregation was horrified.

The minister called at once for the resignation of the mechanical choir and the salesman, in disgrace, left the church and then the town in a hurry. His only explanation was that after arranging the music for the service and placing it in his portfolio on Saturday night, he repaired for

some revelry to Jerry Boyce's saloon. He could only conclude that while he was celebrating, somebody tampered
with the music. All eyes turned toward Bob Edwards and
before long, he too was leaving High River.

* * *

This time he would try Calgary where he had a staunch
friend in the famous Irish lawyer, Paddy Nolan. In the
bigger centre, Bob's weaknesses would be less conspicuous
and his pen would have more scope, or so he hoped. And
sure enough, the Calgary climate suited him well and circulation began to climb.

He roasted the federal government about the two little
boats that made up the Canadian Navy; he fought the
Canadian Pacific Railway for failure to build safe crossings; he was some times close to libel but always escaped
its consequences.

When he wrote that "the three biggest liars in Alberta
are Robert Chambers, Gentleman; Hon. A. L. Sifton
(Premier of Alberta) and Bob Edwards, Editor," Mr. Sifton
threatened action. Bob answered that he, as Robert
Edwards, gentleman, would gladly enter joint action with
Premier Sifton in suing Bob Edwards, editor. The whole
thing began to look so ridiculous that legal action was easily
forgotten.

It would have been easier to recognize greatness in
Edwards' writing had it not been necessary for him to provide such volume of material for his one-man paper. But
he was more than a writer; as a public influence, nobody
in the West was able to better him, and as a humanitarian,
his efforts never ceased. There were two places in early
Calgary where a hungry man could be sure of a meal, one
the Salvation Army and the other, Bob Edwards' suite.

Of his influence upon public opinion, there is lots of
evidence. His stand in the matter of Alberta's prohibition
vote in 1915 is an example. Those on the side of liquor
were sure a drinking man like Edwards would use his powerful editorials to help their cause and they called on him.
It is told that they offered him a big sum, five or ten
thousand dollars, but Bob said, "No, I don't want that kind

of money. I've made up my mind to oppose you and that's all for today. Goodbye gentlemen."

Pretty soon Bob had a visit from the prohibitionists. They hardly hoped that a man with Edwards' record and one who had made so much fun about the subject of drink could be on their side—but they'd find out.

"How much will you pay me?" Bob enquired. The reply was, "We're sorry but we have no money." Said Bob, "That settles it; I'll be with you. Next issue of the old paper will be all for your cause."

The next issue was a masterpiece with column after column of bighting anti-booze editorials. But when the copy came from the printers for proof-reading, the unfortunate editor was in the grip of that enemy against which he had launched a fight. With a grin of temporary irresponsibility, he drove his marking pencil across the copy as if to destroy it. But Edwards had friends who undertook to see the issue published.

There are stories about the "wets" trying to steal or buy all the copies to prevent them going into circulation but Bob's friends were watching and when the famous anti-booze issue went out the next day, the editor was "sleeping it off" in the hospital where he usually ended after a bout with his enemy. But the Eye Opener editorials took the countryside by storm and may have been the biggest single factor in the prohibition victory of 1915.

* * *

Western Canada had few if any progressive thinkers to rival him. He was far in advance of his time. He fought for provincial rights, argued that the natural resources should be owned and administered by the provinces long before there was any agreement on the subject. He was a conservationist when few people were thinking seriously about saving soil and trees and water; he argued for social measures long before the politicians thought much about them, wanted hospitalization benefits and old age pensions. He was even demanding "votes for women" and reform of the Canadian Senate at an early date.

And though he humiliated the politicians, in 1921 he accepted a Calgary nomination for the legislature. Not that he changed any views about politicians—after attending a funeral for a member of the legislature and listening to extravagant words of praise, Bob said, "Now I know what a statesman is; he is a dead politician and what this country needs is more of them."

In his campaign, Bob made one speech of one minute in length and refused to make more. He wrote editorials for a special issue of the Eye Opener but scrapped the whole thing when he decided it would give him an unfair advantage over others in the campaign who did not have their own papers. But with 20 candidates in the Calgary City constituency, Bob finished second and went to the legislature. He sat through one session and died November 14, 1922.

When members of the Men's Canadian Clubs in two western cities were asked to name the prize personality in this part of Canada, a lot of colorful pioneers were nominated but the one to draw the highest number of votes was Bob Edwards.

CHAPTER VIII

RULER OF RUPERT'S LAND: GEORGE SIMPSON

AS THE GOVERNOR of the Hudson's Bay Company in the northwest for nearly 40 years, short, Scottish, Super-man Simpson was the virtual ruler of a far-flung fur empire extending from Red river westward to embrace half of the present Canada.

When the two old rival companies in the fur trade amalgamated in 1821, a strong leader was needed and it was then that George Simpson's authority struck Rupert's Land like a hot tornado.

Some of those around him said he was a dictator; some whispered that the man was too amorous, had fathered 70 sons between the Red river and the Rocky mountains. But even the critics had to admit he ruled with justice, skill and a fascinating touch of pomp. Those who worked with him, worked hard and liked it.

"The Governor and Company of Adventurers of England Trading into Hudson's Bay" were in the West from 1670 but about a hundred years later, horny-handed Canadians with Scottish names were coming from Montreal, pressing into company territory and intercepting the Indians on their way to trade at the Bay. These Montreal pedlars made big profits, incorporated as the North West Company and built forts and trading posts at strategic points. This intrusion, the older company resented bitterly, especially after furs began to dwindle. Competition became so keen that ethics suffered and liquor became a feature of trade.

Relations between the two companies went from bad to worse until, encouraged by the colonial office, they got together and consumated a union. The new organization demanded a resourceful leader acceptable to both groups; he should be a Britisher to suit the Hudson's Bay people and a Scot to humor the North-Westers. Moreover, he should know something about the fur country.

George Simpson, sent by the London office of the Hudson's Bay Company a year earlier to take over if Governor Williams fell into the hands of the opposition, was the man. He was 33 years of age, born where Atlantic waves washed the west coast of Ross-shire, born with the cloud of illegitimacy hovering over him.

Taken by his grandfather, he was raised in the atmosphere of the Scottish kirk. For 10 years he was a clerk in London, serving a firm of West Indies merchants, senior member of which was Lord Selkirk's brother-in-law.

* * *

In accepting the assignment in far-away Rupert's Land, Simpson knew he was embarking upon a dangerous mission. Union was being discussed but feeling was at such pitch that throats were in constant danger of being cut.

He arrived in the far Athabasca department with 15 canoes loaded to the waterline and immediately caught the spirit of the fur trade. He acquired a half-breed wife "according to the custom of the country," fought a "cold war" with Simon McGillivray of the other company and extended his trading posts.

The strength and wisdom of this five-foot, seven-inch Scot were quickly recognized. Andrew Colville, in whose London office Simpson was a clerk, now dominated the Hudson's Bay Company and in his opinion, Simpson was the man to carry union into effect. The legal aspects would not be troublesome but the practical job of welding two hostile organizations into a smoothly operating trading company promised difficulty.

It was Simpson's resolve to rule with justice and firmness and from the beginning, he won respect. At Red river he tried to help the settlers and give the Council of Assiniboia, over which he presided, some reasonable responsibilities.

Perhaps he wasn't sympathetic to farming in the fur country but he tried earnestly to gain more security for the settlers, agreed to buy their surplus products and in 1831, started a successful experimental farm close to the Assiniboine river, three and a half-miles west of the forks. To that farm Robert Campbell brought the sheep survivors from the long drive starting in Kentucky, in 1833; and to it came the famous imported English stallion, Fire-Away.

Breed history will relate the Governor's name with other experimental importations of livestock. The first purebred cattle to set feet upon the soil of the West were two Ayrshire cows and a bull, brought with the Thoroughbred stallion, Melbourne, in 1848.

And the first Aberdeen-Angus cattle on the continent were a bull called Orlanda and heifer, Dorthea, sent by the Earl of Southesk as a gift to Simpson when the latter was living at Lachine, Quebec, in 1860.

* * *

From the beginning of Simpson's association with Red river, he was anxious that settlers would find a commodity for export. Grains were too bulky for canoe transportation and flax, wool and tallow were considered. He aided the Red River Wool Company but in spite of its £1200 capital, it failed.

Then, in 1833, the Tallow Company, capitalized at £1000 was organized and 473 cattle were branded "TT" for Tallow Trade. But storms, feed shortage, bad management and wolves combined to ruin it. Hence, Simpson's announced willingness to buy the supplies needed by the company from the settlers, relieved the uneasiness about markets somewhat.

Fortunately, Simpson loved to travel because, to keep in touch with his trading empire, he had to do it. When he went on tour, it was with a hand-picked crew of paddlers. He might have sentiment for Highlanders, especially Orkneymen, but to handle his 18-feet-long canoes, he wanted the husky, chanting French and French half-breed voyageurs.

To be chosen for the Governor's personal canoe was the highest possible honor, a tribute to stamina and courage. But nobody accepted the assignment for its rest value because Simpson's super-men were expected to paddle 16 and 18 hours a day.

How he escaped labor troubles will puzzle present day readers. There is record of only one major upheaval, it being when Simpson and party were crossing Lake of the Woods and the Governor was nagging for even more speed than usual. One of the big voyageurs, unable to restrain himself longer, seized the offender, ducked him in the lake and set him back in the boat, dripping, cold and humble.

Said one of his men, "He's nae big but tough as a Highlan' stirk."

For a period in his life, Simpson started each day with a dip in lake or stream, winter as well as summer. He expected his men to be as well-conditioned as he was. Freight brigades and inspection missions had to operate with punctuality that would fill a modern train dispatcher with envy. When his personal canoe was leaving Edmonton House, the paddlers were reminded of the day and hour the party was expected at Fort Garry or Norway House.

* * *

His canoe trip from York Factory on the Bay to Fort Langley near the mouth of the Fraser River in 1828 was an example and fortunately, Archibald Macdonald was along to record the events. Two canoes with nine carefully selected voyageurs in each departed at one o'clock, a.m. on July 12; a seven-gun salute and cheers from company men sent the travellers on their way and the canoemen broke into song. Fully provisioned with what were considered essentials, the party had pemmican, guns, tents and "wine for the gentlemen and spirits for the voyageurs." The Governor would decide when each would be dispensed and how much.

At Norway House there was more cannon fire and cheering, also at Cumberland House, Carlton, Edmonton, Chippewayan and so on. As for the Governor, he'd look more like a kid-gloved diplomat from the Court of St. James than a fur trader.

Approaching a post a halt would be called to allow the men to clean up and don their best sashes. As the canoe came near, residents of the post would hear music, "music from Heaven," strains from Colin Fraser's bagpipes.

Then as canoes came gliding into view, spectators saw the be-tartaned piper standing at one end, a crew of seasoned paddlers bending in mechanical unison and the stout figure of the Governor with top hat, cloak and gaiters, standing erect and dignified at the bow. It was something for natives and others to remember but, unfortunately, there were no press photographers to catch the spectacle.

The private piper was not there by accident. In 1826 Simpson made request to the London office for a piper and the next year Colin Fraser from the Highlands was hired at £30 per year. He arrived late in 1827 and thereafter piped George Simpson up and down every navigable stream in the West, until advancing years reduced his respiratory pressure and he devoted himself to the fur trade, remaining with the Company until his death in 1867.

At each post visited, the Governor examined company records, sat to judge local disputes and admonished his men to be diligent in service and the Indians to obedience and temperance. He had strong ideas about the evil in liquor and when, on one occasion, he saw a drunken Indian and a keg of company rum nearby, he seized an ax and sank it into the wooden staves to let the contents waste on the ground. Drunkenness among his own people, he would not tolerate.

That western trip in 1828 may have been the first in which canoemen went all the way down the Fraser and through the canyon. Nobody enjoyed it and Simpson's views about transportation changed. The "dangers whitened the countenances of the boldest, even our dark Iroquois who is nearly amphibious." The scribe's further comment was that of a man thankful to be alive, "I should consider the passage down to be certain death in nine attempts out of ten."

Arrival at Fort Langley was 90 days after leaving Hudson's Bay, 14 of the days being spent at posts. Most days of travel began at 2 or 3 a.m. and took the party 40 or 50 miles on its way. Perhaps the terrifying trip down the Fraser produced prejudice but Simpson was no booster for the west coast or its climate. It was not a fit place for his traders to remain for more than two years at a time; after such period they should return to Fort Garry for a spell to recuperate.

When in England in 1830, the Governor married, this time in the most acceptable ecclesiastical manner. There remained the problem of finding another man for the native lady in Rupert's Land who considered herself his wife, but she was ultimately assigned along with a dowry, so it seems, to a willing taker and everybody was satisfied.

* * *

The ensuing years produced new problems in the fur trade. Beyond the Atlantic, silk toppers were replacing the elegant beaver hats and to add to Company worries, Russian traders were encroaching from the North upon Hudson's Bay Company fur country.

But in August of 1838, the Governor of Rupert's Land accompanied by John Henry Pelly, Governor of the Company, went to St. Petersburg, where Simpson, acting for the Company and Baron Ferdinand for the Russians, signed the first international trade agreement affecting Western Canada.

Success and loyalty gained a knighthood for Simpson. But that didn't demand retirement. He wanted to go round the world and on March 3, 1841, he left London for that purpose. He was in his 55th year but he was fearless.

The first part of the trip was via Montreal and the water route of the fur trade but at Fort Garry, joined by Chief Factor Rowand, wheels were adopted. With three horses and a cart, travel to Fort Edmonton was at a rate of 50 miles a day. Simpson hadn't changed a bit.

At Edmonton a large group of Indian chiefs, Blackfeet, Bloods, Piegans and Sarcees, were present to see the Governor. Though painted and beaded to honor the great man, the chiefs were not forgetting their own needs, hoping that by his blessing, "their horses might always be swift, that the buffalo might instantly abound and that their wives might live long and look young." Nothing of importance was overlooked.

Simpson saw the Pacific ocean for the third time, crossed to Siberia and on to St. Petersburg. There the Russians dined him with caviar and he countered by offering Fort Garry pemmican, which may explain why Russia has been suspicious of the West ever since. Anyway, from St. Petersburg he returned to London, completing the world tour in 19 months and 26 days.

* * *

Quite understandably, Simpson was a fur trader more than an agriculturist and his pessimism about farming did his judgment no credit. When a committee of the Imperial House of Commons examined the Hudson's Bay Company monopoly in 1857, Simpson was called as a chief witness.

He insisted that Rupert's Land had no future except in furs, his reason for so thinking being "poverty of the soil." Fortunately, the parliamentarians were not convinced and Captain John Palliser was already commissioned to conduct a study. Simpson's views about the future of farming now seem laughable but it must be remembered that many others shared his views at that time. On most other matters his judgment was good.

But Simpson was getting old; eyesight was failing. The spirit, however, was unchanged. Even in the months before his death on September 7, 1860, he was determined to visit Fort Garry and actually travelled as far as St. Paul before being persuaded because of illness to turn back. He ruled for nearly 40 difficult years without any major trouble in Rupert's Land. That record speaks for itself.

CHAPTER IX

MAN FROM MISSOURI: HENRY WISE WOOD

ONE of the best contributions from the state of Missouri to the new province of Alberta was Henry Wise Wood whose record of farm leadership in his adopted land calls for the highest honor. An important factor in the political and economic life of the West, this humble and earnest man should be forever remembered for his part in the formation of the Wheat Pools and his promotion of farmer co-operatives in which he believed implicitly. For 20 years he held the confidence and enjoyed the loyalty of western farmers and to many of them, Henry Wise Wood was "Wise Old Henry."

What a force he was in his adopted province! Somebody observed that between 1916 and 1930, Wood was the most influential person in Alberta. For 15 years he was president of the United Farmers of Alberta and for many of those years he was also president of the Alberta Wheat Pool.

Had he so desired, he would have been premier of Alberta when the group of which he was the head was swept into power in 1921. The fact he refused the coveted office at that time must be seen as proof of high purpose—he was not motivated by personal or selfish ambition.

Public office came to him without seeking; he was not

an opportunist, not a radical or fly-by-night, and never bitter or unfair. Man of mild and kindly character, he simply developed a conviction that farmers were carrying too many non-producers on their backs and that by co-operation they could improve their positions without injury to anyone having a legitimate and productive occupation.

Wood looked and acted like a senior professor of economics. Even more than an economist, however, he was a philosopher, doing his best thinking as he assumed a characteristic pose, straight-stemmed pipe in one hand and a burnt match in the other. More often than not, a lighted match went out before it made contact with the tobacco.

Matches were his chief luxury and his friend Lew Hutchinson recalled him setting waste paper fires in his office in the Lougheed building in Calgary on at least two occasions. Each time however, the blaze was extinguished before it was out of hand.

* * *

Although few farm leaders have a better claim to a place in Canadian history, this one spent only the last half of his life in this country. He was 45 years old, a family man, married more than 20 years when he came to locate at Carstairs, Alberta. In Missouri where he was born, his farming enterprises were successful and it was not for any reason of failure that he made the move.

From boyhood years, Henry Wise Wood was a student, always a reader, ever an admirer of the philosophy of Emerson, the poetry of Burns and the democratic ideals of Lincoln. Indeed, as others may have observed, he shared more than ideals with Abraham Lincoln; he had Lincoln's slow but resolute manner, Lincoln's lean and gaunt body and Lincoln's awkwardly long legs that sometimes threatened to part company.

Like the great American statesman, too, Wood had a dry and salty sense of humor. When a certain overbearing representative from Saskatchewan attended the annual meeting of the Alberta Wheat Pool, boringly explaining his substitution for a senior official detained because of a quarantine for smallpox, Wood remarked dryly: "Well, we'd rather have you than the smallpox."

61

There was one obvious physical difference between Lincoln and Wood, however; Lincoln could comb his hair while Wood, as most western people remembered him, had nothing to comb, or practically nothing.

It was a desire to go into cattle ranching, coupled with a general restlessness that brought Wood to Alberta. Very well he might have remained to enjoy the relative comfort of his Missouri farm. If it were opportunity in public life that he sought, he could have accepted a nomination to run for a seat in the state legislature.

But the idea of ranching was with him from school years and while still in his teens, he drove a mule team all the way to Texas, expressly to get work and experience as a cowboy. For three years he rode the Texas range and loved it. From then on, talk about the grasslands of Western Canada fired his ambition.

In 1904, he visited the North West Territories and was convinced and said he'd be back. One year later, just as Alberta was being created a province, Henry Wise Wood arrived at Calgary and continued on to Carstairs where he secured land.

* * *

As it happened, his land was good for wheat and he decided to farm for a while before going into ranching. Moreover, since Canada was now the land of his choice, he believed he should seek his Canadian citizenship as quickly as possible.

"No use holding either a membership or a citizenship," he said, "unless one is going to use it," and when, in 1909, the United Farmers of Alberta resulted from the amalgamation of Society of Equity and Alberta Farmers' Association, Farmer Wood was ready to assume a member's responsibility.

From the beginning, his ideas were firm; while he believed that a farmers' organization would be most effective if it remained out of politics, he insisted that every good citizen should be politically active. In the campaign preceding the "reciprocity election" of 1911, Wood was out working for "free trade" candidates.

Already he was a marked man in the farm organization.

Reasoned judgments had not gone unnoticed and in 1915, just 10 years after his arrival in Alberta, he was elected vice-president of the provincial body. Within the year, the UFA president died and Wood became acting president and then president.

It was a trying time for agriculture and there was growing sentiment for direct political action as farmers saw themselves being caught between controls and rising tariffs. Wood repeated that his organization must speak courageously but with justice and his attitude won the support of the provincial government. Hence, many of the reforms he sought were granted.

But should these organized farmers attempt to go it alone politically? Wood said, "No." In the first place, he contended, lack of adequate leadership would be a crippling handicap. He had seen it happen across the line. Better that farm organizations become strong within the ranks of the old parties rather than start a third party.

The man was in a good position to practice what he preached; having been appointed to the Board of Grain Supervisors in 1917, it is believed that he could have been minister of agriculture in the Union government at Ottawa. But the choice was to remain, to pilot the destiny of his beloved United Farmers of Alberta.

But however much he was personally opposed to his organization going actively into politics, Henry Wise Wood was ready to bow to the democratically determined will of the membership. He was worried about the rising demand for direct participation—no denying that—but when the association declared its decision, made in its own democratic way, Wood stood ready to give the new policy all the energy he possessed.

When Alberta's Premier Stewart called a snap election in 1921, Wood forgot about his summerfallowing and gave his full time to the campaign on behalf of the farm movement. And then came the surprise—triumph beyond anybody's dreams. When the new party won 39 out of 61 seats in the province, it was a Henry Wise Wood victory as much as for the UFA.

Now there was the problem of selecting a premier. The

high office was Wood's for the taking and public opinion would have supported him, but at the meeting of newly-elected representatives, the humble and dedicated Wood declined to be a candidate for the premiership and Herbert Greenfield was chosen.

* * *

Wood had other pioneer work to do. The next important chapter in his life was wheat marketing and the organization of the wheat pools. Again his leadership stood out like an elevator on the prairie horizon. He served as a member of the Canadian Wheat Board of 1919 and had faith in the soundness of the board principle. As he saw it, the Wheat Board was a form of farmer co-operation, government-sponsored, and he was anxious that it be continued. But in 1920, after marketing one crop, the board was being discontinued and the Winnipeg Grain Exchange was about to reopen.

Prices were declining and farmers were unhappy. From some circles the cry was for guaranteed prices, from others, for another wheat board. Wood refused to endorse the request for a fixed price, saying that farmers opposing tariff protection for industry, could not or should not ask protection in another form.

"In co-operation and self-help we'll find the solution," he said, adding, "If the government will not provide a wheat board, the farmers of these three provinces can create their own, just as the fruit growers of California created their own marketing pools."

That was in 1920 but the West was not ready for all that was suggested and implied. A year later, Wood repeated his confidence that a contract wheat pool controlling most of the crop in the western provinces would bring relief to a situation growing worse almost daily.

When hope of obtaining another wheat board had vanished, Wood concluded that growers were sufficiently annoyed to really get behind a huge pooling effort. His United Farmers of Alberta executive voted to go ahead with the plan for organization but doubted if sufficient time remained to ensure a proper sign-up in that season of 1923. Most executive members favored waiting until 1924 as Saskatchewan and Manitoba had decided to do. But farmers were restive and Aaron Sapiro from the United States had already been invited to Alberta to tell how it could be done.

The outcome was a decision to undertake a whirlwind campaign, hoping to sign up 50 percent of Alberta's wheat acreage by September 5. On that date, the actual acreage signed to five-year delivery contracts represented about 45 percent of total but the decision of the Alberta Wheat Pool, of which Wood was chairman, was to go ahead anyway.

And so, Alberta, with Henry Wise Wood at the helm, led the way and in the next year, Saskatchewan and Manitoba organized and the inter-provincial body known as the Central Selling Agency was formed. There were problems, lots of them, but they were surmounted and after two or three years, the three provincial pools controlled the sales from 15 million acres of wheat and jointly represented the largest grower-controlled co-operative in the world.

* * *

Wood retired from the presidency of the United Farmers of Alberta in 1931 but continued as president of the Alberta Wheat Pool until 1937. By the latter date the Pool was a very much different organization; it had survived the mistakes of 1929 when an all-too-high initial payment was made in the face of declining prices. Henry Wise Wood's Wheat Pool had changed in character but the old man had lost none of his faith in self-help for farmers' ills.

And he was still the philosopher. A few former supporters may have turned against him but there was no need to become excited about the reactions one could expect, especially if a person were sure he was in the right. Reply to one who deserted and become noisy about it? "No," Wood said, "there's nothing to be gained by fighting futility any more than fighting a skunk with its own methods."

Honors came to Henry Wise Wood. He was the recipient of the Cross of St. Michael and St. George, a tribute to his leadership and in 1929, the University of Alberta conferred upon him the honorary degree of Doctor of Laws. Emerging in the new academic robes, he was heard to say,

"This is just like putting show harness on an old Missouri mule."

Henry Wise Wood died in 1941, age 81. In a splendid treatment of the man, author William Kirby Rolph said: "In the history of Alberta, Wood's career was as important as that of Mowat in Ontario and Howe in Nova Scotia."

CHAPTER X

PADDY WAS AN IRISHMAN—PADDY NOLAN

WITH a name like Paddy Nolan and a birthday on March 17, there could be but one logical and decent land from which to spring. And a super-abundance of Irish wit and good humor left no doubt whatever. Sure, and Patrick James Nolan was born in Limerick, Ireland, and the year was 1864.

It was a most fortunate thing for the infant community of Calgary when the young lawyer decided to locate there and it wasn't long until Nolan's presence at any western gathering brought as much joy as a chinook arch in a winter month. For a generation, the mere mention of his name brought smiles of pleasant recollection to the faces of old-timers and the re-telling of some Paddy Nolan story: "Do you mind the one about Paddy when he was defending the horse thief . . ."

In addition to being a famous wit and the best company on the frontier, he was a great lawyer by any standard. The late Right Honorable R. B. Bennett pronounced him the "greatest jury lawyer I have ever known." Any accused who had Paddy Nolan on his side breathed a sigh of relief and hope; his friend, Bob Edwards said, "All the best criminals go to Paddy Nolan."

R. B. Bennett probably knew more about the theory of

law but Paddy Nolan knew more about human nature. One may find amusement in trying to picture Bennett and Nolan on opposite sides of a certain court case; Bennett, as usual, laden with imposing law references, turns to his student assistant saying, "Boy, give me Phipson on evidence." A few minutes later he commands again, "Boy, give me Lewin on trusts." Nolan considered the show was being carried a little too far and, rising to present his side of the case, turned to a young fellow present, with the words, "Boy, give me Bennett on boloney."

With unending demand for his services in law, Nolan might have been wealthy but he was better as a lawyer than as a collector and there were important legal cases for which he sought no payment, the famous McGillicudy libel case, for example, in which Bob Edwards of the Eye Opener was plaintiff and represented by Paddy Nolan. Payment was refused in that instance and settlement was made ultimately with a box of cigars—not very choice ones either if any one judge from the good natured banter passing between the two noted personalities.

* * *

In his academic career, the Nolan brilliance was evident. From Trinity College in Dublin, Paddy graduated with honors in classics and a gold medal for oratory. To the University of London he went for law and in due course was called to the English Bar. In 1889 he stepped off a train at Calgary, a total stranger and one with an Irish green about him. Why he came to Calgary, he never knew, except that he wanted to go somewhere in a new country. In the year in which he arrived, he was admitted to the Bar of the North West Territories and was the ninth legal light to be so enrolled.

Paddy Nolan was a stranger when he stepped off the train but he wasn't strange for long. Personal magnetism coupled with a recognition of talent made people beat a path to his office which was, for a long time, next to that of A. L. Sifton, another lawyer, one who became chief justice for Alberta, then provincial premier and a federal cabinet minister.

As an after-dinner speaker, there was no one to rival

68

Paddy Nolan and when he relaxed in the rotunda or the bar of the old Alberta Hotel, men congregated about him like cows around a salt-lick. Calgarians recalled the dinner arranged by Pat Burns, a sumptuous meal, after which a world traveller told about a tour through Europe, through Austria-Hungary in particular. Paddy Nolan was called upon to thank the host of the evening. He said a traveller might go through Austria-Hungary but "Pat Burns would never let anybody pass through Calgary-hungry."

And in entertainment of a public nature, nothing in early Calgary rated higher than a court-room session on a morning when Paddy Nolan would be defending Mary Fulham, better known as "Mother" Fulham. The lady, it should be explained, was a keeper of pigs for which she gathered hotel garbage. Now and then she departed from the accepted ways of sobriety and now and then she felt obliged to use her good Irish fists to defend her garbage monopoly against competitors who also had pigs. Anyway, if Mrs. Fulham and Paddy Nolan were to appear in the same court, the seating space was bound to come far short of demand.

One of the famous Mother Fulham stories has been told with different interpretations. In one version, Paddy Nolan had the supporting role but it was actually Dr. H. G. Mackid who figured in it. The lady had injured a knee and, meeting Dr. Mackid on the avenue, enquired what she should do toward faster healing. The kindly doctor suggested they step inside a nearby drug store where he would examine the injured part. That they did. A stocking was rolled down, exposing not only the bruised knee but an exceedingly dirty limb. Spontaneously, the astonished doctor muttered audibly, "I'd bet a dollar there isn't another leg in Calgary as dirty as that one." But the lady replied quickly, "Put down your money, doctor; that's a bet." With that she rolled down the other stocking and held out her hand to collect a dollar from the doctor. There was no doubt about it; she won her bet and the druggist was there as a witness.

Paddy Nolan was at his best on defence, with a jury to which he could make his inimitable appeal. So successful was he in defending cattle rustlers that the stockmen became alarmed and took steps to retain him for prosecution. Convictions did increase for a time but Nolan was not happy on that side and soon returned to defence.

While he created no end of fun in and out of court, he never did it to hurt any undeserving person. Sympathies were as tender as his body was big, but he could resort to some ingenious techniques. Defending a certain widow accused of conducting a lottery on her dead husband's watch, Nolan was hard pressed for convincing evidence. Knowing the defence was sure to be weak, he obtained a couple of the raffle tickets, some days before the case came to court, visited the judge who would preside, and casually mentioned the poverty of a widow of his acquaintance.

"Perhaps, Mr. Judge," Paddy said quite innocently, "you'd like to give her some help by buying a couple of these tickets."

In the court, Lawyer Nolan, with an Irish twinkle in his eye, said, "even my learned and Christian friends in this room would not refuse to help a poor widow." Nobody except the counsel for defence knew why the judge was embarrassed but the accused received nothing worse than suspended sentence.

Paddy Nolan liked to go to Fort Macleod, a hundred miles south of Calgary, and made business trips there quite often. Swapping stories with Harry Steadman and "Kamoose" Taylor and others who were his friends was a fine experience. But many of the Fort Macleod stories were "tall" ones and difficult to rival, leading Nolan to say of the place, "Fort Macleod is an outlying point and the men I know there can out-lie those of any district in the North-West."

When crossing the river on one trip to Fort Macleod, the stage coach tipped and Paddy Nolan, all 275 pounds of him, received a ducking. With wet clothes and no dry ones big enough to fit his huge frame, he yielded to the only alternative and appeared in court with a Hudson's Bay blanket wrapped about his huge frame.

It may have been on the same occasion that he was defending a Fort Macleod interdict found with a bottle of whisky. Again there seemed nothing upon which to base a defence but Nolan never gave up. As the case neared conclusion, Nolan arose to enquire if any responsible person had determined definitely the contents of the bottle in question.

The reply was, "no," and Nolan hastened to point out that whisky bottles have been known to carry strange fluids and suggest that the prosecuting lawyer might sample the contents in the presence of the court. This, the other lawyer considered unethical. The defence then proposed that His Lordship be the judge of the liquid, but this too was declined.

At this point, the presiding judge countered with the proposal that since the defending lawyer knew something about whisky, he might conduct the sampling. That was the opening Nolan was seeking and in reply, said, "Your Lordship, when I consider what that bottle might contain, I wouldn't let it within a yard of my mouth." Certainly nobody was ready to make the experiment after that statement and the case was dismissed.

*   *   *

Ernest Cashel was Paddy Nolan's most celebrated client and all Canada followed the story with interest. It was 1902 and Cashel was wanted for forgery. He was in the Red Deer district, supposed to be buying cattle to stock a ranch but after staying with one Isaac Rufus Belt, neighbors noticed that both men had disappeared. Some time later Cashel was located and arrested but before the police delivered their prisoner at Calgary, the man jumped from a wash-room window of the train and made his escape.

Again Cashel was arrested but in the spring, the decomposed body of Belt was found at the mouth of a creek flowing into the Red Deer. Cashel was now charged with murder, convicted and sentenced to hang on December 15, 1903. But Cashel was difficult to hold. Shortly before the date set for execution, the prisoner produced two revolvers, herded the guards into a cell, freed himself and walked calmly to freedom. At this particular time Nolan was in Ottawa seeking a new trial for his client and as he talked with the minister of justice, making his petition, the government man received a telegram. After reading the message, the minister turned to Nolan, saying with consternation in his voice, "Your man has escaped."

Nolan, they say, just reached for his hat, said, "Thank you sir. Goodbye."

A mighty man-hunt followed and for weeks there was no progress. Cashel was hiding close to Calgary, sleeping in a den hollowed out in a haystack and spending part of his time in a nearby shack. As police made a routine check on the premises, a bullet whizzed past their ears. Cashel was soon surrounded but not until police set fire to straw about the cabin did the convicted man throw down his guns and come out. Even at this stage, Paddy Nolan did not stop working for his client but it was of no avail—Cashel, this time, paid the penalty for his crime.

* * *

Of course, the stories about Paddy Nolan are legion. An oldtimer will tell about the occasion when a visiting police officer from Edmonton developed an evening thirst and proposed to his friend Nolan that they go together to a bootlegger for some refreshments. At the house to which they made their way, nobody was at home but Paddy assured his friend he knew where the whisky was kept. After having their drinks, Paddy produced a dollar from his pocket, left it on the kitchen table and the Edmonton man did the same. Next day, however, the visitor discovered that the house to which they had gone on the previous night was none other than Paddy's own home.

Nolan was appointed a King's Counsel in 1907 and he was a member of the first senate of the University of Alberta, a post he filled until his death in 1913. It was a comparatively early death but the tributes to his memory were many.

Paddy Nolan was a great lawyer and a great Western Canadian institution. "His faculty of keeping a crowd in a sustained roar of laughter for hours at a stretch was a constant source of wonderment," wrote his staunch and loyal friend, Bob Edwards. "He never repeated himself. Paddy's well of fun never ran dry and the rapidity with which he could drive away the blues from the mind of a worried friend was not the least endearing of his qualities."

Chapter XI

HENDAY SAW THE MOUNTAINS—
ANTHONY HENDAY

A S THE provinces of Saskatchewan and Alberta celebrated their Jubilee in 1955, western people were
reminded of another anniversary; it was exactly 200
years earlier that the first white man to gaze upon the
Canadian Rockies was returning to his base on Hudson's
Bay to tell his story of adventure to unbelieving ears. The
man was Henday—Anthony Henday—an employee of the
Hudson's Bay Company and one who found it easier to get
along with Indians than with white men. For his Company,
he was the right man for the task and the long journey
across what is now Manitoba, Saskatchewan and Alberta, to
winter within sight of the mountains, should be seen as one
of the most daring in the history of North American exploration.

As this courageous fellow set out on his dangerous mission in 1754, things were going badly with the great Hudson's

Bay Company, then 84 years old. As long as Indians from the interior were willing to paddle great distances to the Bay in order to trade, company business flourished, but things were changing—traders from New France on the shores of the St. Lawrence river were pushing westward, building posts on the lower Saskatchewan and intercepting the Indians taking furs to the Englishmen on the Bay.

One French post was situated where the Manitoba town of The Pas stands today and another was La Corne's east of where the city of Prince Albert arose. Men of the English company were worried; their trade was being cut off and livelihood threatened. No longer did the Indians of the plains find it necessary to take their furs over the long and difficult route to Hudson's Bay and they welcomed the chance to trade near their hunting ground.

Loathe as the English company was to change its trading policy, something had to be done—either posts must be built far inland where they would compete with the French or the Indians must be induced to resume their long trips to the Bay.

* * *

The time had come, the English officers agreed, for one of their representatives to travel inland—farther than anybody had gone before and visit Indians in the southwest, dangerous as it seemed. Henry Kelsey went into Cree Indian country on the Saskatchewan river and was the first white man to see the plains east of where Saskatoon stands. But nobody was anxious to travel into the country of the Blackfeet, most savage of the western tribesmen. Even the Cree Indians advised against adventures into that more westerly region.

Even the hardy fur traders shrank at the idea but when the Hudson's Bay Company called for volunteers, Anthony Henday said he was ready to go. He wasn't well known, being a comparative newcomer to the company, but he was a robust young Englishman who knew no fear. The Isle of Wight was his birthplace and home and if he had a profession in his years on the island it was that of smuggling. It was an occupation of which people on the south coast of

England took little notice, at least not until a man was caught at it and then they said "farewell," because he was usually outlawed. Anthony Henday had the misfortune to be caught plying his illegal trade and was promptly banished, according to the time-honored tradition.

Whether the Hudson's Bay Company realized the new employee was a smuggler is not clear but it doesn't matter; Anthony Henday was just the man needed. He crossed the Atlantic and was assigned to the humble post of servant at York Factory, the company's post on the cool shore of Hudson's Bay, where James Isham was governor.

Isham was now convinced that the English company had little future on the northern coast unless its traders went inland to get business. He agreed, moreover, that Henday would be a suitable person for the first assignment. No doubt the governor reasoned that the young fellow was not essential in the business organization and one displaying resourcefulness becoming a smuggler would have the best chance of surviving on the remote prairies.

That one venturing single-handed into the far west had only a small chance of returning, didn't seem to worry Henday. He was ready to go and go without any white companions. And so, on June 26, 1754, Anthony Henday left the Bay in a canoe carrying a party of Crees returning after bringing furs to the post. With his Indian companions he got along fine and he and the leader, Conowapa by name, became fast friends.

They passed up the Hayes river and made their way by Cross lake to the Saskatchewan river. Where The Pas in Manitoba stands today, Henday was called by the trader at the French post to explain the reason for his trip. Suspicious that the purpose was in opposition to their interests, the French threatened to detain Henday, even suggested sending him to France. But the Englishman refused to be frightened and with characteristic coolness hinted he'd just as soon see Paris as the distant prairies or the western mountains the Indians had talked about. Finally, Henday produced a "secret weapon"; he presented the Frenchman with a roll of "Brazile tobacco" and all hostility ended.

He and his friends continued on their way, upstream on the Saskatchewan. When the Indians of his party met their families waiting somewhere in the Carrot river country, there was celebrating and hunting and feasting. Henday soon demonstrated he could celebrate and hunt and feast with the best of them and the speed of travel suffered.

There was really no need for hurry anyway. With squaws and papooses and dogs in the party, canoes were now abandoned and the journey was continued on foot, across bushland, parkland and prairie. The travelling arrangement was quite satisfactory, however, because the noble males had their squaws to carry equipment, and Henday, ready to follow any good Indian example, accepted the luxury of a female partner, sort of a human pack-horse.

Wild game animals were abundant. Moose, buffalo and deer could be obtained at any time the need arose. On August 16, according to his journal, he or his friends killed six deer; on the 17th, four deer; on the 18th, several moose, and on the 20th, five deer. Certainly, fresh meat was no problem.

The life of an Indian suited Henday even better than that of a smuggler.

* * *

At some point north of the present city of Saskatoon, the party touched the South Saskatchewan river and crossed on rafts made by stretching moose skins on willow frames. It may have been in the area now marked by the town of Wilkie that Henday met Indians who took him buffalo hunting with bows and arrows. Seven buffalo were the reward and to make the day more memorable, one of the young Indians on the hunt had a brush with a grizzly bear and was mauled seriously.

Henday continued, traded a gun for a horse, and in early October crossed the Red Deer river, somewhere southwest of today's Stettler. At a point, presumably between the river crossing and the place now marked by Olds, he encountered an encampment of Blood Indians—two hundred tents of them. It was the first chance to test his power of salesmanship, the real purpose of the long journey. He sought out the chief's lodge and sat before him on an albino buffalo robe.

Would the tribesmen bring their furs to the English on the Bay? Before the chief had time to answer, Henday made a presentation of tobacco; but it failed to have the desired effect. The chief could think of various reasons why his people should not go to Hudson's Bay; it was too far; it was beyond the buffalo country and his men could not live on fish. And finally, because the trip to the Great Bay would have to be made by canoe, his Indians who had now adopted horses would not fancy it. Moreover, his people were living and eating pretty well and why should they exhaust themselves to gain a few extra knives and beads? On second thought, Henday agreed that his case was weak enough; he couldn't think of any convincing reason either why the Indians should work so hard for a few extra trinkets they were getting along without.

Clearly, he had failed to win his first potential customer but he wasn't unhappy. The mountains showed silvery clear and he was attracted. As for the Indian disposition in this part, it wasn't nearly as belligerent as he had expected. And there was fur in abundance thereabout, even though the Indians were indifferent about taking it to the Bay. He resolved to do some trapping on his own account during the winter. His trapping took him along the foothills in the direction of the place at which Rocky Mountain House was built later.

* * *

With the arrival of spring, this first white man to see that section of our Alberta, loaded his furs on sleighs, said "farewell" to the Rockies which the Indians called Arsenie Watchie, and started out in the hope of finding the north branch of the Saskatchewan river, whose current would carry him half way to his home base on Hudson's Bay. When he reached the river, after passing over or close to ground on which Wetaskiwin was to be built, the ice was still thick. Not wishing to wait for open water, he and a few Indians who were ready to return with him, dragged their sleds over the ice until they came to a place offering birch bark, suitable for canoes.

As Henday paddled his way downstream, he was joined by a few more Indians with furs for trade and by the time he reached the forks of north and south branches of the river, he was piloting a brigade of some 60 canoes loaded with prime skins of beaver, martin and fox. It gave him a feeling of importance and induced him to make a foolish halt at La Corne's post, north of present-day Kinistino, just to pay his respects to the governor.

Henday hadn't seen a white man in almost a year and naturally he would have found it difficult to pass without a friendly call. But the Frenchman had two glasses of brandy for the Englishman and several gallons of the stuff for the Indians accompanying with fur-laden canoes. Next day there was more brandy and by this time the semi-intoxicated Indians were ready to trade their furs with the friendly Frenchmen, forgetting the English on the far-away Bay. It was four days before Henday's Indians were sufficiently sober to take to their canoes and by that time, many of the best furs were the property of the French traders.

It was a mistake to stop at La Corne's fort and one might have expected Henday to avoid repetition of such error, but when the flotilla of canoes reached the other French post, the temptation was on him again and he stopped. Again there was French brandy and again Henday drew his Indians away with difficulty after they parted with more of their good furs.

But notwithstanding the inroads made by the clever French traders, Henday arrived back at York Fort on June 20, 1755, with a fleet of 70 canoes. He had been absent for one year, except for six days. He had seen the Rocky Mountains, had seen the Indians of the southwest who were not as mean as they'd been painted, and completed a journey of over 2000 miles, most of it in exceedingly strange country.

The report Henday brought back to his governor was both good and bad. The country through which he passed was attractive; the mountains were majestic and the Indians though savage were reasonable enough. But about persuading any substantial number of those remote Indians to bring their furs over the long water course to the Bay, Henday was not hopeful. If the English wanted to trade with distant Indians, they must go to meet them and either escort them back or set up trading posts right there in the fur country. Company policy did change but not rapidly. Nineteen years later, the Hudson's Bay Company established Cumberland House on the Saskatchewan river, and then many other inland posts.

* * *

There was one part of Henday's report the staid officers of the company refused to believe, the part about Indians riding horses. They just laughed and no doubt discounted the rest of his story because any one inventing such a yarn would distort other description. As a matter of fact, the first horses were seen in the valley of the Bow river only a few years before but the Indians were quick to adopt them for hunting and fighting and Henday saw them, beyond a doubt.

Yes, just over 200 years since the first white man completed an expedition across this mid-western section to view the grandeur of the Rocky Mountains. It's a brief history but it becomes increasingly apparent that no part of the continent has a more colorful story—colorful because of colorful people who were a part of it.

CHAPTER XII

THE KEEPER OF HOTEL FORT MACLEOD
HARRY TAYLOR

THE town of Fort Macleod in southern Alberta is different. In size it is like many other western communities but in age and tradition it is surpassed by none. It was the first urban centre in the southwest and is still the windiest. In its origin, "The Fort" was the western headquarters of the North West Mounted Police who came in 1874, but while still an outpost on the plains it became the cowboy capital of Canada and the focal point of bull-team freighting in pre-rail years.

There, early citizens saw the big units consisting of eight, 10 or 12 pairs of oxen, driven tandem and hauling heavy freight wagons loaded with 16 or 18 tons of freight, to and from Fort Macleod. No less colorful than the teams were the heavy-drinking, hard-swearing drivers or "skinners," one of whom, to illustrate the magnitude of the outfit he handled on the Fort Macleod-Fort Benton trail, said there were so many pairs of oxen strung out tandem that the team in the rear was walking in manure up to its hocks all the time.

Among the personalities that became an essential part of the old town was hotel keeper Harry Taylor, best known by the name "Kamoose," Indian equivalent of "thief." Exactly how he came by that title, nobody has explained.

Anyway, Kamoose Taylor was versatile; otherwise he wouldn't have been able to include the occupations of miner, missionary, whisky trader, hotel operator and rancher in one lifetime. He was an Englishman, born on the Isle of Wight in 1824. In the year 1848 he sailed around the horn, landed in California to dig gold and then went on to British Columbia by pack train to add a bit of excitement to the Cariboo gold rush.

According to Sir Frederick Haultain who began his practice of law at Fort Macleod, Taylor, along with John Glenn who broke the first sod on Fish Creek, came through the Jasper Pass to Fort Edmonton in 1863. During the last four days of that journey the travellers had no food but at Edmonton they bought a bag of potatoes from the Hudson's Bay Company, begged some butter from the Catholic mission and acquired a young pig by means never explained, and started south for Fort Benton.

* * *

A soldier of fortune such as Taylor could not overlook the opportunities in whisky trading in the country through which he was travelling and he returned to Bow river. Others had similar ideas and Healy and Hamilton of Fort Benton built the notorious trading post, Fort Whoop-Up, about a day's ride east of where Fort Macleod was to arise.

Two cupfuls of well-diluted whisky were paid for a buffalo robe and a gallon would buy an Indian horse. Transactions were conducted through a wicket in the heavily built stockade and thus trader and Indian didn't necessarily come together. Such an arrangement was in the best interest of the trader's health and as further precaution, a few cannons were mounted and some pigeon-holes cut in the walls for muskets. Outside the fort walls there was nothing to restrain murder and other crime which went with Indian drunkenness

But such debauchery was to end. Almost immediately after the Mounted Police under Col. Macleod began to build quarters on an island in the Old Man river, the whisky business slumped. Some of the traders fell into police hands, some went south with the birds and others elected more respectable though less profitable pursuits.

One of the first traders to run afoul of the police was Kamoose Taylor. When the law overtook him, he was south of Fort Macleod, nonchalantly transporting two four-horse loads of whisky and buffalo hides. The goods were confiscated and the fine was $500. The repentent Taylor agreed he had been foolish and announced he was seeking a new occupation. Saying farewell to his past, he operated a stopping place at Fort Calgary and in 1881, built a hotel in the old town of Fort Macleod. Now, he was on the best terms with the police but every time he saw mounties in buffalo coats, he was sure he could recognize some of the furs they took from him.

Three years after starting the hotel at Fort Macleod, the short, plump, educated, witty and kindly Englishman rebuilt on the new townsite and continued to make himself the life of the frontier community. Frequently he was in mischief and sometimes a resident had the urge to punch him. He wasn't much for good clothes and 'tis said he never owned an overcoat while he operated the Macleod hotel; when obliged to go out in cold weather, he just took a customer's coat off a hook in the lobby and put it back when he returned.

* * *

He didn't like it, however, when chickens were removed from his hen-coop. A chicken or two disappeared every night for awhile in a winter season and a new padlock on the hen-house door failed to stop the loss. It wasn't a weasel or skunk because no feathers remained, and the window for ventilation was too small to admit a man. It was a mystery but Taylor decided to keep a watch one night.

Sometime after midnight, he saw it; an Indian lit a fire behind the chicken-house and proceeded to warm the end of a long pole. The heated end of the pole was then shoved through the small window and among the sleepy hens. The night being cold, a hen could not resist moving onto a warm place to roost and when two birds mounted the pole, the Indian withdrew the object and placed the hens in a bag. But by this time, Kamoose was upon him and when the suffering Indian was seen next day, the seat of his pants was burned away, suggesting only that he had been forced to sit on the smouldering fire over which he warmed the pole.

*   *   *

Kamoose Taylor was in about everything that happened at Fort Macleod. He had a ringside seat for the opening of the cattle range, the most exciting drama in western history. Fred Kanouse who turned cattle on the range while the buffalo were still numerous, was one of his pals and he knew every cowboy.

It was right there in his hotel that the first ranchers association in Canada was organized. It was in 1883 that the South West Cattle Association was started. Originally, it represented eleven ranchers but in 1896 it merged with the Alberta Stock Growers' organization to form the Western Stock Growers' Association.

At the first meeting in Taylor's hotel, assembled cattlemen accepted the bylaws of the Choteau Association in Montana as a basis, bylaws which allowed officers to raise both hands in voting while ordinary members raised only one. But the Canadian association was not ready to accept the Montana rule with respect to mavericks.

The new secretary, who did not have any cattle of his own, moved that "mavericks go to the Crown." Somebody enquired what it meant and was informed that "the Queen would own the cattle." The representative from the Waldron Ranch is reported to have exclaimed with feeling: "Well, the Queen will need a hell of a fast horse if she's going to get any cattle off my range." The motion was defeated.

*   *   *

But it was the hotel that brought special fame to Taylor

and the town. Over the door of that rough and ready western resort hung a sign, reading: "In God We Trust; All Others Cash." Customers could buy shelter, food, drinks and stamps, three-cent American stamps selling at 25 cents each. For some years, the only mail connection with the outside world was through Fort Benton, Montana, and there was no law to stop Kamoose from making a profit on the stamps.

Bullet holes in the walls and tables of the bar-room were numbered and indexed so that nobody could claim credit for shots to which he was not entitled. In the restaurant of the hotel, nobody argued about the quality of food without being invited to try the grub at Fort Benton a couple of hundred miles away. But the proprietor offered no apologies. Why should he? Had not English peers and noblemen eaten there? When Lord Latham, Lord High Chamberlain in Queen Victoria's time, and Alexander Stavely Hill, backers of the Oxley ranch, visited the southwest, they dined at Hotel Macleod. Not wishing to risk so delicate a situation to clumsy helpers, Kamoose proceeded to wait on the English gentry, himself.

With dirty towel over his shoulder and head held high, he strode forth to take the dinner orders.

"Soup, sir?" asked Taylor, and Lord Latham enquired: "What kind is it?" The reply was, "Damned good soup, Your Lordship."

One thing he refused to do was shine a nobleman's shoes and when one of the aristocratic guests left his shoes outside the bedroom door at night, inviting a shine, he had to search for them on the following morning in the litter at the end of the hall to where they had been swept.

Nor was cleanliness one of Kamoose Taylor's virtues. A roller towel served everybody, the accepted theory being that Taylor had four towels, one for each week in the month. A complaint would be greeted by the remark that "twenty other people are using it and it's good enough for them."

* * *

Kamoose Taylor and Fred Pace were in competition for hotel business and there might be doubt about which served the best meals and biggest drinks; but in point of originality, there was no doubt. The code of rules posted to govern conduct at the Macleod hotel was something without parallel and for the well-kept copy, dated September 1, 1882, from which the following items are taken, the late Senator Harry Mullins who had managed the Cochrane ranch, must be thanked.

(1) "Guests will be provided with breakfast and supper but must rustle their own dinner.

(2) Boots and spurs must be removed at night before retiring.

(3) Dogs are not allowed in the bunks but may sleep underneath.

(4) Candles, hot water and other luxuries charged extra, also soap.

(5) Two or more persons must sleep in one bed when so requested by the proprietor.

(6) Baths furnished free down at the river, but bathers must furnish their own soap and towels.

(7) Jewelry or other valuables will not be locked in the safe. The hotel has no such ornament as a safe.

(8) The proprietor will not be responsible for anything. In case of fire, guests are requested to escape without unnecessary delay.

(9) Guests without baggage may sleep in the vacant lot.

(10) Meals served in bedrooms will not be guaranteed in any way. Our waiters are hungry and not above temptation.

(11) All guests are requested to rise at 6 a.m. This is imperative as sheets may be needed for tablecloths.

(12) No tips to be given to any waiters or servants. Leave them with the proprietor and he will distribute them if considered necessary.

(13) The following tariff subject to change: Board $25 a month. Board and lodging with wooden bench to sleep on, $50 a month. Board and lodging with bed, $60 a month.

(14) When guests find themselves or their baggage

thrown over the fence, they may consider that they have received notice to quit."

That was the spirit of Hotel Macleod and the spirit of Harry "Kamoose" Taylor and some other amazing people who walked the streets of the old town with him, ex-mountie and mischief-maker Dave Cochrane, half-breed police guide Jerry Potts, professional stage-driver "Polly" Pollinger and others of their ilk who seemed to be created for a frontier town. They were men who seemed to straddle two worlds, having seen the buffalo disappear and the domestic herds come in. They knew the West before it was domesticated and never completely lost their love for the old order.

* * *

In March, 1892, Kamoose Taylor quit the hotel and moved to his land—half farm, half ranch—about three miles from Fort Macleod. There he spent some of the happiest years of his life, raising a few cattle, growing some crops, tending his garden, entertaining friends who delighted to call on him, and proclaiming the infallibility of the Conservative party. He died at the home of his son in Lethbridge on March 23, 1901.

"He may have been somewhat lacking in theoretical religion," wrote F. W. G. Haultain, premier of the North West Territories, "but in the religion of humanity he was an able exponent and hundreds can testify to his extreme generosity." (Lethbridge News, March 28, 1901.)

CHAPTER XIII

POET OF THE QU'APPELLE VALLEY
STANLEY HARRISON

STANLEY HARRISON of Fort Qu'Appelle called himself a farmer but people had reason to wonder when one engaged in writing, sketching, bird-watching and racing Thoroughbreds would find time for the menial operations. Actually, there wasn't much time; just when he'd be ready to begin seeding or harvesting, along would come a schoolboy or neighbor with a robin or meadowlark whose broken wing required expert attention and farming operations would have to be suspended.

The home farm was the one he got in a horse trade in 1914—a thousand dollars and a Hackney horse he happened to be driving at the time, was the price. For reasons not difficult to comprehend, the Valley had better farmers but neither the district nor the West had a more devoted student of flowers, birds, poetry and horses.

This refreshing fellow came from Yorkshire, was born there in 1889. When he and brother Roland came to Canada, it was to buy a fruit farm in British Columbia but a Fort Qu'Appelle banker they met in Winnipeg argued convincingly that young Englishmen should get practical experience before purchasing. As a result Stanley hired himself to a Valley farmer at $10 a month and a few weeks later rode his first racehorse in a contest on the Fort Qu'Appelle street. The street terminated at the river and the boy's ill-mannered mount refused to stop, plunged into the water and swam to the other side. The rider's clothes were dampened but not his enthusiasm.

Came the First World War and Stanley Harrison responded to the call. Three times he was wounded and when home on leave, the armistice was signed. Perhaps now he'd become a public servant, work for the Soldier Settlement Board or something of the kind. But the answer was, "No, I'm going back to live on my little farm at Fort Qu'Appelle and read and write and raise horses."

It was as a horseman, a breeder of Thoroughbreds, that most western people came to know Captain Stanley Harrison. He judged at horse shows across the country and for years, he and his horses attended the race meets. Something noble and cultural about horses! Harrison said so and proved it. "The story of the horse is the story of civilization." He repeated the sentiment in verse:

"He shared the battle-wrath of ancient kings;
Assailed the walls of Babylon, arrayed
With hosts of Cyrus, scorning flame and slings
With lofty mien and spirit unafraid.
Clear through the song of history throbs the beat
Of swift and dauntless hooves in thundrous flight
To wrest some epic victory from defeat
And turn the darkness of despair to light.·
His brave 'Ha, Ha,' has mocked the stricken field
Where hope forlorn had triumphed over might.
No fear of peril would his courage yield
As barrage shells screamed through flame-split night;

And when at dawn the signal trumpet blew
Death's call—he did not fail the rendezvous."

The loss of his horse in the First Great War was the loss of a dear companion. Who reads his lines written at Passchendale in November, 1917, could have no doubt:

"Never shall I forget the first time I saw him there in the hills at home. Head uplifted, his brilliant eyes regarded me with kindly dignity. Ah, but he was superb! About him was a great shining, like a naked sword tempered in beauty and strength. Beneath his coat of rippling silk one sensed the soul of rhythm, and courage like white fire . . ."

"Nor that last hour shall I forget. Even as I caught his low whinney I knew the wings of Pegasus had touched his shoulders. There amid the rumble of guns, Death had beckoned. But there, too, was something greater than death, shining down through the long long trailing centuries of Time . . ."

"Beyond the cannon-mist I thought I saw him again, imperishable as all true beauty, one with the wind and sun, one with the glory of life—aye, and the glory of death."

"Remember him.
Somewhere in God's Own Space
There must be some sweet-pastured Place
Where creeks sing on and tall trees grow;
Some Paradise where horses go,
For by the love which guides my pen
I know great horses live again."

As women inspired Robert Burns to write his finest poetry, so horses sparked the pen of Stanley Harrison. Horses were fellow creatures for which his affection was natural. "How lovely and gentle are the little blood foals," he wrote. "In their babyhood I get my reward; to watch them playing like sprites in a sunbeam is a very real joy always."

And so the story about Harrison and his mare, Delia D, must be told. It was love at first sight. Harrison and a friend sat in the rotunda of the Kings Hotel in Regina one day in 1911, when a team hitched to buggy was driven by. Conversation stopped and Harrison leaped to his feet, saying, "Did you see that off mare? Excuse me, Mac, I must overtake her."

As good fortune would have it, the driver pulled up at a hitching post near the post office and there stood Harrison's dream horse, a beautiful chestnut, 16 hands, every inch a Thoroughbred, reared in Kentucky and pedigreed. Yes, the owner was willing to sell but he wanted $175 and Harrison had only five. He paid what he had and promised to have the balance by nightfall, even though he had to rob a bank to get it.

When the boys went to war, Delia D was placed in the care of a brother. She raised one foal and late in the war years strayed away. Another year went by. Captain Harrison came home in the fall and received a report that a mare resembling Delia D had been seen 15 miles away and had died beside a strawpile, leaving a most dependent chestnut baby, just two months old. Harrison could not rest.

He had no trouble finding the strawstack; there were the bones which dogs and coyotes had picked clean, and there was the wretched filly, dwarfed, reduced to a skinfull of bones, almost dead on her feet. How she had survived after being orphaned at such tender age, nobody could know, but day after day she had foraged for feed and returned at night to lie beside the bones of her mother.

Stanley Harrison had wet eyes when he saw the dejected thing but in its head he recognized it as Delia D's baby. Local advice was to shoot the emaciated wretch but he couldn't shoot anything that had done so valiantly to survive.

"Deadest thing I ever saw standing," one man commented, but the wee thing was placed on a stoneboat and brought home to the Stockwell barn where she was given the best of feed and the name Redwing. She began to improve. She and her older brother became pals, more than pals, and when the stunted filly was scarcely three years old, she gave birth to a foal to which was given the name Dusky.

It was another bad experience for the stunted young mother but the foal was vigorous and later when she began to show racing form and the unmistakable spirit of her dam, Dusky's name was changed to Merry Minx and she went on to win important futurities and become a distinguished performer on Canadian and American and Cuban tracks.

What a mare was Merry Minx! She was one of the few Thoroughbreds to survive an epidemic of fever that struck Harrison's horses in Cuba; she came out of a freight train accident, bruised and bleeding, but went on to Winnipeg and won her race. She was a worthy grandchild of Stanley Harrison's dream horse. "She was true and game and I loved her for it," he said. And she helped swell the purses won by Delia D's offspring to well over $40,000.

* * *

Harrison raised a lot of good Thoroughbreds and between the First World War and the second, he imported about 30 from England. It was a fortunate day when, in 1934, he secured the great stallion Pensweep which almost certainly inspired the verses entitled, The Stallion. That noble horse is in every line:

"With upflung head he watched the mares race by
To distant fields. His form a superb mould
Of life intense, and turned to breathing gold
By magic touch of Sun's weird alchemy.
Moist nostrils wide, his neigh rang shrill and high,
Voicing allure as beautiful and old .
As love itself, by myriad tongues retold
To shy wild hearts beneath a springtime sky . . .
Magnificent, he wheeled in futile wrath
And lip upcurved took solace from the wind;
Then flashing hoof sped o'er impounded path,
To stop, mid-flight, in attitude resigned.
His brilliant eyes now lit by leaping fire
Of lust in leash and passionate desire."

And then there was Bendy. "Oh Bendy, yes, a lovely mare with the heart of a fighter. She was swift and kind and belonged to the Delia D family too. She taught me one must love a Thoroughbred, not for what it does in the eyes of the world but for what it is in itself. She won three races in three starts and then fell on the track and broke a leg. They would have shot her but a gardener's wife who fed her carrots intervened, shielded the filly's frightened eyes from the sun and begged to give her a chance to recover. Bendy went to hospital and after six months she was all right except for one short leg and a stiff pastern. She was through racing but Bendy might have a career as a family mare. At first she was dogged by ill luck, dead twins, a dead single and then twins again. But her luck changed and she gave us five winners in a row. When Bendy grew old, we were not just man and horse; we were old friends."

* * *

Stanley Harrison's horses brought him thrills every day; even a drive in the snow was good for a poem and his Thoroughbreds triumphed over Saskatchewan's winter in The Cutter Team:

"Loose the bridles, let them go
Into wide and trackless snow.
Sleigh bells peal and runners lift
Over waves of blizzard-drift:
Spinning vapour clouds and clings
To the buckles, bars and rings;
Frosted white from throat to hip,
Beads of ice on lash and lip;
Heads upflung and mettle-crowned,
Limbs that spurn the swirling ground.
How those stifles bulge and flow
With each mighty driving blow!
Here goes life and fiery heart,
Winter's weary woes depart,
Vanquished by the blood that sings
Through the veins of equine kings."

A visitor to the Harrison farm had to inspect the horses, and then the birds, mostly canaries. The latter had cages but generally the cage doors were open so the wee things had the freedom of the house. Sure, they roosted on china cabinet and chesterfield and some extra housekeeping was necessary but Mrs. Harrison was good-natured about it and the birds enjoyed living. And the wild birds received as much attention as the tame ones.

"Never a wild wing cleaves my dawn-lit sky,
Never a leaf unfolds, nor sunrise flames
But mem'ry sings their laughter and their love."

When he went hunting, it wasn't with a gun. Long before he had sold his gun and bought a pair of binoculars. "How men can murder those lovely wild creatures is beyond my understanding." He found birds which were not supposed to exist in Saskatchewan. When he reported a mocking bird near home, a bird editor said "fantastic," but later, when two of that species were shot in the Qu'Appelle Valley, and proof was acknowledged, Harrison was furious. "Just to think," he said, "they had to shoot my friends to prove they existed. Not all the murderers have been hung."

His bird hospital became a community institution. School children and others brought injured birds and half frozen birds and Harrison would set broken wings and patch up gunshot wounds. There were as many as 18 birds in the hospital aviary at one time and Harrison discovered that many of the recovered birds refused to leave his stoop.

One of the little creatures with broken pinion was a bluebird and it refused to leave. And so, Topaz the bluebird moved into the Harrison house and took up quarters in the sunroom. From one of Harrison's letters: "Topaz is alternately on my shoulder pecking at my pipe and down close to the typewriter, making ribald remarks at the flying keys."

No bluebird should have to live without a mate, so a hunt was instituted and a bluebird's nest was discovered. One young bird was removed and in due course it too moved into the Harrison home to live with Topaz. Birds had no fear of the man. "I've discovered the purpose of those small round holes in storm windows," he said, casually; "they're to let the chickadees into the house in winter."

Perhaps he wasn't a master farmer by the score card but no one on the land was more fully and richly in tune with nature. Love of the land claimed him when he first saw the West. "I seemed to fade into the land itself . . . I knew a happiness that choked me."

Years ago one of his friends said, "Harrison the horseman will some day be better known as Harrison the poet."
His verses were exactly what Saskatchewan needed. The
Harrison hand which drove horses, pitched hay and repaired
broken birds, used a pen with the skill of a scholar and the
sympathy of one who knew the 'delight that comes on small
wings.' Proof is from the poem, Things I Love:

> "I love the sound of summer rain
> Murmuring through the drooping grain;
>> The gloaming mist,
>> The ridge sun-kissed,
> The low wild notes of a bird's refrain.
>
> I love the lines of a Thoroughbred—
> Clean-cut limbs and high-flung head;
>> A birch canoe,
>> A cornflower's blue,
> A drowsy sun in his fleecy bed.
>
> I love to think of the open trail,
> A throbbing screw or a scudding sail,
>> The morning haze,
>> A comrade's praise,
> The scent of hay in a new-mown swale.
>
> I love the song of the eager skate,
> A winter fire in an open grate,
>> The fireside talk,
>> A twilight walk,
> The kildeer's call when the hour grows late.
>
> I love the light in a woman's eyes,
> A singing lark in the quiet skies,
>> A crooning stream,
>> My secret dream . . .
> Of such is memory's paradise."

People elsewhere wanted him to move to Kentucky and
they wanted him in the East. He knew he could make more
money by moving and he'd get away from Saskatchewan

winters but his answer was, "No; I love the West and here I remain to breed horses and watch the birds."

"Tonight is almost full moon and I am sitting under a georgeous oleander that is lovely with scented blossoms," he wrote to a friend. "Through the wind comes the sound of rustling leaves wet with evening dew, and beyond my view, in the heart of the bluff a bird is singing divinely, the sweetest of all our common songsters, the little mocking-bird. Good night and good luck. If you get opportunity, do come down while the things that are worth while are at their best."

CHAPTER XIV

"MAJOR BILLY" OF BELL FARM
W. R. BELL

THE famous Bell farm at Indian Head, Sask., was a bold experiment in large scale operation—first of its kind in the North West Territories—and the man in whose mind the idea originated was William Robert Bell, better known at "The Head" as "Major Billy."

As the rails were laid westward, thousands of land-seekers flocked into the country to file on quarter-section homestead farms. It was Bell's reasoning that if a small farm could be made to show a profit a big farm should return big profit. It sounded logical enough, at least until somebody proved otherwise. It was for Bell to conduct the mighty trial, settle "whether large crops of grain can or cannot be grown here." (Nor-West Farmer, Feb., 1884.) And though his big farming enterprise did not survive long, it was a worthy landmark on the trail to imposing western achievement.

Behind the Bell Farm's Bell was United Empire Loyalist stock. Born at Brockville on May 28, 1845—same day his lumberman father lost a valuable raft of lumber on Lake Ontario and saw it float away toward the Gulf Stream—

William Robert grew up thereabout, attended school, captained the Brockville lacrosse team and joined the army to fight Fenians. He was a good soldier and after taking part in several skirmishes, he was decorated for bravery and retired with rank of major.

Like many men forsaking military uniforms, this one wasn't sure what he wanted to do or where he wanted to be. He went to Minnesota, then Winnipeg and westward. It was 1881 and the Canadian Pacific Railroad could carry him as far as Brandon but no farther. With a soldier's feet and legs, however, he was not stopped by lack of rails and he continued into the Territories.

Studying soil as he travelled he was most impressed by what he saw around a point marked only by an Indian skull suspended on a post and there he caught a vision of a big farm organized with some co-operative features. Back he went to Winnipeg, bubbling with enthusiasm.

Winnipeg friends and some English investors were impressed by the idea of a farm having unprecedented size and before a year elapsed, the Qu'Appelle Valley Farming Company was formed. By this time the route of the transcontinental railroad was known and Bell's choice of land was a block 10 miles square, extending seven miles north and three miles south of the point at which Indian Head was being located. A good bargainer, Bell obtained most of the land from the CPR and Hudson's Bay Company at one dollar an acre. An arrangement was made with the Canadian government to get the homestead land within the block and that gave Bell complete control of 100 square miles, except for land held by three squatters, one of whom proved especially tenacious, refusing to leave and refusing to sell.

As managing director, Bell organized his farm as he would a field force resisting Fenian attacks. Bell was the unchallenged officer commanding while Superintendent A. M. Rutledge had the duties of a captain, and farm foreman McLary, brought from Brockville, was like a first lieutenant. By 1884 there were eight assistant foremen and numerous bookkeepers, timekeepers and so on. One feature entirely new in agriculture: workmen could acquire equity in the farm by remaining in service.

* * *

No grass grew under Bell's feet. He was on the ground early in '82 and although there was no land ready for crop that year he brought oxen from Winnipeg and set his men at breaking with walking plows. In that first year of operations 2700 acres were broken and made ready for seed. When Angus MacKay arrived that season the Bell farm breaking was the first he saw west of the Manitoba boundary. Ox-drawn plows were working on the particular section which later became the Dominion Experimental Farm.

The spring of 1883 opened early. The company's 160 horses and oxen were put to work in mid-March and 12 broadcast seeders were in use. But an early spring was exactly what Major Bell wanted because there were endless jobs to be completed that summer, grain storages to be provided and stables, fences and cottages to be built. Twenty-two five-room cottages for married workers were erected that season, also a fine stone house and stone barn at headquarters. And more sod was broken.

In the month of June, Bell sent 40 three-horse sulky plow units to do the breaking and total cultivation was brought to 6000 acres. Some of the furrows of that season were so long that teamsters made only one round per day; they ate noon lunch at the far end of the furrow and barring breakdowns, were back to the starting point at night.

The first crop was reasonably good. Two outfits did the threshing and wheat averaged 20 bushels of No. 1 Hard per acre. The new storage bin with capacity for 30,000 bushels was full and bulging. Wheat was worth 88 cents a bushel at Indian Head or $1.25 for seed purposes.

When shareholders assembled for the annual meeting in Winnipeg on January 9, 1884, a fine spirit of optimism prevailed. The president mentioned dry season and early frost but attributed company success in escaping the latter to good seed and early planting. He reported scores of miles of fencing, six miles of trees planted for windbreaks, dams, roads, buildings and so on. Then, with typical western boldness, he took to forecasting "next year's crop," said it would be 120,000 bushels of wheat on the company farm. That the Bell farm expenditure for the year was $162,346.66 and from its beginning was $244,719.96, didn't seem to worry the confident directors.

Everybody was happy, even the men working for a big wage of $35 a month. Married men were provided with cottages and fuel in the form of wood hauled from Hurricane Hill reserve, 17 miles away. To do temporary work, Bell hired Indians, with the squaws performing the heavy toil and the braves collecting the wages.

The Major believed in feeding his men and horses well. The workers didn't get grapefruit for breakfast but they got all they could eat of vegetables, dried apples, rice, syrup, home-made bread and "rattlesnake pork." That pork from Missouri river pigs was highly regarded, even though the pigs' diets were supposed to include snakes. But while the food was good, the water was generally bad. Wells were shallow and in the fall when crops ripened, water in the wells did the same. But people hadn't heard about Bacillus coli and nobody died.

* * *

The year 1884 saw favorable growing conditions until close to harvest time when a heavy frost did severe damage. Nevertheless, spectators saw 45 "self binders" at work in one big field and they looked with some misgiving when all the binders and a small army of workmen were held stationary for several hours waiting for a trainload of overseas visitors who wanted to see the newest thing in harvesting. The machines were a sensation. According to a reporter present, the binders were doing "great execution in a wheat field expected to yield 30 bushel per acre." He mentioned also that the train to Indian Head had travelled at 35 miles per hour.

Seven steam-driven outfits threshed 130,000 bushels of grain that fall of 1884 but on account of frost and wet weather the sample was poor, some of the wheat was so damp it could not be marketed. Troubles were increasing. After erecting a grist mill in the hope that flour would sell more readily than wheat, there was the disappointment of discovering that flour sent to Montreal returned little more than the cost of freight. Some damp grain spoiled in storage and the balance was fed to pigs, 300 home-raised swine and 400 more which were bought.

Altogether, it was a poor year and financing became difficult. Directors now concluded that too much money was being spent but how could they stop it at this point? With all the self-assurance of a professor of economics, the Major could tell the cost of producing every bushel of wheat but in the face of obvious losses, it was poor consolation. The studies showed that wheat delivered at the Bell farm elevator had cost seven cents a bushel for labor, three and six-tenths cents for horse power, three and three-tenths cents for maintenance of laborers, and 20 cents for seed, depreciation and interest at eight percent. It totalled 34 cents a bushel but a lot of the frozen wheat wasn't returning that much.

Adding to the troubles of that year, 22 horses were stolen from the farm barns one night. Next day a posse of 10 men attempted to follow the thieves south but only an aged horse abandoned by the fleeing culprits was found. George Speerman, the new foreman, with five others set out for a more extended search and after an absence of three weeks, returned with 12 of the horses but not the guilty men.

Later in the year, however, a covered wagon drawn by a team of white mules called at the farm. The two men present aroused Bell's suspicion and the police were notified. They were arrested for illegal entry into Canada and in the wagon was found a horse halter bearing the Bell farm initials. The Major bought the confiscated mules and wagon and later sent the outfit to the Riel Rebellion of 1885 where it served as a field ambulance for General Middleton's forces.

The fighting up that way changed many things. Settlers' lives were in danger and the call for men and teams took priority over farming. Before the crop of 1885 was planted, Bell sent 50 teams to haul freight to the Duck Lake area. A man and team would earn $10 a day and that was more than they could make growing frozen wheat. And at General Middleton's request, Bell went to Qu'Appelle as transport officer, and farming was at a standstill.

"Major Billy" of Bell Farm: W. R. Bell

The troops knew Bell as a kindly but firm officer. He could find a horse and saddle for a person needing them but he had no patience with anyone shirking duty. When teamsters near Touchwood went on strike, Bell, knowing that delay would mean food shortages at the front, hitched a pair of ponies to a light wagon and drove all night. With two pistols in his hands, he talked to the striking teamsters, reminding them that this was war. Fifteen minutes after his arrival the freight was moving again and Bell headed back toward Qu'Appelle. One of his horses dropped dead on the trip but the soldiers got their rations.

When the war was over and the troops were returning east, General Middleton and his staff were entertained at the Bell farm where they saw stylish saddle and carriage horses which were the pride of Major and Mrs. Bell, 250 cattle, 900 pigs and more farm equipment than they had seen before—seven steam threshers, 45 binders, 40 seeders, 80 sets of harrows and numerous wagons and things.

* * *

The year 1886 was another dry one. The only good crops in the country were on land which had been fallow the previous year when most of the horse power was doing army duty. Angus MacKay had managed to keep the weeds down on his land and some of the Bell land was cultivated. It was a notable demonstration of what a year's holiday could do by way of moisture conservation. It was the beginning of the practice of summerfallowing.

But there were many reverses and on such a big farm the impacts seemed to be doubled and trebled. By 1888, some retrenchment was ordered. It didn't mean that Bell was quitting. The records show that in 1893 he was president of the Indian Head board of trade and, at the same time, harvesting 70,000 bushels of grain. But the big farm was being broken into private farms, big ones and small. A large piece was acquired by Lord Brassey who had been identified with the company and he operated it as the Sunbeam farm. And a section was bought by the Canadian government for the experimental farm.

Actually, Bell was thinking about experimental farms

and agricultural colleges long before either were established in the West. In 1885, a college building was erected and Bell went to England to secure students and a "noted professor." There is reason to believe the professor he wanted to be principal of his "college" was the well-known Primrose McConnell whose name had appeared on the Bell farm visitors' book.

That Visitors' Book, with dates ranging from 1884 to 1895, would be a study in world personalities, and fortunately, it has survived the years. English peers, Austrian counts and Anglican bishops were coming and going much of the time. At least a third of those names appeared must have worn monocles, and there were times when a session of the British House of Lords might have been convened right there at Indian Head. Some came to hunt, some to see the wonders of Bell farm and some to enjoy the Major's hospitality.

The last signature in the visitors' book was made on December 1, 1895.

The crop had been severely damaged by frost and it was then that Major Billy retired from active participation on the land to which he had brought notoriety. But he didn't retire; he went to Ireland, plunged into the development of the Irish peat bogs for fuel. Next, he went to the Bahamas and became interested in lumber, and finally, back to Winnipeg.

Still he didn't really retire. He was interested in a coal mine in Alberta and a gold mine in the east. And prior to his death in Winnipeg in 1913, he was working on a galvanized iron granary, patented with some new ventilation features for use in western wheat fields.

He was an athlete all his life, a member of the first Canadian team to take part in the Wimbleton rifle competitions, an inventor and a man of brilliant personality. But it was his farm, as big and as broad as his imagination, that won world attention. And while it was not a financial success, it was an important experiment with land, climate, seed, methods, machines and other things and it did much to attract attention to the prairie soil.

CHAPTER XV

SITTING BULL ON CANADIAN SOIL

F OR lovers of Canadian scenery, the Cypress Hills in Saskatchewan's south-west offer special attractions. In the midst of a vast sea of level prairie, the Hills rise as an island, distinctive in topography, climate, flora and fauna. And for those who have discovered the charms of western history, there'll be added delight in the beautiful valley setting of old Fort Walsh, Mounted Police post for some years after 1875.

There, the police cemetery, the big trees and the very soil beneath the visitor's feet seem to whisper secrets about frontier adventure. In studying the rebuilt Fort Walsh, now a horse-breeding station for the Royal Canadian Mounted Police, one cannot escape the association between the old post and that Indian bad-boy of some score years ago, Sitting Bull. The center of association is the rebuilt log structure in which was held the notable conference between Assistant Commissioner A. G. Irvine of the police, General Terry of the United States Army and Sitting Bull, in which the Sioux war chief was urged to take his hungry tribesmen back to the United States whence they came.

But why was that much-feared Indian on Canadian soil? The answer: to escape vengeance of the "long knives" or United States soldiers. It was Sitting Bull who led the Sioux Indians in that tragic fight known as the Custer Massacre beside the Little Big Horn river in Montana in 1876, where General George Custer and his American soldiers engaged a big band of Sioux and were cut down, every one. Custer was foolish; it was his hankering for military glory more than good judgment that drew him into that battle, the last major victory for the North American Indians. The triumphant Sioux, knowing the United States Army would seek revenge with an overwhelming force, fled northward and crossed the "Medicine Line" into Canada.

Part of the tribe came to Wood Mountain in what is now the province of Saskatchewan late in 1876 but it was in the following spring that Sitting Bull and the main band followed. The Manitoba Free Press of March 5, 1877, carrying news that Sitting Bull had crossed the Canadian boundary at Wood Mountain with a large group of warriors and over a thousand horses and mules, sent a wave of fear over the prairie communities. The very name of Sitting Bull was enough to strike terror in the hearts of people who read the accounts of Custer's last stand. Settlers shuddered to think that here was a ruthless killer with a strong following of warriors and altogether some 5000 hungry and disgruntled natives, proposing to take residence in the new homestead country.

But was Sitting Bull the ruthless scoundrel that many people had him painted or was he quite a reasonable and wise Indian whose love of freedom would induce him to fight for it?

*　*　*

To the Indians, birth dates and birth places were unimportant—not worth remembering—and in failing to keep his vital statistics, Sitting Bull was no exception. Hence, information about his origin is only approximate. Presumably, he was born somewhere in the Dakotas, about the year 1834. Throughout his life he was frequently on the Canadian prairies and as much at home there as farther south. At first he went by the name, Sacred Stand, but it wasn't appropriate for a fighting man and, after proving himself a warrior, the name was changed.

His first fight of consequence was at the age of 16. After taking an enemy Assiniboine prisoner, the young warrior received a leg injury from which he remained lame. The prisoner and prisoner's horse were sent back to the Sioux camp as trophies of war and thereafter, the young brave was known as Lame Bull or Sitting Bull.

Many years later, when held as a prisoner at Fort Randall in Dakota Territory, the aging chief was induced to sketch the story of his life as he remembered it. The first sketch, crudely drawn, showed that initial conflict with the Assiniboines in which he captured a warrior, and another engagement that netted him five Assiniboine women, all of whom he fed and released to return to their people—at least, that was his story. The battle with General Custer, however, Sitting Bull refused to sketch.

Sitting Bull was still a young man when courage won him leadership and he became war chief. After the battle with Custer, he was on the defensive more than ever and hoped to get a better deal on the Canadian side. Upon arrival at Wood Mountain, he at once sent word to Assistant Commissioner Irvine at Fort Walsh that he wished to hold a talk. Irvine and a few of his men set out by wagon, no doubt a bit anxious about how to approach the notorious Indian. Instead of meeting hostility, however, the Mounted Police officer was greeted with outstretched hand.

Displaying a silver medal his grandfather received for fighting for King George III at the time of the American Revolution, Sitting Bull wanted permission to remain and strengthen his claim to Canadian residence. At the same time, the squarely-built Sioux admitted worries about food for his people; the buffalo numbers were dropping rapidly at that time and the Indians were hungry.

Irvine couldn't promise permanent sanctuary in Canada but assured the Chief that as long as his people behaved themselves, they need not worry. With such re-assurance, Sitting Bull led his people to a spot 20 miles east of Fort Walsh for a Sioux sun dance, where they made their petitions to the Great Spirit and young men in breechclothes danced until exhausted and qualified for the high rank of "brave."

Still, no Canadians were happy about the prospect of 5000 Sioux Indians as steady boarders and even the people in the United States had a lingering feeling of uneasiness. Americans concluded that until Sitting Bull and his band settled down to a peaceful way of life on a reserve, settlement of Northern Montana would be delayed. And so, there began a long series of attempts to persuade the Chief to return.

* * *

In a Calgary collection of private papers left by Commissioner Macleod of the Mounted Police is a letter to his wife, dated Fort Walsh, October 12, 1877, which reads: "My Dear Mary; I have just got back to this place with Sitting Bull and a lot of his chiefs. It was quite a job getting them this far, they are so very suspicious. However, here they are, safe within the fort, about 25 of them. I expect General Terry at the Boundary on Tuesday and am going out to meet him myself . . . Jim."

But the proud Sitting Bull refused to shake hands with the United States general. He did not trust the "long knives," and that conference and some others failed. Whether it was fair criticism or not, the Sioux Chief accused the Americans of turning the buffalo herds as they migrated northward and in so doing, trying to starve the dependent Sioux Indians into submission.

As long as the Indians were hungry, they were likely to be difficult. The most tense moment in Mounted Police dealings came when Major Walsh was called to settle a dispute over stolen horses. The Indians lost horses and suspected theft. The Police were unsuccessful in solving the problem but the Indians located the animals with privately owned horses near Willow Bunch.

Since the Police had not found the horses, the Indians decided their own people should be able to arrest the men who were holding the lost stock. That's exactly what they did and held two men prisoners. Young Mounties sent to the Indian camp decided against trying to force the prisoners' release but the display of weakness annoyed Walsh and with only an interpreter with him, he set out for the Sioux camp.

At first Sitting Bull refused to release the prisoners, arguing that he was capable of administering justice, but Walsh, facing the Indian mob, stepped up to the Chief, siezed him and told him he was a prisoner of the police. Strangely enough, there was no violence and Sitting Bull, filled with admiration for the policeman's courage, smiled and said, "All right; you can take your white men."

But the food situation grew worse rather than better. Buffalo numbers continued to decline. The Indian plight was desperate. The Mounted Police did what they could but the Indians were many. Father Hugonard, priest at the Mission in the Qu'Appelle Valley, witnessed their destitute state.

He had just received 24 bags of flour from Fort Ellice and Sitting Bull's people camping nearby, heard about the supplies. Within hours, the priest had visitors—a whole yard full of mounted men, decked in feathers and paint and carrying guns. The priest tried to be friendly and Sitting Bull and 20 head men entered the house.

They wanted flour—had to have it to save their people. The priest explained that the flour was not his personal property and therefore some payment would have to be made. Then the bartering began. Sitting Bull offered his blanket; five other chiefs offered short pieces of wood, each of which was to represent a horse; and others offered watches taken from the soldiers who fell in the Custer affair. But as the priest discovered, the watches were out of order, the Indians having removed the wheels for use as ear-rings.

107

But in spite of the sad state of the watches, the Indians got their flour and it helped briefly. Again the Mounted Police proposed that the Indians would be better off if they returned to the United States. The Chief was adamant —still hoping his people would be recognized as Canadian Indians, still suspicious that a powerful United States force would exact vengeance. By this time, he had developed a fine respect for the word and counsel of Jean Louis Legare, trader at Wood Mountain. The French Canadian's dealings with the Indians showed him friendly and fair and Sitting Bull said, finally, "I will ask Jean Louis; if he says it is safe, I will return with my people."

Jean Louis' advice was to return and surrender to the United States officers at the boundary. That, Sitting Bull agreed to do and about midsummer, 1881, as the railroad was being built westward across Manitoba, the Sioux Indians broke camp and, accompanied by Legare and a few Mounted Police, moved southward.

* * *

A few tribesmen were left behind and they were finally granted a reserve. But Sitting Bull and the main part of his band were back on United States soil and Canadians breathed sighs of relief. It had to be admitted, however, that during four years in what is now Saskatchewan, the Chief with a bad reputation behaved himself very well.

When Major Walsh wrote his annual report for 1880, he had a good word for the Sioux: "The conduct of these starving and destitute people, their patience and endurance, their sympathy, the extent to which they assisted each other and their strict observance of all order, would reflect credit on the most civilized community."

For the white settlers on the Canadian side, Sitting Bull's departure marked the end of a chapter but the storms of life were not over for the fugitive Sioux. Sitting Bull and his people were allotted a reserve in the Dakotas. For people with their wild, free spirit, it was hateful to be settling on a limited reservation and Sitting Bull found it as terrible as any. It was difficult to love the white people who had made him a fugitive for years and in 1890, there was another wave of resentment. He was accused of fomenting hatred among his people and an order was issued for his arrest. It wasn't an order an individual with Indian ideals of freedom could accept readily and on December 15, 1890, Sitting Bull was shot to death in his resistance.

Some of the reference books say he was a bad Indian whose life was one of murder. But as the Police and others knew him in Canada, he was quite a reasonable gentleman whose strong and courageous views about freedom, really made him a good Indian.

CHAPTER XVI

LIVINGSTONE IN DARKEST ALBERTA
SAM LIVINGSTONE

WITH 14 children and a mountain range bearing his name, Sam Livingstone, resident of Calgary before there was a Calgary, can never be forgotten. When a party of Mounted Police rode north from Fort Macleod to build a fort at the junction of Bow and Elbow rivers in 1875, squatter Livingstone was there to greet the men— probably the only spectator as Mounties drove stakes in the ground where a city was to arise.

Surviving pictures show Sam Livingstone as a man everybody would want to know—buckskin jacket on his broad shoulders, long hair suggesting a 40-year boycott of barber-shops, and a kindly face partially buried in whiskers. The one time he had his hair cut, he caught a bad cold. What the whiskers couldn't hide was a twinkle in his Irish eyes, the twinkle of a man who once resolved never to spend two birthdays in the same place.

But after roaming over much of the North American

110

continent, he did settle down, the Canadian foothills, a growing family and farming opportunities round about, combining to change his mind. And so Sam Livingstone became one of southern Alberta's first farmers, grew oats, barley and livestock on land later occupied by the Chinook race track and the man-made lake behind Glenmore dam. There the old soldier of fortune built a home, broke the first sod for miles around and had the nerve to plant fruit trees.

After a man has lived long in the wilds where such civilizing conveniences as calendars are unknown, it must be understandable and pardonable if he forgets his age. In Livingstone's case, either he forgot the year of birth or chose the popular frontier custom of disclosing as little as possible about the past. This much is clear, however: he was the son of a parson of the Church of England and born in that bit of old Ireland of which Thomas Moore wrote, "Sweet Vale of Avoca! How calm could I rest; In thy bosom of shade, with the friends I love best."

At the age of 16, Sam Livingstone left home, sailed from Liverpool to test the newness of America. What he did in and about New York where he remained for a while is not clear but 1849 found him with a party crossing the continent by wagon-train to join the search for gold in California. In other words, he was a "Forty-Niner."

If he discovered much wealth in California, he certainly didn't hoard it. This affable young fellow had more interest in adventure than in wealth. He travelled south into Mexico and eastward on the plains to hunt buffalo. While on one of those prairie hunts he had his first serious brush with Indians. It is not clear whether he offended them or they, like some less savage modern males, couldn't resist a scalp with long blonde hair. Anyway, the pursuit by red men was said to last six weeks and it was in the retreat northward that Livingstone saw Canadian foothills for the first time. It may have been this occasion, when he outdistanced his pursuers, that he scratched his name on rocks in the mountains, an action which led to the naming of the Livingstone range in the Rockies.

Then another gold rush—this time to the Cariboo country in the British Columbia interior. Sam Livingstone couldn't resist a gold rush and even in his later years, when he wanted relaxation or holiday, he went panning gold. But he didn't stop long in the Cariboo. Within a year he continued northward to the headwaters of the Peace river and made his way downstream, not knowing where he'd stop. But there was hardship on the journey and rations were inadequate, leading him to remark he hoped he would never again have to live on coyote meat and hawk soup.

Along the way Sam traded with Indians when there was opportunity and this took him to Fort Edmonton, Victoria which was northeast of Edmonton, and south into the foothills. According to George Edworthy, the tall and erect frontiersman met Rev. John McDougall at Fort Edmonton about 1865. Sam, at that time, was trading and keeping pigs, no doubt the first representatives of the swine race in that part. About the same time, too, he met Miss Jane House, member of an old Red river family and granddaughter of Jasper House for whom Edmonton's Jasper avenue was named, and shortly there was a wedding, with Rev. George McDougall officiating.

Now that Livingstone had a wife, travel had to be curtailed, at least limited to those freighting trips he made now and again with a string of Red River carts to Fort Garry and sometimes south toward Fort Benton. A cart trip to Fort Garry would now only keep him away about four and a half months.

About 1873, he opened a trading post in the Jumping Pound district, west of the confluence of Bow and Elbow rivers. But Sam Livingstone was nothing if he wasn't versatile and when he wasn't trading he was doing something equally exciting.

During the first winter after the Mounted Police came to Fort Macleod, he contracted to furnish buffalo meat to feed the newcomers. When meat supplies were adequate, he'd haul freight for the police. Freighting trips into Montana at that period afforded varied experiences, some not comforting to contemplate.

At one point he was commandeered for vigilante court duty. A suspected cattle rustler had been captured and the six self-appointed officers of law-enforcement, called vigilantes, were divided in their views about punishment; half of the group voted for hanging the offender without further delay or ceremony, while the remaining three members were not quite as impetuous. Livingstone was ordered to be the seventh member of the jury and on his vote the course of action would be determined.

Sam considered carefully and on his deciding vote, the suspect was released. Quite probably, the man was a criminal but Livingstone's merciful judgment was one that brought its own reward a short time later.

It was this way: Sam was proceeding northward toward the Canadian border, his carts loaded with freight for Fort Macleod. A lawless band of mounted men swooped down upon him and held him up at point of gun. What the gunmen had in mind will never be known—probably robbery or murder—but at the moment of greatest tensity, the leader of the badmen recognized the Livingstone whiskers and long hair and exclaimed: "That's Sam Livingstone; let him go." To be sure, Sam was delighted to go. The gang leader was the man whose life he had spared from a countryside hanging.

* * *

Livingstone, who had seen much of the western world, had an obvious preference for the country about the confluence of Elbow and Bow rivers. It would become a great agricultural country, he believed, and when the Mounties dropped into the valley of the Bow to build Fort Calgary in 1875, Livingstone was on the spot, preparing to build a homestead home. Sam was there first and might have insisted upon his squatter's rights but he was a strategist as well as a trader and withdrew in favor of the law, selecting and building on an alternative site north of the Elbow and a few miles back from the mouth. His first buildings were on a flat beside the river, now flooded by water held behind Glenmore dam, and his first cultivation was on an island in the river.

Later, the pioneer took a section of land on the other side of the Elbow and built a bigger house to accomodate a bigger family. In that log house, a portion of which stands today west of Chinook race park, the last of Livingstone's 14 children, six girls and eight boys who grew to maturity, were born. Most of the children were taught by private teacher who lived under the Livingstone roof. And the big house was one that dispensed hospitality to all comers including Canada's governor-general, the Marquis of Lorne, and scores of travellers who remained nameless.

Sam Livingstone found himself a neighbor of the Sarcee Indians. Of course, nobody knew the Indians or understood them better and he was on good terms with them. On one occasion he was suspected of being too friendly with them. It was just after the fighting started at Duck Lake in 1885 and Sam seemed to know a lot about Indian conversations and manoeuvres.

The white settlers about him whispered that Sam must be sharing confidences with the insurgents. Police were told to watch him; "he may be siding with the half-breeds and Indians and plotting to help them." But such fears were groundless as the police soon discovered; Sam Livingstone had merely been "eavesdropping" on Indian smoke signals. He knew the Indian language and Indian signs and smoke signals about as well as the natives did.

It is really not surprising that squatter Livingstone with so many children to feed, became the first tiller of the soil at Calgary. He was serious and progressive about it, owned the first mower and hay rake in the country, having carted them in from Fort Benton. Then he introduced the first threshing machine and drove it by horsepower. He raised pigs and his cattle, increasing to over 300 head, carried one of the oldest brand marks in the province, "Quarter Circle L," used in recent years by George Edworthy of Calgary.

When Charlie Jackson, as Calgary's first dairyman, began peddling milk on the streets, using a five-gallon can and a dipper of uncertain capacity, the product was from cows borrowed from Sam Livingstone. And Livingstone was almost certainly the first to plant fruit trees in what is now

114

Alberta. The Calgary Tribune of April 1, 1887, reported: "Mr. Sam Livingstone informs us that all the fruit trees he set out last year show signs of life so far."

When Calgary's first agricultural society, parent of the present exhibition and stampede with annual attendance exceeding half a million, was formally organized on August 22, 1884, Sam Livingstone was among the directors. Sending exhibits of grains and vegetables to the East to convince skeptical folk there about the capabilities of western soil and climate was a major project with the young agricultural society and when one of the first displays was sent to the Toronto exhibition, Sam Livingstone accompanied it.

To the Easterner who visited the display, the most fascinating feature about it was Sam, himself. He could tell most convincingly about gold rushes, buffalo hunts, long-distance freight trips lasting months, about how it felt to be chased by Indians brandishing scalping knives, and about the richness of the western soil. The eastern people listened with intense interest and observed that the story-teller looked like a man uneasy to get back to his domain beside the mountain river.

Somebody commented that Sam Livingstone was a practical fellow who never lost a day from sickness in his life, and when he had to die, "he did it up in a hurry." On October 8, 1897, he drove to Calgary for a binder repair, took ill on the street and went into the Windsor Hotel where he died almost immediately. Even then, his long hair was a bright gold in color and to the last he was active and vigorous. Had he lived a few months longer, he'd have heard about the gold rush to the Yukon, his years notwithstanding, he'd want to go.

In reporting his death, the papers gave his age at 67 years, but members of his family were sure he was 70 at least. However, it didn't matter about his age—more important that he was an attractive part of the Old West, the trail blazer, courageous and kindly. Nothing could be more fitting than Livingstone as a name for a range of the Rocky Mountains.

CHAPTER XVII

THE NAME IS CAMPBELL
GLEN CAMPBELL

IF EARLY Manitoba had anything resembling a Tom Mix or Gene Autry, the distinction would go to one who ranched and farmed close to the Riding Mountains, Glen Lyon Archibald Campbell, six feet four, built in similar proportion, soldierly in bearing, magnetic in personality and daredevil in nature.

Anyone with the ability and versatility to command a war-time battalion, make pretty speeches in the House of Commons and manhandle a bull moose, must be seen as a candidate for western honors. But the story about Glen Campbell cannot be separated from that of his father. If an adventuresome spirit is hereditary, Glen Campbell could not have escaped it. The father, Chief Factor Robert Campbell, was one of the exciting characters in the service of the Hudson's Bay Company, one who chased sheep from Kentucky to the present site of Winnipeg and pursued the fur trade into the far reaches of the northwest where the foot of white man had never before made a mark.

Robert Campbell was born in Perthshire in 1808 and

there he grew up on a sheep farm. When 22 years old he applied for the post of sub-manager of an experimental farm being started by the Hudson's Bay Company in the 18-year-old settlement at far-away Red river. The position was awarded to him and, after 48 days at sea, he stepped ashore at York Factory beside Hudson's Bay, from where it was still a four-week trip to Fort Douglas on the west side of the Red river. Robert Campbell was at journey's end on September 22, 1830.

The Selkirk Settlement was a small world apart in which peace reigned intermittently. It had two mail deliveries a year, a church minister or two, one doctor and no lawyer. Governor George Simpson of the Hudson's Bay Company ruled about as well as could be expected in unorganized territory. As for the new experimental farm, it was about three miles west of the forks of the two rivers and Chief Factor McMillan, a distant relative of Campbell, was supposed to be in charge. Upon Campbell's arrival, practically all the farm responsibility was given to him.

Anxious that settlers should become as secure and self-sufficing as possible, the Company was determined to put sheep to the test for the second time. Twenty-one Merino sheep were brought with the settlers in 1812 but dogs, coyotes, Indians and poor care accounted for losses and failure. Now, Campbell was told to hold himself in readiness to travel south with a party to buy sheep. It would not be the first time a Campbell had travelled southward and crossed a border in search of sheep but this time, the trip could be made by daylight.

The purchasing commission consisting of 10 men, saddle horses and two carts loaded with provisions, left the settlement on November 8, 1832. As they might have suspected their travels were a mixture of good fortune and bad. They escaped various Indian war parties, one of which followed for three days, but they missed the late season Mississippi river boats which might have sped them on their way. Abandoning the carts, Campbell's party took to sleighs and then canoes and reached St. Louis, some 1500 miles from home, after 56 days of travel.

117

But no sheep were available there so the party divided to continue the search farther on. Finally, sheep were located in Kentucky and a band was bought at prices ranging from five to seven shillings per head. After several months, men and sheep—1370 sheep and lambs in the flock —started the long and tedious overland journey to Red river. Ten or eleven miles a day was the usual speed but there was trouble ahead—no end of it.

There were flies and maggots to worry the sheep and there were rattlesnakes to claim a few. But worst of all was the dreadful scourge of spear grass. In June the sheep were suffering so much from the spears that the shepherds decided to stop and shear, hoping that the removal of the wool would reduce the severity of the menace. But shearing made no difference and sheep died or had to be destroyed daily.

By early July only half the sheep remained and on August 11, the count was down to 295 head. The long and perilous drive which started in Kentucky on May 2, ended on September 16 when 251 sheep survivors reached the Selkirk Settlement. Regardless of the extent of its success, this undertaking by pioneers of Western Canada was probably the longest and most ambitious sheep drive in history.

Campbell continued in charge of the sheep for a time and then, in May, 1834, he was transferred from the experimental farm to the fur trade. The Company wanted a courageous man for the Mackenzie river district. "Don't get married," wrote Governor George Simpson, "we want you for active service."

Indeed, Robert Campbell's years in the northwest were filled with activity. He established post after post for the Company, overcame Indian hostility, discovered and named a few rivers and cultivated the friendship of "a fine looking Indian chieftainess about 35 years of age." Moreover, he nearly starved during some of the winter months but nothing prevented exploration and business expansion.

* * *

When Campbell finally confessed to an interest in marriage the Governor, anxious to keep him on the job without any waste time, volunteered to hand-pick a bride for him in Scotland and bring her out. Campbell, however, made it clear that he preferred to make his own selection, even though he had to snowshoe a big part of the way to Scotland. He left Fort Simpson on November 30, 1852, travelling on foot and by the following March 13 he was beside the Mississippi river, 3000 miles from starting point.

Scotland, when he finally arrived, looked good to him but nothing loked as attractive as the lassie he wanted to marry. Parents said she was too young and perhaps she was; but Campbell knew she'd outgrow such a handicap and promised to wait. Six years later she sailed from Liverpool and on August 5, 1859, married Robert Campbell at Norway House.

Early in 1863 the Campbells were transferred to the Swan river district, with headquarters at Fort Pelly and there, on October 23 of that year, Glen Campbell was born. He was a robust youngster and from the time he could walk, about as fearless as a kodiak bear. When he was seven years old, mother and children went to Scotland where Mrs. Campbell died and the motherless children were taken by an aunt in Perthshire.

Glen attended Glasgow Academy and Merchiston Castle School in Edinburgh. It was a good education but when schooling was completed he lost no time in returning to the scenes of his childhood in Manitoba. He was 19 years old and already planning to be a rancher. Realizing a need for practical experience in his chosen field, he drifted to Montana where he learned to ride and shoot and cowboy with the best of the range men. Then, after a couple of years, Glen Campbell returned to raise cattle on the Riding Mountains where he and his father had secured land not far from Gilbert Plains.

About home, those people who enjoyed hunting flaws in human character found the young Campbell a good subject. They said he was wild, that the curse which fell upon the Campbells when they murdered the MacDonalds at Glencoe had fallen squarely upon Glen. What he really had was boundless energy and a dislike for convention.

His urge to experiment led him to bring some of Scotland's West Highland cattle to graze on his hill pastures. The shaggy, hardy specimens which he and his father imported from the heather-covered hills of Western Scotland were the first of their kind in all of Western Canada and they took to the Riding Mountains like hot pigs take to mud. The trouble was that after fraternizing with the Manitoba elk, they became almost as wild and some had to be shot in the hills in order that their meat be recovered.

Some of Campbell's Highland cattle were sold to Fred Stimson of the Bar U Ranch in the Canadian foothills, about 1886, and in 1894, Campbell sold two carloads of his Highland cows and heifers to E. D. Adams for his ranch southwest of Calgary. The Highland breed failed to gain a permanent place in the Canadian cattle country but Campbell's pioneer experiments with it had lasting value nevertheless. The animals were slow in maturing and relatively light in weight but they were hardy and some of the best steers to come out of the foothills in the 90s were four-year-old half Shorthorns from Campbell cows.

Then came the Klondike Gold Rush, attracting venturesome men everywhere. Glen Campbell, determined to go, sensed a north country demand for pack horses. Always an able horseman, he bought ponies and bronchos of a type considered suitable for the miners and took them to Skagway and farther. Horses not sold at Skagway were taken over the Chilkoot Pass and on to Dawson City. It was a terrible undertaking as the bones of an estimated 3000 horses scattered along the "Trail of '98" would indicate. At one point, Campbell's men ran short of rations for themselves and were reduced to boiling the sinews of their snowshoes. But Glen Campbell didn't scare easily and he forgot hardships quickly. The spirit of the man was demonstrated in Winnipeg when, faced with a serious operation, he refused anesthetic, said he wanted to watch.

* * *

So conspicuous and colorful a citizen could not expect to escape politics. In contesting the Dauphin constituency in the provincial elections of 1892 and 1896, he was beaten by his Greenway opposition but he was elected to the legislature in 1902 and again in 1907.

The politics of Campbell's day were inclined to be rough and pioneers around Dauphin have told about one of his opponents who sought to smear Campbell's character; the straight-laced fellow said there were just two kinds of Campbells, "the bloody Campbells from Glencoe and the lousy Campbells from elsewhere." Glen Campbell had no intention of debating his past or anything about clan traditions but when it was his turn to speak at the joint candidates' meeting, he confessed he had made mistakes but, "at least I never broke my leg when being thrown out of a bar-room."

The other candidate sprang to his feet and amid waving of arms and display of wild temper he said he never had a leg broken from being thrown out of a bar-room; in fact, he had never been in a bar-room. Glen Campbell replied calmly, "I only said, 'I never had my leg broken by being thrown out of a bar-room'." The audience roared with laughter and was drawn unmistakably to Campbell.

In 1908, he resigned from the legislature and was elected to the House of Commons. At Ottawa, he created one sensation after another. He was a good speaker but a bit unpredictable. After listening to a speech in which an eastern member used endless big and ill-chosen words, Glen Campbell rose in his place and made a speech in Cree Indian, mixing a little Latin with it.

But the members of the House of Commons listened with unusual attention when Glen Campbell related a hazardous ride on the back of a Riding Mountain moose. He came out of a tree, lighting on the animal's neck, and notwithstanding frantic antics on the part of the bull to shake the parasite off, the powerful young rancher made his hold secure and reminded himself that he had no hope of dismounting in safety while the moose's strength remained. Glen Campbell braced himself for a long ride— long enough to completely exhaust the bull. It was a new experience for a bull moose but Campbell's plan worked all right—many miles away the moose fell exhausted and Campbell had a long walk home.

* * *

When the First World War broke Glen Campbell was no longer a young man, but in opposition to medical advice, he was determined to go. At that time he was chief inspector of Indian agencies for Canada. The life of a soldier was not new to him; he had served with Boulton's Scouts in 1885 and was raised from the ranks to a captaincy on the field.

At the outset of the Great War, he volunteered to raise a western battalion, completed the recruiting of the 79th, a Brandon unit, then started another, the 107th. Campbell then went overseas and into the trenches in France. Wherever he was, the giant rancher leading his men was an impressive figure, and men in the ranks were never asked to go where Lt.-Col. Glen Campbell would not lead. But life in the trenches disagreed with an old kidney disorder and Glen Campbell died over there in October, 1917. He was buried in a Canadian cemetery in France.

It was part of his philosophy that nobody should let himself get too busy for some play. Hunting was one of his pastimes and few people could equal his skill. When he hunted coyotes, his aim was to kill without making a bullet hole in the pelt. When he mounted to a saddle, it took a very superior horse to unseat him. And when the boys at the local school needed a new football, it was to Glen Campbell that the need was communicated.

In his broad-brimmed hat or out of it, he was the hero of his frontier. And in the Riding Mountain country, the Indians, the oldtimers and those who were boys when he went to war, still talk about "Big Glen." He was educated in Scotland and buried in France, but he was born in the West of Canada and there his heart was, always.

CHAPTER XVIII

PRINCE OF WESTERN SHOWMEN
GUY WEADICK

A T High River, not long ago, they buried that prince of western showmen, Guy Weadick, one whose name is forever linked with the development of rodeos and stampedes in Western Canada and elsewhere.

It was a funeral service not soon to be forgotten. Bad roads failed to prevent a big attendance as people came from far and near in the cattle country; Guy's favorite saddle mare occupied a place of honor in the procession and seemed to understand the meaning of, the riding boots reversed in the stirrups; and the soloist sang "My Little Grey Home In the West." It was just as Guy Weadick would have ordered it and his last resting place was that section of the continent which came closest to his heart.

In any parade of western personalities, there must be a place for that tall, lean cowboy, voted by at least one group of observers seated comfortably in a plush room of a Calgary hotel, as "the most romantic figure to ride across the Canadian range." Nobody carried a western hat or high-heeled boots or colored shirt any better and nobody was more loyal to the traditions of the range. He helped Tom Mix to get started, called Will Rogers and Charlie Russell by their first names and, in many ways, seemed tailor-made for association with their kind at Hollywood. But he elected to do his cowboying on the bigger and greater stage of the western grass country.

He was not a native son, did not take up residence in Canada until his maturity. But as an adopted son, he quickly became a part of the land of his choice and scarcely could anyone have become better known.

Guy Weadick was born at Rochester, New York, in 1885. His people were Irish in origin and the family traditions were in the profession of law. Elders hoped to see young Guy become a practicing lawyer and become wealthy but they were disappointed. The lad was fascinated by stories of the West and he was determined he'd be a cowboy.

Before he completed public schooling, Guy's mother died and a short time later, the boy ran away from home. Which way did he run? Anyone who knew him would be able to guess; for a boy who dreamed about life in a stock saddle, there was only one way to go—west. He was in Montana a while, learned to ride and rope and talk the cowboy language. In 1904, in company with a horse buyer, he saw Canada for the first time, having crossed from Montana and stopped at the Blood reserve, south of Fort Macleod. The visit was brief but Guy had a premonition he'd be back for a longer stay. In the very next year he was back in Alberta, this time sharing blankets with that negro cowboy, Will Pickett, the man who introduced "bulldogging" as a rodeo event.

Story has it that Pickett's first bulldogging was unplanned and unwelcomed. As he stooped to pick up a pouch of tobacco on the ground, a petulant Texas steer spotted him as a perfect target and charged. There was no time to plan a scholarly defence and the negro, sensing his only chance to survive the wicked onslaught, seized the big critter by the horns and wrestled him to the ground. When Pickett did it as a public act at Calgary some time later, springing from a galloping horse to grab a pair of long horns and throw the steer, it was the first time a Canadian audience had witnessed such a display.

With Guy Weadick as manager, the Pickett show was taken to Airdrie and other Alberta points. Encouraged by public interest, Weadick and Pickett added bucking horses to their show and went on to Winnipeg, but that city was disappointing. Negotiations with the Winnipeg Exhibition failed and the two barnstorming showmen decided to make their own arrangements. They quartered their rodeo stock at a Winnipeg park, presuming everything would be safe in that respectable old city. But even Winnipeg wasn't entirely free from rustlers in that period and when Weadick and Pickett went to give the animals their morning feed, cattle, horses and saddles were gone; thieves had taken everything.

Weadick was described as a "one man show," even in those years but he couldn't stage a rodeo without a horse.

One show had failed but another was about to begin —the search for stolen property. The cattle were located at the stockyards and it was learned that a band of horses was being driven southward at a fast pace. Weadick and Pickett took train to Emerson, crossed to United States territory, picked up the trail of horses near Pembina and finally located the stolen animals in a livery stable not far from there. The thieves were arrested and jailed but recovery of the horses was complicated by legal red tape and the two showmen decided to go on to Chicago for a holiday. Actually, the fates were being kinder than Guy realized; at a wild west show in that city, he met Miss Flores La Due, a performer later accorded a world championship for fancy roping.

For the first time in days, Guy found it easy to forget the loss of his rodeo stock. Miss La Due was a fancy roper, sure enough, but more than roping was fancy about her. Guy became attentive and before long he threw his lariat neatly over the lady and she became Mrs. Weadick.

* * *

Together the Weadicks went to bigger things in show business—Broadway, a tour of Europe, Buffalo Bill's Wild

West Show, and so on. Good stories have been told about Guy's escapades in Europe. One with the cowboy reckless-ness of Weadick could scarcely travel across that continent without disturbing the calm of the Old World.

From a Paris stage, so it is told, Guy joked about the exorbitant price he was obliged to pay for a shave and the Parisian barber, taking the remarks as a reflection upon his honor, challenged poor Guy to a duel. The cow-boy, never one to walk away from a challenge, said, "Sure, I accept on one condition—that I choose the weapons." The challenger agreed and Guy said "Fists." Evidently the barber had never considered a fight at that level but fists were the instruments of combat and, while nobody was killed, anyone knowing Weadick would have strong views about the probable victor.

There is another story, about Guy making a reckless boast that he could take his saddle horse to the top of the Eiffel Tower. A Frenchman offered a bet that it couldn't be done and Guy covered it before realizing the difficulties. Details about how the man from west of the Atlantic over-came the physical and diplomatic obstacles are lacking but he said he won the bet and established a new altitude record for horses in that section of Europe.

Back on North American soil, the Weadicks rejected an invitation to go into movies, but when Miller Brothers, Oklahoma ranchers, staged their Wild West Show in West-ern Canada in 1908, Guy and wife were riding and roping in it. The show in Calgary gave Guy some new ideas. He talked with H. C. Mullen, livestock agent for the Canadian Pacific Railway, and they agreed that Calgary would be a good place for a big annual, cowboy field day, one at world championship level.

Nothing came of the discussions for some time but Weadick and McMullen kept in touch with each other and in March, 1912, Weadick was back in Calgary. He had a pal with him, a young fellow, not well known at that time, Tom Mix by name, just killing time before going with Cummins' Wild West Show.

Between McMullen and Weadick, Calgary heard much

about the proposed rodeo. It would have historical and entertaining value, they contended, and it could become a frontier classic. The major problem would be in financing. Business people were interested but not to the point of risking their own money in it. Obviously, both cost and risk of loss would be high.

At this point the "Big Four Cattlemen" appeared in negotiations. George Lane of the Bar U Ranch was most receptive and told McMullen as they sat in the old Alberta hotel that he would talk it over with "a couple of friends." The friends were Pat Burns and A. E. Cross and very next day a request was made to the Calgary Exhibition for the use of Victoria park. Things moved along with encouragement and A. J. McLean came in with Lane, Burns and Cross and together they backed the project to the extent of $100,000. Their one stipulation was that the show must be a good one and all competitions fair and honest. It was settled; George Lane would be chairman and Guy Weadick, manager.

Weadick began work on a rodeo blueprint and what a plan he drew! Two hundred Mexican Longhorn cattle were secured from a herd imported by Gordon, Ironside and Fares and grazing on the Blood reserve. The sum of $15,000 was set aside for purchase of the wildest horses available and 300 really mean ones were obtained from A. P. Day of Medicine Hat. Day, incidentally, was to be arena director. Then, with Frontiersman Fred Kanouse in charge, a replica of notorious Fort Whoop-Up was erected to make the old whisky traders feel more at home when they visited the Stampede. And every member of the original force of Mounted Police who could be located, was invited to attend at the expense of the organization. Prizes were big—$20,000 in all—unprecedented at that period.

The dates were September 2 to 7 and Weadick publicized it as the greatest show of the age; and as it got under way, it was living up to claims made for it. The street parade was such as Western Canada had never witnessed. Contestants came from everywhere and competitions were for "world championships." Most of the major wins were taken by rodeo-experienced cowboys from the United States but not all. There was rejoicing when Tom Three Persons from the Blood reserve won the championship for bronco riding.

The Duke and Duchess of Connaught were special guests and artist Charlie Russell was there with paintings. It was a rousing success. But in spite of triumph, Calgary didn't repeat the event for some years. Guy Weadick roamed about the continent, promoted and managed a big rodeo in Winnipeg in 1913, saying: "The money is here; come and get it. The best man wins irrespective of where he comes from or what his color may be." A cowboy vaudeville in London, England, was a part of the Weadick enterprise at that time and he introduced the stampede to New Yorkers in 1915.

* * *

At length, the Calgary Exhibition directors recognized opportunity in the stampede as a feature and in 1923 the cowboy classic was merged with the regular show and Weadick was named to manage the rodeo section. In this capacity he continued until 1932. There was some unpleasantness in connection with his ultimate separation from the Exhibition and Stampede but that was forgotten in a short time. But before leaving the Calgary post, Weadick bought a ranch on the Highwood river, above Longview, about 35 miles west of the town of High River. He called it Stampede Ranch, a proper name to which no one had a better claim. To it he retired to ride the range, run cattle, entertain guests from many parts of the world, and write his stories. Sure, he "wouldn't give a damn for a man who couldn't spell a word more than one way," but he had something to write about.

People at High River have their own way of doing most things and on August 9, 1950, after it was known that Guy and Mrs. Weadick were going south for reasons of health, they planned an unusual picnic. It was a "Guy Weadick Picnic" and friends from far and near gathered to pay tribute to two famous citizens. Indian chiefs from Canadian reserves and across the Montana boundary were there in brightest clothes and cattlemen from prairie and foothills ranches and business men from Calgary and neighboring towns made it an impressive gathering.

Chief Simon Big Snake spoke for the Stoneys, Sarcees, Bloods and Piegans, saying, "We have known Mr. Weadick since big show of 1912 . . . As long as rivers flow and grass grows green, we will not forget him." Then, after the Blackfoot chief presented beautiful beaded gifts, there were other presentations, among them a gold cigarette case containing a cheque for $10,000 from "a nameless group of friends and admirers." Of friends, no one had more.

He was "Mr. Cowboy" of Alberta and on his funeral day, somebody quoted a verse from the pen of the great cowboy artist, Charlie Russell, and sent in an early letter to his friend Guy Weadick:

> *"Here's hoping your trail is a long one,*
> *Plain and easy to ride,*
> *May your dry camps be few*
> *And health ride with you,*
> *To the pass on the Great Divide."*

CHAPTER XIX

FIGHTING FARMER FROM SINTALUTA

THE "Great High Priest" of Canadian agriculture for many years was Saskatchewan's W. R. Motherwell, whose story holds a lesson for everybody. As his province's first minister of agriculture and, later, as Canada's minister of agriculture for nearly 10 years, Motherwell had opportunities in nation building but no amount of administration and responsibility could draw him away from the soil for which he had an enduring love. In certain farm circles he was dubbed "Statesman in Overalls," because of the dignity he continued to bring to the working clothes, just as to a Prince Albert coat and to his office in the House of Commons.

It has been suggested before that the story of this young homesteader who arrived on the prairies by ox-team in 1882 and became the wise and unselfish spokesman for agriculture could very well be prescribed reading for young people, across the West at least.

"W.R." as he was known to neighbors before he became "Honorable W.R." and Doctor Motherwell, was precisely what the homestead country needed. He belonged to a vigorous and self-reliant strain or he wouldn't have gone homesteading in that year when rails were being laid west of Brandon. The robust manhood seen on the frontier brought him pride but, at the same time, he had strong views in support of co-operation. Most of the time, a gentle person, yes, but how he would fight for a principle. He'd fight for farmers' rights and it was just such an encounter in 1901 that led to the birth of the Farmers' Movement; he'd fight for conservation of soil and trees, for his views about temperance and for anything he believed to be right.

A political associate recalled one of his last fights in Ottawa. It was against Prime Minister Bennett's redistribution bill which was about to pinch Mr. Motherwell's constituency seat. Adding force to his objections, he brought his cane down upon the Prime Minister's desk with such force that the cane broke in a dozen pieces and he added caustically, "I may still have a seat but no place to put it."

* * *

Just why this man who ultimately had the clearest voice in Canadian agriculture came to the remote homestead country is not clear. As a bright young fellow just out of the Ontario Agricultural College, he didn't have to go homesteading. He might have returned to farm with comparative comfort in the home district in Lanark county in Ontario. With college diploma tucked under his arm, he might have accepted professional work in the settled east. But decision was to go west to the end of the railroad and perhaps further.

He halted briefly at Winnipeg to earn some needed dollars, working for the Canadian Pacific Railway, and in the spring of '82, he was driving a pair of sulky oxen and a cheap wagon westward from Brandon. Every time the oxen stopped to graze, Motherwell was examining the soil, wondering how much farther he should go. A hundred miles or so along the trail he swung the "bulls" northward and crossed the Qu'Appelle valley. Finally, close to where the village of Abernethy was to be located, he resolved to stop and farm.

131

The first chore was to build a sod hut for himself and another for the oxen. Then he began to break sod but there was embarrassment about that. He was a little ahead of the survey and evidently his calculations were not strictly accurate because, before noticing a mistake, he plowed up all of one road allowance and part of a neighbor's land.

The error wasn't serious, however, because there was lots of land. More important was the fact that his first crop was frozen and almost a total loss. The need for livestock was more apparent than ever and Motherwell went to Ontario, returning with some grade cows and a purebred Shorthorn bull. Homesteaders for miles about drove to the Motherwell place to inspect the bovine marvel, a bull with a pedigree certificate, and at the first Indian Head fair, the splendid brute captured prizes totalling $10. That was a lot of money and homestead neighbors wondered how the owner would spend so much. But he surprised them all and according to his telling, be bought a wedding ring and quit baching.

* * *

Came the Riel Rebellion and homesteader Motherwell turned to freighting between the CPR and the scene of fighting. He needed all the money he could make that way because farming wasn't rewarding. There were two major difficulties, one frozen crops and the other, trouble in selling a crop when it was harvested. Homesteaders were being gypped when they marketed their crops; they had trouble getting service from the railroad and the people who bought the grain took unfair advantage. Motherwell's part in the campaign for justice is one of the interesting chapters in his life.

It was this way: Farmers wanted to avoid the heavy work of shovelling grain into cars by hand and, to encourage elevator construction at country points, the railroad company offered practically monopoly privileges to anyone who would build. It worked well until operators began to take advantages which monopoly made possible. Farmers were at the mercy of the buyers and obliged to sell grain at whatever prices and on whatever grades were offered.

Prices appeared too low, dockage excessive and weights

unjust. Complaints caused the government to intervene and the Manitoba Grain Act, intended to regulate the whole grain trade, was passed in 1900. Thereafter, any farmer who was dissatisfied with offers from an elevator would at least have the right to load the grain by hand, just as he did before elevators were provided.

But in the next year, the farmers found themselves in as much trouble as ever. When they wanted to load by hand as a protest against elevator treatment, they were denied freight cars and were back in the clutches of the elevators. Obviously, there was collusion between the elevators and the railway and with a big crop in the country and elevators full, the farmers were worried and irritated.

Late in the fall of 1901 a few farmers came together in Indian Head to talk things over. Motherwell was among them. Some days later, he and neighbor Peter Dayman burned midnight coal oil together and agreed the time had come for farmers to organize and take a stand. That same night, Motherwell drafted an invitation to farmers round about to attend a meeting at Indian Head on December 18, at which a proposal for the formation of an association of grain growers would be considered.

On that particular date, as it happened, the premier of Manitoba and the premier of the North West Territories were at Indian Head to take part in a debate about changing boundaries of Manitoba and farmers for miles around were in town. The farmers held their meeting first and with Bill Motherwell as provisional president, they took the first step in organizing the Territorial Grain Growers' Association. The farmers were enthusiastic and a month and a half later, the new body held its first convention at Indian Head, with Motherwell being confirmed as president.

* * *

Now, the 1902 crop was a big one and, when the season for delivery came around, it was quite evident that farmers were going to have the same trouble—perhaps more of it than ever. Railway cars were not being distributed fairly according to the Manitoba Grain Act and while elevators could get cars for loading, farmers couldn't.

Motherwell and Dayman went to Winnipeg and secured

133

pretty promises that things would be better. But they weren't better and Motherwell and his fellow-officers decided to take action. They brought suit against the elevator agent at Sintaluta and charged failure to allot cars justly. It was a test case, quite obviously, and as revealed rather recently, the farmer named in the case was W. H. Ismond who lived three miles north of the Motherwell farm.

The hearing announced for Sintaluta became the talk of the countryside and on the appointed day, farmers from far and near came to town. They hardly dared think they could win against a mighty railroad company but they wanted to be there anyway; at least, the farmers' case would get an airing in public. But strange as it seemed, the farmers did win their case and the station agent was fined $50. The railroad company appealed, and lost again. The homesteaders were the victors in the most widely publicized legal battle of that time and Motherwell was their leader. The Grain Growers' movement spread pretty fast after that and Motherwell's faith in co-operation was vindicated.

* * *

His popularity spread like the new movement itself and in 1905, he was persuaded to stand for election to the new provincial legislature. He did stand and won easily and became the first minister of agriculture for Saskatchewan, a cabinet post he retained for 13 years, during which time his department had to be built, the agricultural college at the University of Saskatchewan was being created and important farm policies had to be defined for a rapidly developing province.

For Saskatchewan they were 13 important years. Then, in 1921, Mr. Motherwell was elected to the House of Commons and immediately, Prime Minister Mackenzie King invited him to join the cabinet as Canada's minister of agriculture. It was an excellent selection because Motherwell understood the problems of farming in both East and West. Many of the agricultural services offered today were introduced by him, grading services, for example, and the search for rust resistance in grain varieties.

The University of Saskatchewan made him Doctor Motherwell and nobody deserved an honorary degree more completely. In 1930 he retired from the office of minister of agriculture but remained to represent his constituency in parliament for another 10 years. By that time he was 80 and said, "When a man drops out at the age of 80, people can't say he's a quitter."

Fact was that nobody could ever say William Motherwell was a quitter. Had he been of feeble heart, he wouldn't have stayed with the homestead after a succession of frozen crops; he wouldn't have remained with his Territorial Grain Growers to see the movement become mighty and he wouldn't have remained in politics to become Canada's agricultural leader.

And even after his retirement from public life, his interests were as broad as ever. If anything, his life-long concern for the welfare of soils increased. To him, the very life of the nation was wrapped up with agricultural soil and he pointed out time and again that the great expanses of fertile farm land capable of supporting crops and livestock are Canada's richest treasures. "You must make these soils last forever," he would say. "Nothing can take their place."

A letter written shortly before he died at the age of 83 was a dramatic plea to one of his friends to miss no opportunity to preach the message about preserving our soil resources, our water and forests. He was wishing he were younger to start a campaign to grow more grass to hold and rejuvenate soils. That letter, written exactly 60 years after he ox-teamed his way to the Qu'Appelle valley, carried the message of an ardent guardian of the soil, "passing the torch" of conservation to others who would accept it.

In 1902, grain merchants in Winnipeg called him the "Fighting Farmer from Sintaluta," but he earned other and more dignified titles, best of all, "The Grand Old Man of Canadian Agriculture."

CHAPTER XX

THE RIGHT HONORABLE "R.B."

THE West furnished one Canadian prime minister, Richard Bedford Bennett, better known as "R.B." and ultimately, "Viscount Bennett of Mickleham, Calgary and Hopewell." Actually, he was called by many names and not all flattering but, call him what they would, he stood as one of the finest examples of success by dint of sheer determination. Story has it that he made a youthful declaration that he intended to be a great lawyer, a millionaire and a prime minister. Whether that was really his three-point goal or not is hard to say but "R.B." was a man unusually determined in purpose and such sweeping ambition must seem entirely plausible. In any case, his story is one with which Canadians should be familiar.

Perhaps it is too soon to make a final appraisal of his statesmanship. That must be left to the writers of history and they're never in a hurry. But all who knew him would testify to his strength of character, high ideals and personality distinctiveness, all of which he carried into his political life. If, as we've been told, he promised his mother he would never take intoxicating drink, no power on earth could induce him to swerve from the resolution. At a certain Calgary reception for the Prince of Wales, when guests were instructed to charge their glasses and drink a toast to His Royal Highness, at least one of those present drank it in water—R. B. Bennett, of course. And when one of his political campaign managers told him that a supply of whiskey was needed or a certain group of votes would be lost, Bennett replied, "It's unfortunate, but they'll have to be lost."

Those who were close to him would tell that he was a temperamental fellow and sometimes he was annoyingly impatient and irritable. Perhaps he was a lonely man. He became a man of wealth and was generous with his gifts to needy people and institutions but, even as a millionaire, he did not outgrow the frugal habit of saving bits of scratch paper and pieces of string.

And sense of humor? Yes, he had it but his humor was of an intellectual type and often it went unnoticed. In his dress he was immaculate, seemed "tailor-made" for a morning coat and wing collar. Folk said he was the first man to appear on a Calgary street wearing a frock coat and top hat—and he may have been the last in many years. In addition to having the first plug hat, he had one of the first automobiles, with which he crashed into the Imperial Bank on Stephen avenue, wrecking his magnificent one-cylinder car, and though he owned other cars, he never again drove one.

* * *

As one might have guessed, "R.B." was a Maritimer in origin, a New Brunswicker to be exact. His people were of United Empire Loyalist stock and the father operated a small shipyard at Hopewell Cape on the Bay of Fundy. There the boy was born in 1870 and there he went to school. But even as a lad he wasn't an average specimen. Being unusually devoted to studies and Sunday school, he had no time for sports. Even then he was a serious fellow and at the age of 16 he left home to attend normal school at Fredericton.

A school at Irishtown, near Moncton, provided the first job with pay but teaching was only a stepping stone to Dalhousie university, and law. On graduation he went to Chatham, N.B., to become a junior partner to K. J. Tweedie, later Premier Tweedie in his province. An interest in politics was immediately evident and young Bennett was elected to the Chatham town council. It was during years there that he met and formed lasting friendships with John and Jennie Shirreff, through whose devotion Bennett inherited a controlling interest in the E. B. Eddy company.

But how did it happen that this young man became a Westerner? It was like this: Senator James Lougheed of Calgary wanted a bright young lawyer for junior partner and Dean Weldon of the Dalhousie law school told the Senator about Bennett, explained how this recent graduate had championed the cause of an old trapper who had been jailed for poaching furs. Believing the old man to be innocent, Bennett, with no hope for reward, took the old man's case through to the Supreme Court and won his release. Said Senator Lougheed, "that boy'd make a good Westerner."

And so, early in 1897, Richard Bennett stepped from a westbound train onto Calgary's muddy streets and set his law books out in neat piles in Senator Lougheed's office. At once the natty young lawyer created a stir, especially among mothers of eligible daughters. What the ambitious mothers couldn't know at that time, however, was that this particular bachelor had a skin no feminine dart would ever be successful in piercing.

Almost at once he was in politics. Shortly after arrival, he and Senator Lougheed went to a political meeting in downtown Calgary at which Frank Oliver from Edmonton was speaking. Midway through the lecture, the newcomer Bennett interrupted to offer a correction and ask a question. The reception to this interjection was mixed. Some voices called, "Put him out," and others demanded that he go to the platform to make his comment. He ended up taking the platform and making the best speech of the evening.

That led to his nomination and election to the legislative assembly of the North West Territories in 1898, retaining the seat until the provinces of Saskatchewan and Alberta were formed in 1905.

        *   *   *

At Regina, where the Territorial meetings were held in those years, folk called him the "Boy Orator," and sometimes, Richard "Bonfire" Bennett. It was obvious that he belonged in politics; he loved the smoke of political battle; he was an effective debater—none better at that time.

He lost in the first provincial election in 1906, but in 1909, Calgary sent him to the provincial legislature and in 1911 to the House of Commons. In the legislature, he led the opposition. He opposed the selection of an Edmonton site for the provincial university and in criticizing the government's railway policy, he established a record in oratory that most people hope will never be broken or exceeded—a speech lasting exactly five hours. There is no information about the number of suffering legislators to remain in their seats for the full five-hour treatment; but one thing sure, though of ill-chosen length, the quality of the speech would be high.

Bennett was a great and thorough lawyer but it was in the field of federal politics that he rose to the most distinguished heights. As in most political adventure, disappointment mingled with success. In a reconstructed Meighen government at Ottawa in 1921, R. B. Bennett became minister of justice, but in the general election of the same year, his Conservative party suffered set-back and Bennett, running for the Calgary West seat, was among the defeated. In the elections of 1925 and '26, however, he was elected with big majorities, and at the national convention in Winnipeg in 1927, Bennett was chosen to lead the Conservative party of Canada.

With characteristic vigor and thoroughness, he began rebuilding the party and in the election of 1930, the Conservatives were victorious and Bennett became Prime Minister of Canada.

The five years, 1930-35, during which he headed the government, were difficult. They were depression years and, in the West, drought was an added tragedy. Unemployment, mounting debts, and country-wide suffering in those grim times led many people to changes in political viewpoint. Bennett's philosophy changed, too, and by 1935, he had plans for some major economic reforms. Speaking to the people of Canada on January 4, 1935, he disclosed a four-point reform program to reduce unemployment, give support to health insurance and a remodeled old age pension plan, gain a better distribution of wealth through taxation, and provide uniform laws governing minimum wages and maximum working hours. He had faith in capitalism as the best system for a vigorous people but he saw defects and wanted to correct them.

"I am for reform," he said, "and in my mind, reform means government intervention." And then there were phrases, typically Bennett: "I nail the flag of progress to the masthead. I summon the power of the state to its support."

It was an election speech, sure enough, but in the election following, the tide of public opinion was running against the Bennett administration. Canada had been sick and even the Prime Minister admitted it, "sick unto death," but given the right treatment, there would be complete recovery. He was confident.

As Prime Minister, he worked hard and ruled with firmness. But when the votes were counted in 1935, his party was defeated and R. B. Bennett became leader of the opposition, a position he held until 1938 when he resigned to retire from public life. In the next year he went to England to live in a country home on Juniper Hill, near Mickleham in Surrey, and be a neighbor of his old friend of New Brunswick years, Lord Beaverbrook.

In his leaving Canada where he acquired wealth and fame, many people were disappointed; but he, too, had been disappointed and may have had a little resentment in his heart. His administration in the depression years was criticized severely; the term "Bennett Buggy" was a sarcasm and personal wealth made people feeling the full sting of depression, say with scorn in their voices, "He is a rich man!"

To the fortune he created by his own efforts was added a big share of the E. B. Eddy pulp, paper and match interests of Hull, Quebec, which he sold in 1943. How did he come by those interests? Jennie Shirreff, his friend of early years at Chatham, married E. B. Eddy in 1894. She inherited her husband's fortune and by the terms of her will, 1007 of the 3000 shares in the company were left to her brother and 500 to her "friend for the past 30 years," Richard Bedford Bennett. Mrs. Eddie died in 1921 and when her brother died in 1926, his Eddie shares passed to Mr. Bennett, giving him a controlling interest in the rich company.

But nobody could say the Bennett wealth wasn't used for worthy purposes. In 1943, a million dollars were presented to Maritime and western universities. Dalhousie, from which he graduated in law, received three-quarters of a million; Mount Allison received a substantial gift and the University of Alberta was given a hundred thousand dollars to provide scholarships for students from Calgary and district. Being cautious with his money was natural to him; he never spent frivolously, but he was not mean. In political adventures, he preferred to pay the cost of his campaign from his own purse and thus be asured of independence. Gifts and charities were made quietly, as such should be made. He was the sort of man who would work vigorously to convict an offender and send him to penitentiary but, as it happened on one occasion, when he discovered there was a widowed mother concerned, he supported her quietly for several years.

Some folk said he had no sentiment. That was not so. No mother had a more devoted son ,and on entering the House of Commons, he wrote to his mother, saying, "All I am and all I ever expect to be, I owe to you." And on trips to Calgary in later years, usually his first calls were to the children's wards in the hospital and the Woods Christian Home.

In 1941, this noted Canadian living in England, was raised to the peerage. He became Viscount Bennett of Mickleham, Calgary and Hopewell. One more of the goals he set for himself was achieved.

There at his home in the English countryside he died

on June 27, 1947. Richard Bedford Bennett had lived a full life and demonstrated a resolute determination with qualities of inspiration about it. The inscription on a Bennett monument in Calgary's Central park says, "His devotion to Canada and the Empire was steadfast and enduring."

Those who were on his side in politics and those who weren't, agreed to his fine intellect, memorable debating power and well-won place among the great sons of Canada.

CHAPTER XXI

REGINA'S DAVIN

THE East had its famous orators, like Joseph Howe and D'Arcy McGee—spellbinders and able men. Somehow, it has been overlooked that the early West had them, too, one of the most brilliant being Nicholas Flood Davin who started the Regina Leader and was the paper's owner and editor from March, 1883, until March, 1887.

In the House of Commons, where he sat to represent the constituency of Western Assiniboia for 13 years, and out of it, he was a controversial figure. Some people called him "Mr. Tempest," because of the political storms he was able to foment with striking regularity. But for clear thinking and bold speaking, Davin had no peer in his time. And when he adopted the West and the community of Regina, he was ready to fight their battles, single-handed if necessary.

He met his death under tragic circumstances in October, 1901, and now, a little over half a century later, only a few citizens show interest when his name is mentioned. But that only increases the importance of recording something about the dashing journalist, orator and Member of Parliament who left vivid marks upon the youthful and impressionable face of the prairies.

143

Before adopting Canada, Nicholas Flood Davin was an Irishman, born in Tipperary in 1842. When the father, who was a country doctor, died, Nicholas Flood's hope for a good education seemed to vanish and, reluctantly, he left school to learn the trade of an iron-worker. By a stroke of good fortune such as only a young Irishman could anticipate, a distant relative with means was attracted by the boy's obvious literary talent and offered to help him gain further education.

The lad resumed studies, graduated from Queen's college at Cork and in 1868 was called to the English bar. Friends said he would make a good lawyer but for reasons they could not comprehend, his inherent interest was in journalism and gradually he found himself doing more writing and less legal work. As war correspondent for the Irish Times, he was sent to cover the Franco-Prussian war and won praise for his work until wounded and sent home.

* * *

It was his talent as a descriptive writer that brought Davin to Canada. As a special assignment he was to report on the interest Canadian people had in joining the United States. Canada was in the grip of political and economic trouble and there was, unquestionably, a fairly strong body of sentiment favoring annexation to the neighboring nation.

He was in Canada for the express purpose of reporting the situation for the English papers, but at a Toronto meeting at which the merits of seceding to the United States were being debated, he was invited to speak. Perhaps a reporter should be without prejudice but there was no question about where Davin stood on the issue and he wasn't one to hide his views. The opportunity to address a meeting was one he waited for and he waxed eloquent. To the embarrassment of the publicized and featured speakers, Nicholas Flood Davin's forcefulness and Irish humor completely won the audience.

Immediately there were other demands for him to speak at meetings. Catching a vision of Canada's destiny, his decision was to remain in the country. Sir John A. Macdonald heard about him and sent a message of encouragement. It influenced him to accept a nomination prior to the general election of 1878, to run in an Ontario constituency. There he was defeated and probably that was fortunate because, had the result been otherwise, he would never have adopted the West. Several non-political assignments followed, one of them to Washington, studying the organization of industrial schools for Indians.

But in 1882, Nicholas Flood Davin was in the West—to stay. Early in the next year, Regina was named the capital of the North West Territories and about the same time, Davin started the Regina Leader as a weekly paper. The primitive community was not quite ready for an editor with the Davin touch and may not have appreciated him fully. Before long, however, it was evident that Regina needed a fighting spokesman, especially when Winnipeg papers embarked upon a campaign of bitter criticism of the site chosen to be the territorial capital. The editorial exchanges of that period make interesting reading, even today.

The Manitoba Free Press of September 11, 1882, said: "That Pile of Bones lacks every one of the essentials for a city, or even a modest market town—wood, water, drainage facilities, a surrounding agricultural country—is a fact which no amount of booming will remove. . . . At the present moment the creek is not more than 12 inches deep. . . . Every stick of wood for fire or building purposes will have to be brought in by railroad or dragged a distance of from 15 to 20 miles. . . . It may be trumpeted and boomed without end, having no solid basis, it will topple to pieces like a house of sand. . . ."

The Winnipeg Sun, September 16, 1882, added in somewhat more self-righteous terms: "We feel sorry for Regina. It got a bad name. . . . The place itself, it would appear, is not as black as it has been painted."

Davin explained, as soon as he had opportunity, that all the mature editors had quit Winnipeg and the office boys were writing the editorials. When the Winnipeg Sun carried the view that Regina was dead and "the town beyond resurrection," Davin replied in tones of sadness: "Poor, God-forsaken, bankrupt Winnipeg."

The man was noted for his short and caustic remarks, conveying as much as most longer speeches. "A cabinet of antiques," he said of a group in government in which he had no confidence. And when one of his acquaintances made the statement he could govern Canada as well as Sir John A. Macdonald, Davin snapped: "Phipps, if you had a secretary, you could govern the universe."

* * *

The appearance of the Regina Leader did much for the new town and the homestead districts for a hundred miles or more on all sides. Editor Davin became the self-appointed champion of the prairie settlers. He told Ottawa what was wrong with immigration and homestead policies and what should be done about the administration of Indian affairs. He demanded better representation for the West and almost at once his paper's circulation soared to 5000.

The paper carried news, the editor's views on every important topic, and some needed humor for frontier consumption. From the very first issue, dated March 1, 1883, readers were assured that, "The humblest will receive justice at our hands and the most powerful can expect no more." Among the items of special importance in that first issue was one about schools: "The first school has been started in Regina . . . we hope to see at an early date a noble school house in Regina. Meanwhile we wish Miss Laidlaw all success."

Then there was an item of cheer concerning Moose Jaw: "Our advice from Moose Jaw describes the ambitious town on the banks of the creek of that ilk as going ahead. It now contains 30 houses and four stores . . . Moose Jaw is 40 miles from Regina; Hamilton is 39 from Toronto. There is therefore room enough for Regina and Moose Jaw in this portion of the North-West." Not as serious were editorial observations to bring smiles to homesteader faces on the plains, that "a man in St. Louis who has been drunk for 20 years, died within a few hours of sobering up. What a terrible lesson to those who are thinking of sobering up." And concerning matrimony: "Marrying a deceased wife's sister is not an infraction of divine law but it is, nevertheless, an attempt to dodge the responsibility of two marriages by having but one mother-in-law."

When Davin wasn't writing copy, he was making poetry

or practicing the art of politics. He seemed to be created for politics. He looked the part of statesman and his platform manner was captivating. A resident of early Regina recalled attending a political meeting at which Davin spoke for three full hours and "nobody in the audience left the hall."

* * *

In 1887, he was elected to the House of Commons for his constituency of Western Assiniboia, a riding covering a big part of what was later the Province of Saskatchewan. He was one of four members from the North West Territories, the others being W. E. Perley for Eastern Assiniboia, D. H. Macdowall for the District of Saskatchewan and D. W. Davis for the District of Alberta.

Somebody suggested that if the West of that period had six Davins to represent it, the Canadian capital would have been moved to the banks of the Wascana. But even with the gifts of oratory and statesmanship, nobody won political contests easily in that period of hard-fought campaigns. In the election of 1896, when Wilfrid Laurier came to power, Davin won his seat with a majority of one vote, that crucial ballot having been cast by the returning officer.

Three days after that election, Davin was still trailing and believed beaten but there was still one ballot box to come in over the trails from Blackstrap Coulee, up near Saskatoon, from where Dr. Willoughby was bringing it. In due course, the Blackstrap box arrived and the result gave Davin a slight advantage but there was a re-count and the vote was declared "a tie." It was then that the returning officer, Dixie Watson, exercised his right, cast a deciding vote for Conservative Davin who took his seat on the opposition side in the House of Commons.

If powerful and sustained oratory could have achieved it, Davin should have won any election, easily. To him, it wasn't a speech unless it lasted two hours, and it wasn't a good one unless it was well prepared, polished and loaded with fancy phrases. But in the general election of 1900, the great orator was defeated, defeated by Walter Scott, the ambitious young Liberal, to whom he had sold his Regina newspaper.

147

Important as Davin's contribution was to public life, there were those people who wished he had devoted more of himself to the enrichment of Western Canada's literature in that period. He had the talent for poery as well as prose and left just enough to prove the point. Deep sentiment lay in his verses:

And lovely memory searching through,
Found no such stars in the orbit past,
As the glad first greeting 'twixt me and you,
And the sad, mad meeting which was our last.

He was in Winnipeg just about a year after his political defeat, when he met his death, October 16, 1901. Some lines written several years before, suggesting emotional strain and fatigue not commonly recognized were repeated:

As for me, I'm time-weary,
I wait my release.
Give to others the struggle;
Grant me but the peace.
And what peace like the peace
Which death offers the brave?
What rest like the rest
Which we find in the grave.

Nicholas Flood Davin wasn't fully appreciated by the people about him. It was easier to be impressed by his capacity for controversy than by brilliance, poetry and oratory.

CHAPTER XXII

CLAD IN BUCKSKIN

THERE'S nothing wrong with the name Waterton gracing the lovely national park in Alberta's southwest corner but good reason could have been given for calling it Kootenai National Park or Kootenai Brown National Park in honor of that buckskin-clad scholar and adventurer who selected the location for his home and became the first park warden.

His real name was John George Brown but the Indians called him "Kootenai" and that name suited him better and linked him forever with that part where prairies and mountains meet. When Brown looked down upon the place of almost undescribable beauty, he said: "This will be my home." It was the climax to travels on four continents and as the first white man to settle thereabout, he believed with some justification that he had a proprietary claim to the nearby mountains and lakes. Obviously, nobody had a better claim.

Legend has intertwined itself in the story of his life. It's to be hoped nobody will ever insist upon separating all the facts from the fiction. Perhaps no such separation is possible. He was born in the Old Country, close to Balmoral castle and, as a boy, played with children from England's Royal household. According to story, he had the additional distinction of having punched a certain prince on the nose to cause royal blood to drip from it. Formal education was completed at Eton and Oxford and then, entering the Imperial Army, he was posted to the Queen's Lifeguards.

One thing certain, the days were never dull when John George Brown was about and that applied to both the earlier and later parts of his life. Whether fighting, hunting or making love, he did it with convincing vigor and sometimes the consequences were unhappy and unhealthy ones for him. It's told that while still in the Lifeguards, John George Brown became "too friendly" with some of the ladies of the Royal Court and he was unceremoniously posted to India where his charms would be less of a threat to palace decorum.

* * *

In India, this tempestuous soldier didn't escape public attention for long. Nobody expected he would. There was a private shooting affray and Brown decided to be travelling again. This time he took ship to South America but his stay was brief. Perhaps it was safer to be moving. He went north on foot, made his way along the Isthmus of Panama and continued northward to San Francisco.

There is but scant information about his activities in the United States but it is believed that he tried his hand at river-boating on the Mississippi and the more hazardous occupation of scouting for Indian hunter General Custer. Happily for Brown, however, he quit the scouting some time before that tragic year in which Custer and his United States soldiers were cut down by Sioux Indians at Little Big Horn.

Attracted by lingering reports about gold in the Fraser river area, Brown headed northward into what is now British Columbia but he wasn't lucky at mining. Inquisitive fellow, he wanted to see the country to the east of the Rocky Mountains and with guns on his belt and pack horses loaded with supplies, he negotiated the mountain passes and emerged to see a panorama of lakes and trees and grassland that gave him at least fleeting ideas about settling down—fleeting because with a few angry Indians on his trail, he didn't remain long for meditation or scenery. In the interest of safety, he continued eastward to Fort Garry but he could not forget the lake setting beside the mountains.

It was 1865 and in that area now marked by the city of Winnipeg, there wasn't much to do except hunt and trade. But a bit of leisure paid well at that time because he was attracted by a French half-breed girl he met on the United States side of the line and married her. Together they travelled about the prairie country and in 1868, Brown proposed returning to the unforgettable wonderland beside the mountains and settling down.

There, in what is now the Waterton National Park, Brown and wife squatted, built a log cabin and cultivated the first land to be worked in southern Alberta. Apart from some small areas planted at a few northern fur posts, it was no doubt the first cultivation in all the country enclosed by the present boundaries of Alberta. Brown has been called Alberta's first homesteader but that is not an accurate statement because there was no provision for homesteading for some years after he settled. Actually, he was a squatter but, having cultivated land, one could call him the first farmer.

* * *

Strange as it may seem, this scholar with an Oxford education and an officer's rank in the Imperial Army, felt settled for the first time in his life. He let his hair grow to shoulder-length, wore buckskin clothing, hunted and explored, went overland as far as Duck Lake and Fort Garry now and then, and, during the troubled period of the Riel Rebellion, he acted as guide for the Rocky Mountain Rangers.

But no matter where he travelled, he always returned and proclaimed that he wouldn't exchange his cabin beside the lake for Balmoral castle and the Tower of London thrown in. For the Indians with whom he traded and associated he accepted the new name, "Kootenai" and thereafter hardly anybody recognized him as "John George."

Everybody who came to the southwest soon got to

151

know him, to be sure. They knew him as "that hunter and scholar fellow down by the lake," or "that squawman whose cabin is full of the works of Shakespeare and Tennyson," indeed he lacked nothing in distinctiveness and he was "that short-tempered fellow who was there before the mountains grew up," and "that Oxford man whose vocabulary would fairly wither the grass when he's mad."

As for the gun he carried constantly, he knew how to use it and shot with deadly accuracy, as those who hunted with him in the mountains discovered. There were times, too, when he had difficulty in restraining his shooting instincts and on one occasion, friends had to intervene to keep Brown's fingers away from the trigger. He had been packing supplies to a camp in the mountains, packing flour and sugar and beans. In the course of travel, the sack containing beans was snagged by an overhanging branch and the precious beans began to leak out. With the bean sack empty at the point of destination, the camp cook, not realizing the folly of inviting Brown's anger, accused him of stealing the beans and caching them away for his own purpose. Such an insult could not be ignored and Brown reached for his gun. Fortunately there were woodsmen who came between Brown and the cook while somebody explained that he had seen the evidence of a leaking bean-bag along the trail. Then an apology from the frightened cook brought hostilities to an end.

He was in exactly the right location for one of his tastes. He hunted in the mountains, explored for mountain passes, ran buffalo on the prairies and traded with Indians of both the open country and mountain valleys. More than that, he was the first or one of the first white men to identify oil within the bounds of the present province of Alberta. The oil he recognized was not very abundant but it was sufficient to spark the first western oil boom, in 1901. Repeatedly, he asked the Stoney Indians to be on the alert for a fluid that smelled like kerosene and looked like diluted molasses. Some seepages were discovered not far from the lakes and a company was formed to develop the strike. But, as time was to prove, there wasn't much oil there and the boom was a brief one.

More important was Kootenai Brown's part in connection with the birth of cattle ranching. When Senator Cochrane drove north from Fort Benton early in 1881, sizing up the opportunities for running a big ranch herd, he met the two men best able to furnish advice—Kootenai Brown and Fred Kanouse.

Said the Senator, as he stopped on the prairie to give his team of bronchos a rest, "I propose to bring a big herd of cattle to these parts. How do you think they'd do?" The frontiersmen assured the eastern capitalist that he was driving over grass favored by the buffalo, that where buffalo flourished, cattle would do the same. But Brown had a word of warning that went unheeded for some years—the need to put up hay for bad winters. Most winters, he said, would be entirely favorable for grazing but he believed a cattleman should be prepared for that occasional season when chinook winds didn't come and snow blanketed the range.

In the year in which the big herd of Cochrane cattle —3000 head—was driven from Montana, Kootenai Brown's wife died and he buried her beside the lower lake. A couple of years later, he married again, this time to a Cree woman whom he secured after some prolonged negotiations. She was an attractive person and Kootenai's fondness for beauty went far beyond mountain scenery.

It was when a band of Cree Indians came to trade that he saw this maiden for the first time. She was the daughter of the chief, which only added to the difficulty of winning her. But bashfulness was not one of Brown's failings. He made the chief an offer of two horses as a fair price for a wife but the old man who was no novice at trading, shook his head. Brown raised his bid to three horses and the chief was still adamant. Brown said, "four horses," and it was evident the old Indian was becoming interested. Finally, with the extravagant bid of "five horses," the deal was finalized and Kootenai Brown had a new partner.

She was a good wife, this Cree woman, and Brown knew it. The worst thing about her was the name, something like Chee-Pay-Qua-Ka-Soon, meaning Flash of Blue

Lightning. For his own convenience, Brown shortened the long name to a handier size, called the lady Neech-e-mouse, meaning "loved one." But the old frontiersman made certain that all other people who came that way showed proper respect for his wife and called her Mrs. Brown.

* * *

In 1895, the federal government took steps to set aside Kootenai Brown's playground for a national park and he was appointed, first as fishery guardian and forest ranger of the park and then park warden. This latter post he held until his death on July 18, 1916. Burial was in the plot beside the lower lake, close to the highway, just where he wanted to lie. And in 1936, a stone cairn was erected there to commemorate the name of that colorful combination of soldier, hunter, prospector, scholar and farmer—first white man to camp in Waterton National Park and first to cultivate land thereabout.

He was one of those sparkling personalities who imparted a bit of his own character to the early West.

W. [erehudct

CHAPTER XXIII

CATTLE KING BURNS

PAT Burns, to whom Manitoba, Saskatchewan and Alberta had early claims, achieved what was once considered impossible—becoming a millionaire without losing a friend. And who would furnish a better success story? Starting with the inconvenience of poverty and the handicap of meagre education, he became one of the industrial tycoons of Canada, a senator and cattle king. For the purpose of the man who took the census, however, Pat Burns' choice was "call me a rancher."

Definitely it wasn't his wealth that was most deeply imprinted in the memories of those who knew him. "Ah, yes," an older member of the community will say, "well I mind Pat Burns—a kind man, and friendly." He may have been the busiest man in his city but he had time for anybody who needed his help. When the wife of one of the plant workers was seriously ill, it was Burns who arranged to have her sent to a famous hospital in the United States.

155

When the little Midnapore church of Pat Burns' particular religious faith needed painting, he sent men from Calgary to do the work; and when the nearby church of "the other faith" suffered by contrast, Burns instructed his workers: "Paint that church too."

Yes, and when a small mascot pig, walking beside a float in one of Calgary's Stampede parades, became exhausted and fell behind, it was Pat Burns, riding in a stylish limousine, who stopped and took the dejected wee pig inside. Pat Burns was like that, portraying the spirit of humility and informality.

It will bear noting how this story is strangely similar to that of another leader in the meat industry, Gustavus Franklin Swift of the United States.

* * *

Pat- Burns was born at Oshawa, Ontario, from good Irish stock. The father was Michael O'Byrne until the name was changed to Byrne and then to Burns. The family moved to Kirkfield where the boy Pat attended school, briefly. Going to the Kirkfield school at the same time was another boy destined to win fame, William Mackenzie who, along with Donald Mann, undertook to build many hundreds of miles of Canadian railways.

Willie Mackenzie was older than Pat Burns but that did not prevent them from seeing a good deal of each other. They participated in at least one famous shirt-tail wrestling match for school supremacy and they worked together on a potato-digging contract near home. According to Pat Burns' telling, the potato enterprise was not without its disillusionment; the Irish-Canadian lad did most of the digging and the Scottish-Canadian collected most of the reward. But the two remained fast friends and when Mackenzie and Mann were building railroads in later years, Burns was furnishing beef to feed the workers.

There were 11 children in the Burns family and things were crowded about the home. Pat and brother John decided to go west and file on homesteads. They saved a few dollars and after working in the bush for a winter and accepting two oxen in lieu of wages, Pat slaughtered the ancient animals and peddled the beef. It was his first venture in the meat business and it increased his resources sufficiently to take him to Manitoba. It was 1878 and Pat was 22 years of age when the brothers made that long trip to Winnipeg, a city which only in that year gained a rail connection with the outside.

In Winnipeg there were reports about good soil around Minnedosa, or Tanner's Crossing at it was called then. They set out on foot; there wasn't much choice. After six days of walking and sleeping out at nights, they selected quarter sections and filed on them at the local land office. There was no point in stopping to operate their new homestead farms at that stage because money was exhausted and they couldn't do much without equipment, wagon, plow, oxen and so on. Their decision was to walk back to Winnipeg, back over the 160-mile trail, and get jobs. That they did and took work building the Canadian Pacific Railway grade east of Winnipeg at a wage of $25 a month.

A year later, when Pat Burns had saved enough money, he bought a team of oxen, bought the wagon and plow every homesteader needed and started again toward Minnedosa. Like hundreds of others at that time, he set about to conquer the prairie sod, build a cabin and live on bachelor fare.

His intentions about settling down to farming were good but he saw so many opportunities of other kinds that homestead duties suffered. Neighbors who had helped build his log shack and stable, watched him with special interest, said, "He's hardly ever at home." He'd haul hay from that quarter section beside the present-day village of Clanwilliam, north of Minnedosa, to Brandon, on a rough trail that became a good provincial highway; he'd haul freight from Winnipeg and he'd do custom breaking with his oxen— anything to make a dollar.

Though he was a source of special interest to the homestead community, neighbors liked the chubby young Irish-Canadian. One of those neighbors when past 80 years of age, recalled Pat's good nature and said, "I never heard anything bad about him except his dancing." Together they had gone to some dances and the old gentleman delighted to tell about the night they became lost when the ox-team got off the winter trail. And one of the dear old ladies of the district recalled with half-hidden satisfaction that young Pat was "an awful tease." Several times he chased her, threatening to kiss her, and with a gleam of speculation in her nice old eyes, she added, "You know, if I realized he was going to be a millionaire, I might not have been so hard to catch."

*   *   *

Homesteader Pat Burns bought a cow, bought her "on time," and sold her at a profit. He bought another and pretty soon the people around there got to know that Burns would buy or sell anything. Then, in 1886, when Mackenzie and Mann were engaged in railroad construction in the state of Maine, Pat Burns took the contract to furnish beef for the building crews. It marked the beginning of big operations for him. The contract was followed by a bigger one to furnish beef for the construction camps along the railroad being built from Regina to Saskatoon and Prince Albert.

With business expanding so rapidly, financing was sometimes difficult and he was obliged to ask for a month to pay when he bought cattle from homesteaders. At the end of a month, he'd have settlement for the beef delivered to the construction gangs and then he would go back and make payment to those from whom he bought the cattle. The Wilsons who settled near Hanley, south of Saskatoon, sold him many cattle that way and Burns appreciated their trust in him. Archie Wilson of Saskatoon told that by Christmas time in that year, Burns was "on his feet" financially and, remembering the friends who helped him, he sent the Wilsons a Christmas present. It wasn't a gift that would look especially delicate beside a Christmas fire-place but it was useful, nevertheless; it was a purebred Shorthorn bull and the Wilsons reaffirmed their faith in Burns, said, "He's a good fellow."

When the grade was being built through Saskatoon in 1890, a thousand workers were eating beef supplied by

Burns and one of his slaughtering plants was on the river bank about west of where the Saskatoon Exhibition Grounds is now located.

Those first railroad contracts were profitable and Pat Burns was ready for another. When work on the Calgary-Edmonton line began, he was again buying cattle, slaughtering and furnishing beef. Calgary became his headquarters in 1890 and he had a shack he called his office on 9th avenue. From that year, also, he operated a slaughter-house in Calgary.

* * *

The foothills community and Pat Burns were good for each other and business expanded rapidly. Cattle were abundant on the ranches thereabout and Burns was good at finding markets for meat. He sold beef to fill Indian contracts; he sold it to towns along the new railway lines and he sold it to mining and lumbering camps in the mountains.

In 1898, when the gold rush was on to the Yukon, Pat Burns was the first to say, "Sure, we'll deliver beef for the miners at Dawson City, even if it is a thousand miles farther than cattle were ever driven before." The cattle for Dawson City beef were sent north by boat from Vancouver, then driven inland over forbidding passes and dangerous wilderness, to be slaughtered beside the Lewes river and their carcasses floated from there down to Dawson. Burns qualified for the reward of a dollar a pound for beef at far-off Dawson City and in the years that followed he sent thousands of tons of prairie beef northward to fill the Alaskan and Yukon needs.

The Calgary plant burned in 1892 but the man built again, built on the East Calgary site where a mighty abattoir loomed in later years. By 1898, the Calgary plant was processing 150 cattle per week and Burns was adding pigs and pork to his trade. Most of the buying he did himself, travelling over a big part of the prairie country and British Columbia. He knew the ranchers and many of the farmers and it was quite natural for him to be attracted by production as well as processing.

159

And so, Pat Burns became a rancher and a big one. By 1912, he had six huge ranches, including the Bow River ranch south of Calgary, one on the Red Deer, one on Milk River, one on the Highwood and a couple near Olds. He was one of Alberta's "Big Four" cattlemen who, in that year, backed the first ambitious Calgary Stampede and saw it achieve success. Burns liked the cattlemen and was never as much at home as when he was with them.

The lady he married was the daughter of another "cattle king," daughter of Thomas Ellis of Penticton, British Columbia. The Ellis cattle roamed over the country at the south end of Okanagan Lake and clear to the International Boundary.

Story has it that Burns first saw Eileen Ellis who was to become his wife when he was sitting in the lobby of a Vernon hotel. A deal with a local cattleman was under discussion when Thomas Ellis and his two daughters entered the hotel and proceeded up the stairway. As Burns noticed the Ellis girls, his conversation ended abruptly. His friend asked. "Who were they?" Burns replied, "I never saw them before." There was a pause and then he added, "You saw the girl on this side? She's the future Mrs. Pat Burns." No doubt the cattleman thought Burns was trying to be humorous but sure enough, the girl did become Mrs. Burns.

But life for Burns was not without its reverses. There were lots of them. He lost hundreds of cattle in the disastrous winter of 1906-07. Fire destroyed his Calgary plant for the second time in 1913. But he refused to be discouraged and gradually his business activities embraced all of Western Canada and beyond, with big plants at Winnipeg, Edmonton, Vancouver, Prince Albert and Regina. He added creameries, cheese factories, coal mines and a score of other things and the business enterprises of P. Burns and Company became known around the world.

And in friendships as in dollars, the Pat Burns of those late years was indeed the millionaire. Calgary, in 1931, witnessed a birthday party for the 75-year-old pioneer. It was a party not to be forgotten by those attending. A two-ton birthday cake was cut to provide 15,000 pieces and

700 people attended from all walks of Canadian life to express their admiration. There was a message from Prime Minister R. B. Bennett: "You have been permitted to take a very great part in the progress and development of Western Canada . . . Your life has been an inspiration to the younger generation . . ." Then there was the announcement that Patrick Burns had been appointed to the Canadian Senate. It was a fitting tribute.

CHAPTER XXIV

LUXTON OF BANFF

NORMAN Luxton, as western as buckbrush and distinctive as Mount Rundle, was long recognized as the oracle of Banff. During his residence of more than half a century there, he published a paper, explored mountain valleys, started and directed one of Canada's leading museums, made Banff Indian Days an institution, and captivated tourists with stories of exploits on sea and land.

This lean fellow with spring in his step and a smile any politician would envy—this son of the frontier who taught the Governor of Samoa to play poker— was born in Winnipeg where his father, William Fisher Luxton was one of the founders of the Winnipeg Free Press and one of those who directed the drive to incorporate Winnipeg as a city. In the first city election on January 5, 1874, the elder Luxton was a candidate for mayor but defeated by F. E. Cornish. It was an election bristling with enthusiasm, however, with 308 names on the voters' list and 331 ballots cast and counted. But not even the defeated candidate questioned the integrity of the mayor-elect who, as one of his first acts in the role of chief magistrate, laid a charge against himself for disorderly conduct on a certain night following election, pleaded guilty, fined himself five dollars and paid the fine.

Norman Luxton's birth on November 2, 1876, coincided with the birth of Western Canada's wheat trade, the first consignment of western wheat for shipment to the East having been loaded on a river-boat at Winnipeg a few days before. The lad attended school in Winnipeg but not without resentment; when he should have been doing arithmetic, he was digging in Indian mounds or hunting along the Assiniboine.

At age 16, he was on his own, clerking with the Indian department at Rat Portage. When he and the Indian agent set out by canoe to pay treaty money to the Indians, the cash box full of currency was in Norman's care—carefully tethered at the end of a strap buckled around his neck because, in the event of mishap in the rapids, the box could be recovered more easily if attached to a floating body.

But the virgin country farther west was beckoning and in 1896, young Luxton was in Calgary, working for the Calgary Herald. Duties embraced a little of everything from business manager to delivery boy and when cash reserves dropped alarmingly, he went out and sold brand books which the Herald was printing at the time. The next venture was mining for gold in the Kootenay area and then he went to Vancouver where he and a partner started publishing a weekly gossip sheet called Town Topics. Following an editorial tirade against Vancouver vice, the ministerial association lauded the paper and circulation and advertising soared. But when the editors publicly criticized the ministerial group for failure to cope with the sins of the city, theological buckshot began to fly at the paper and Luxton's business failed.

* * *

At this point came the great adventure on the Pacific. Daring personalities were drawn together when Luxton met Captain F. C. Voss, a Danish throwback to the seagoing Vikings. A two-man expedition into the South Seas was agreed upon, but first, there'd have to be a boat. From a Siwash Indian, Luxton bought an ancient, 28-foot canoe for eight dollars—a simple dugout carved from a red cedar log and probably at least a hundred years old. In any case, the boat needed some renovating and the new proprietors constructed a small cabin on it, fitted the floating wonder with three sails and christened it Tilikum—the Indian word for Friend.

As the boat left Victoria on May 22, 1901, friends said farewell and then rushed away to mourn for daring men they were sure they'd never see again. Not being in a hurry, the travellers reconnoitred up the Island coast near Nootka and on July 6, set out upon the timeless ocean.

Nobody could say the little boat was overloaded with modern nautical equipment. There was a small sextant with cracked mirror, a pocket compass, a watch for a chronometer and a chart showing the approximate locations of South Sea Islands. For fire-arms, the men were rather better off, having a rifle, shotgun, pistol and an ancient, small-bore Spanish cannon that Luxton uncovered when digging sand for boat ballast. The cannon was there by accident but time was to prove its value.

The mariners had their good days and bad. Weather came in all varieties; food spoiled and before reaching Penrhyn Island, they were out of drinking water. Worst of all, they became tired of each other's company and, at times, sat at opposite ends of the canoe and nursed their guns.

Their course led to Manahiki and Danger Islands. They stopped at Samoa and Ninafou and many other places with funny names. At Apia on Samoa, they heard about President McKinley's assassination, and, being short of money at this point, Luxton set himself up as a professor of all card games and made a contribution to local education as well as the Tilikum cash box.

On one of the 42 island fairylands at which Voss and Luxton called, the native king took a particular liking to the Canadian. A royal message went to Luxton: "King Apow wishes to speak to you." Though worried about the purpose of the interview, Luxton appeared promptly.

"You like our people?" the king asked through an interpreter. When Luxton nodded, the monarch continued: "You will marry my daughter and live here," at the same time pointing to acres and acres of cocoanut trees which would become the property of a royal son-in-law.

Luxton squirmed, knowing that rejection of a royal proposal might induce the king to have him thrown to the sharks. After a moment of hasty thought, he made a speech: "I will never forget such kindness but if I leave Captain Voss before I reach Australia, I will be breaking my promise. One who would break a promise could not be worthy of a princess. But when I return to this island," the diplomatic Norman added, "I will accept your offer."

It was intended as a gentle refusal but to the king it evidently sounded like an undertaking to move into the royal household and Apow's two beautiful daughters, dressed brightly and briefly, were ushered in, with instructions to the prospective son-in-law to take his choice. When Luxton hesitated, the king made the decision and the nuptials were proclaimed. The celebration which followed lasted all night with singing and dancing and drinking of cava. It was an unfortunate misunderstanding but preferable to being supper for a shark.

On another island, Luxton was taken in hand by cannibal natives and escorted to the chief. He could see himself doubled up in a cannibal stew pot and, as islanders gathered around anticipating a feast, knew he must act quickly. Somehow, he persuaded the chief to permit a public demonstration of his racing speed. With temporary freedom, his speed was such as to surprise even himself and he sprinted right to the water's edge, hungry natives in pursuit. Voss had the Tilikum ready and also the cannon. As the fugitives pushed away from shore, a blast from the cannon sent startled natives to cover and the travellers sailed into the sunset.

Things went better for a time and then worse. Away to the west a tropical gale dashed the Tilikum on a coral reef and tossed Luxton on jagged rocks where he lay unconscious all night. In the morning Voss found what he believed to be the dead body and had just located a nice place for the grave when the Canadian came to life.

But Luxton was suffering from effect of the accident and when the boat stopped at Suva, capital of the Fiji Islands, a doctor ordered him to proceed to Australia by steamship. Accepting medical advice, Luxton was first to reach Australia. To complete the trip to Sydney, Voss took a Tasmanian for a mate but another storm swept both the mate and the ship's compass overboard and Voss went on alone. At Sydney, he was reunited with Luxton and looked back upon nearly four months and 7000 miles of ocean travel.

From Australia Voss took the Tilikum on a tour of Australian waters, then through the Indian Ocean to South Africa, Brazil and finally to London, England, arriving September 2, 1904—three years, three months and 12 days out of Victoria. There in London the Tilikum was sold and forgotten until years later when, after a diligent search, it was located, a derelict on a mudbank beside the Thames. The owners, E. W. and A. Byford, agreed to present it to. the City of Victoria, on condition that it be displayed without charge to the public. Arriving back at Victoria in July, 1930, to take a place of honor in Thunderbird Park, the little boat had completely encircled the world.

* * *

From Australia, Luxton worked his way back to Canada and Banff, hoping to regain health. That spot in the Rockies looked better than anything he had seen in the South Seas—grass skirts and all. With some printers' ink still in his blood, he took over Crag and Canyon and began publishing. But he had time for other things—real estate, trade with the Indians and hotel operation. Because Banff needed a hotel which would remain open the year around, he celebrated the official opening of his King Edward Hotel by publicly throwing the keys away in the bush.

For years, it seemed that Norman Luxton was the man behind every Banff project. The Winter Carnival was conceived when he and B. W. Collison played cards with their friends one night in 1909 and for a long time, Luxton conducted the Annual Indian Days, a feature of the Banff holiday season, presented in the best Stoney traditions. For more than 25 years, Luxton judged the Indian events at Calgary Stampede. He knew the Indians as few other white people did—celebrated with them, hunted with them.

When his Banff business declined sharply, he took his trading post to Morley and was there when the influenza epidemic struck in 1918. "Where are your people?" Luxton asked an Indian boy who came to the post one morning. The reply was: "All dead." Investigating at once, Luxton found the report exaggerated but some were dead all right and others were helpless and dying. The Indian agent was among the sick and something had to be done quickly. The trader took charge, organized burial gangs and fed the sick from supplies in his store. Medicine was not his specialty but he administered aspirin and whiskey from his pre-prohibition stock and sick Indians began to recover. There being no written orders for supplies from his store, there was no settlement and the trading business failed but the Indians did not forget.

Not many white men could win and hold the confidence of two jealous tribes of Indians but Luxton did it. The Blackfoot tribe made him Honorary Chief White Eagle and the Stoney tribe named him Chief White Shield. Said one of the tribesmen: "White Shield will protect us."

He rejected the chance to marry one "princess" but he did marry another— daughter of the pioneer rancher and trader, David McDougall. To the Stoneys, Miss McDougall was "The Princess" and she became Mrs. Luxton in 1904.

Nobody knew the West, the mountains and the pioneers better than Norman Luxton. For one year he was president of the Southern Alberta Old Timers' Association. He canoed from Jasper right through to Rainy Lake in Ontario and knew all the connecting streams. He knew Louis Riel and admired his determination to improve the lot of his half-breeds. Yes, and it was Norman Luxton who suggested to Hon. Frank Oliver that the Canadian government should buy the thousand buffalo owned by Michael Pablo in Montana, and then, upon instructions from Mr.

Oliver, opened the negotiations which led to the great herd being brought to Wainwright.

One of his magnificent monuments will be the Luxton Museum at Banff, inside which a hundred thousand people signed the visitor's book last year. Through the years, his trading post resembled a museum more than a place of business. As two friends chatted one day in 1953, Mr. Eric Harvey of Calgary, said: "What are you going to do with all those splendid specimens?"

Norman Luxton confessed with a sigh that he didn't know what would happen to them and at once, the man from Calgary said: "Let's build a museum." The result was the Luxton Museum, housed in an elegant log building erected on a choice site beside the Bow river and backed by the Glenbow Foundation. The Luxton Museum is one of the finest things of its kind in Canada.

CHAPTER XXV

HE NEVER LOCKED HIS CABIN DOOR:
H. F. DAVIS

FOR anyone who will follow the trail to the top of the hill overlooking the town of Peace River, there can be double reward, first in the panorama of Canadian scenery which no lover of the out-of-doors could ever forget, and then the gravesite of that pioneer whose name became a legend in the North, "Twelve-Foot" Davis.

The promontory, now marked by the grave, a thousand feet above the town, was a spot close to Davis' heart. There he delighted to stand as thousands of visitors and tourists have stood since, to feast upon the magnificence of the mighty Peace river, with Smoky discharging into it not far away, to look down upon the great expanse of riverwater, islands and rugged country reaching to horizons more distant than most people have known.

For the person who visits that place today, the panorama is no more fascinating than the gravestone, shaped to resemble a poplar stump, the inscription pretty well telling the story:

"H. F. Davis
Born In Vermont, 1820
Died At Slave Lake, 1893
Pathfinder, Pioneer, Miner and Trader
He Was Every Man's Friend
And Never Locked His Cabin Door."

That's the epitaph. It's in error, inasmuch as Davis did not die until the turn of the present century but that's a detail of small importance at this point. What is important is that he lived to make things easier for the people about him and his reputation is not to be forgotten.

It should be explained that Twelve-Foot Davis whose name has become synonymous with friendliness and northland hospitality, was not 12 feet tall. As a matter of fact, he was a short man—only thing big about him was his heart. He must have been a powerful man because, on one occasion, he carried a sick Indian in his arms for five miles, and he would pack a load of 200 pounds over the portages, back in the days when bringing trade goods from Soda Creek on the Fraser river, to conduct his bartering business at Dunvegan, Peace River Crossing and Fort Vermilion on the Peace river in what is now the province of Alberta.

* * *

But what's the story behind this character of the Canadian northwest? If he wasn't a big man, how did he come by the name "Twelve-Foot?" Originally, he was from south of the border. As a young man he was among the adventurers who crossed the continent by wagon to search for gold in California. It was the year 1849 and Davis was a "forty-niner." Just what fortune he met in that western state, isn't clear but when the gold-rush was on to the Upper Fraser river in what was shortly to be called British Columbia, in the late 50s and early 60s, Davis was among the wealth-seekers trekking northward. He was at Barkerville in the Cariboo area when mining and the vices accompanying a gold-rush were at their peak.

But Davis, still a young man, was using his head more than his shovel. As he surveyed the claims on Williams creek where the richest strikes were secured, he made some mental calculations, figured that two of the pioneer claims were incorrectly staked and exceeded the size at which they were registered. At night he measured the gold-laden claims and confirmed his hunch—they were too big by 12 feet. Acting quickly, he filed on the 12-foot strip close to discovery claim and it proved profitable. According to story, he took something like $20,000 worth of gold from the runt-sized claim and from that time forward he was "Twelve-Foot" Davis.

Davis sold his mine and temporarily he was rich. He might have remained a wealthy man but there were people on every hand who wanted money or needed it more than he and rather quickly his fortune was depleted. He went back to trading, found it more to his fancy than mining for gold anyway. At first, he was trading along the Fraser river but discovered that the farther back he went, the better the trade. Before long, Davis was loading freight canoes on the Fraser, taking them upstream and over the height-of-land into the Parsnip river, and thence down the Peace river to Dunvegan or beyond.

Each cargo of furs taken in exchange for trade goods had to be transported out of the country by freight canoes over the same difficult route. To travel from Dunvegan to Soda Creek with a shipment of furs required two months and the return journey with a load of trade goods took just as long. In later years, however, Davis shortened his trade routes a little, used Edmonton as his base and made a trip a year to that place.

* * *

With passing years, Davis became one of the best known and most loved figures in the North. Ultimately, he might have retired amid greater comfort farther south but it was his choice to remain in the area of the Peace river, amid the scenes and people he loved. And as he loved them, the folk with whom he did business, certainly loved him. Honest dealing and a friendly interest in every-

171

body, whether Indians, Eskimos or some other race, were inherent in the Davis character and other traders and trading companies found it difficult to compete with him.

Davis kept no books and no records, but memory never failed. Trappers would willingly turn a season's furs over to him and wait until the trade goods came in, perhaps months later, to take settlement. Travelling in the North, a person will hear stories like that of the Indian who left some beaver skins with Davis and died before receiving settlement. Ten years later, so they'll tell you, the Indian's son came to trade. Davis looked enquiringly and asked; "Was Johnny Split-toe your father?"

When the reply was "Yes," Davis said, "Before your father died, he left some beaver skins with me. I'll pay you now."

Surpassing all else in practical importance, northern travellers knew there would be food and shelter for them if they could reach a "Twelve-Foot" Davis cabin. Always there was a cache of food where it could be found, some flour, a bag of pemmican and tea for whoever might come that way. There would be some extra blankets and an open door, whether the owner of the cabin was present or not. He was known to leave his home camp for trips into the remote fur country with less than a safe amount of food for his own use, in order that sufficient supplies could be left behind for any hungry and weary traveller who might stop during his absence. Race and color mattered not at all and the Davis provisions saved human lives—nobody could estimate how many.

* * *

Late in his life he was asked how he explained the fact of so many friends. Davis, uneducated and whose grammar would never win a school prize, replied, "I dunno; maybe it's 'cause them fellers all needs smiles and they all needs grub, an' I keeps a good stock of both. And so, I just smiles at 'em and feeds 'em." He might be illiterate but his philosophy was both sound and practical, an excellent reminder of what resources in food and good will can do in winning friends for either an individual or a nation.

Just prior to his death, a woman missionary in the North asked the little old man if he was afraid to die.

"No mam," he replied. "I'm not afraid. Nobody is mad at me. I never killed nobody, never stole from nobody; I never hurt nobody intentional; and I always kept my shacks open for tired and hungry people. No mam, I'm not afraid to die."

Though he couldn't read and couldn't write, he possessed qualities of the heart far more impressive on the northern frontier than even the finest of scholarship could have been.

He died at Grouard, beyond Lesser Slave Lake and was buried there. But his friend Jim Cornwall, another who knew and loved the North, had once heard Davis confess a hope to be buried at that scenic spot high above Peace River Crossing. Cornwall, likewise an early trader near Peace river, having started a post at Lake Saskatoon in 1898, resolved that the Davis wish would be carried out. Some years passed but the Cornwall memory was good and arrangements were made to move the remains to the favored spot. That much carried out, the stone of Cornwall's designing and ordering was placed there where it seems to be on the "top of the world," and inspiration to all who will pause and ponder.

"Twelve-Foot" Davis wasn't a farmer at any time in his life; he never homesteaded. Though he drove dogs, he never drove oxen. Still, he was a pioneer in the newest section of Canada's agricultural empire and he had an impressive vision of agricultural development many years before the first settlers drove north from Edmonton or Edson to cultivate the Peace river soil.

He was blind in his latter years but that, somehow, didn't prevent him seeing with his mind's eye. He could see his old home in Boston; see the grandeur of the Peace river from his favorite look-out above the "Crossing." And then he managed to see, away in the future, strange developments in that section of the North of which he was much a part. To the country beside the Peace, still isolated and unoccupied for years after his death, he could see

173

settlers coming. With prophetic vision, he saw people coming to cultivate and make homes and increase Peace river productivity. He said so; he saw schools, churches, roads, fields of grain and pastures stocked with cattle where only fur-bearing animals ranged before.

"Twelve-Foot" Davis' vision didn't come from school or university; perhaps it was the reward for a gentle and generous nature. Anyway, he said he was sorry he couldn't live to see the day when Canadians would discover the goodness of Peace river country, that it is a good place in which to live. If he had survived, he'd probably show the least surprise that the wheat championship of the world has been won rather many times by growers in that which was long considered a "land of ice and snow," Davis' beloved Peace river country.

It's to be hoped the stone bearing the inscription and miniature sermon about a humble little man in the western "backwoods" will stand to repeat its message for a thousand years. "He was every man's friend and never locked his cabin door."

Chapter XXVI

EDITOR AND HORSE THIEF:
PETER J. McGONIGLE

AS PIONEERS with good memories will agree, he was one of Western Canada's fabulous personalities—Peter J. McGonigle. In the period after 1905 when the provinces of Saskatchewan and Alberta were created, he ranked among the best known citizens in the prairie country. Folk who gathered at the livery stables talked about Peter McGonigle. Nearly everybody read about him, following his fortunes and misfortunes with as much interest as is now shown in favorite hockey teams. His behavior was not always exemplary although that did not seem to affect his following and popularity.

But while nearly everybody read about Peter McGonigle, nobody saw him in the flesh. The fact was that Peter never actually lived. He was a mythical character created by that equally amazing person, Bob Edwards, editor of the Calgary Eye Opener.

175

Even today, however, there need be no apology for treating Peter J. McGonigle, Esquire, as though he were as real as Bob Edwards made him appear, and following the poor soul through some of the tribulations that made him famous and some that proved a threat to the calm of Empire relations in his time.

For the purpose of the record, Peter McGonigle was an editor. Yes, he presided over the Midnapore Gazette and wrote the "Society Notes" and other ribald features for the miniature metropolis of Midnapore—a few miles south of Calgary—with a master hand. But an editor must be a man of many parts and Peter was versatile, having several sidelines including bootlegging and horse stealing.

The sidelines being more profitable than editorship, took more of his time and contributed more generally to his fame. But whatever may have been his status on the voters' list, McGonigle and the Eye Opener accounts of his escapades brought more publicity to his alleged village of Midnapore than the most active chamber of commerce could have done.

Years after both Peter McGonigle and his creator, Bob Edwards, had passed from the local scene, a handsome car bearing an American license, stopped at Midnapore while the driver enquired if any members of the Peter McGonigle family were still living thereabout. Unfortunately, there was no McGonigle to whom one could point but, surely, the ghost of the inimitable Peter still hovers about the village.

* * *

Peter McGonigle's first publicity was through the Eye Opener of August 22, 1903, while that paper was being published at High River. Thereafter, Peter was drunk quite frequently, sometimes went to jail but, always, he was cheerful. Often he was the hero in Bob Edwards' fiction and, now and then, he'd lend his name to a local story of fact when it was considered prudent to hide the identity of the real participant.

Notwithstanding his obvious talent in some lines of

endeavor, he seemed to be born for misfortune; even his romances were fraught with peril. One of those affairs, as reported by Bob Edwards, followed Peter's decision to lead a better life. He joined the village church and, having a voice far louder than a foghorn on a Mississippi river-boat, there was an immediate demand that he become part of the church choir. Being an agreeable fellow, our Peter accepted the assignment affably and, the very first Sunday, according to the Eye Opener report, distinguished himself by nearly "shattering the Rock of Ages into a thousand fragments."

That, however, was beside the point. More important, there was a pretty young widow singing contralto and Peter was attracted. By the second Sunday, Peter and the widow were singing from the same hymn-book. Now, it must be explained that at this particular period in his career, when he wasn't writing copy for the Midnapore Gazette, he was turning an honest penny by selling sewing machines.

One evening, he decided that to try selling a machine to the widow would provide an excellent excuse for calling. Accordingly, between eight and nine o'clock, accompanied by his faithful dog, he knocked at the front door of the lady's residence. The greeting was cordial and, on being admitted, Peter ordered the little dog to lie down on the porch to wait for him.

When this enthusiastic editor-turned-salesman was explaining the merits of the sewing machine, the dog sprang from the porch to run after a passing buggy and during the five minutes or so when the animal was absent, Peter McGonigle took his departure. He meandered down to the hotel but finding the bar closed, he went to bed, wondering hazily what had become of the dog.

What he didn't know about the dog was that after chasing a horse-drawn rig down the trail leading to Okotoks, the animal returned to the porch of the widow's cottage to await its master, not knowing that McGonigle had gone home. Faithful dog that McGonigle owned, the brute was still there in the morning when some of the Midnapore citizens going to work at an early hour, saw him lying

asleep at the widow's front door and drew their own conclusions. It wasn't a nice situation.

By 10 o'clock, everybody in Midnapore had heard about
it and poor Peter—his explanations were all in vain. An
officer of the church called at the office of the Gazette and
asked Peter to refrain from returning to the choir. The
unfortunate lady moved to the East where she wouldn't be
haunted by reproachful glances and the unhappy McGonigle
threatened to move his publishing business to some place
like Okotoks or Dundurn.

* * *

But nothing in the McGonigle career brought as much
notoriety to either himself or Bob Edwards as the printed
account of the Calgary banquet tendered to McGonigle on
the occasion of his release from penitentiary where he had
been serving time for horse stealing. The echos from that
famous reception were heard round the world. The spark
that "fired the heather" was the report concerning the
banquet, appearing in the columns of the Calgary Eye
Opener on October 6, 1906.

The report made it clear that the fine affair, tendered
by the Calgary Board of Trade to honor Peter McGonigle
on the occasion of release from Edmonton penitentiary,
was a huge success. Many prominent citizens were present
and Calgary's Mayor Emerson occupied the chair. Letters
of regret were read from Lord Strathcona, Earl Grey,
Premier Rutherford, Charles Wagner, Joseph Seagram, Josh
Calloway and others of similar prominence.

Joseph Seagram wrote: "Dear Mr. Mayor: Though
unable to be with you in the flesh, my spirit is no doubt
with you in sufficient quantities. Wishing Mr. McGonigle
all luck in his next venture. Yours truly, Joseph Seagram."

It was the Lord Strathcona letter that produced the
real fireworks. It went this way: "John Emerson, Mayor,
Calgary. Dear Jack, You don't mind me calling you Jack,
do you old chap? I regret exceedingly that I shall be unable
to attend the McGonigle banquet at Calgary, but believe
me, my sympathies go out to your honored guest. The
name of Peter McGonigle will ever stand high in the roll

of eminent confiscators. Once, long ago, I myself came near achieving distinction when I performed some dexterous financing with the Bank of Montreal's funds. In consequence, however, of the CPR stocks going up instead of down, I wound up in the House of Lords instead of Stoney Mountain. Yours truly, Strathcona."

It was a gay banquet and toast followed hilarious toast. Finally, the guest of honor, the noble Peter J., arose to thank his many friends and explain that had it not been for the ignorance of his lawyer, he might have been acquitted because the horse he was accused of stealing was not a horse at all, but a mare. More than that, the stolen animal died shortly after the theft and it did not seem right that he should have to break so much government stone because of a dead horse.

The people from Winnipeg, through Saskatoon and Regina to Calgary read the story, chuckled as they did many times before when reading the Eye Opener, and thought no more about it. They knew Bob Edwards and thought they knew Peter McGonigle. No local person was surprised that Earl Grey, Lord Strathcona, Premier Rutherford and Joe Seagram were drawn into the story.

Farther from home, however, such a story could be misconstrued and sure enough it was. To the desk of John Williston, editor of the Toronto Evening News, came a copy of the Eye Opener and, knowing nothing of the background, this gentleman was amazed. At once he sensed international news in the account of Lord Strathcona and Earl Grey paying tribute to a notorious horse thief. Being the Canadian correspondent of a daily paper published in London, England, he at once prepared a story and cabled it to London.

Reading his morning paper over a pleasant cup of tea, somewhere outside of London, Lord Strathcona's eyes fell upon the story from Canada and, to his horror, noted he was quoted as having praised the ex-convict, McGonigle. This was preposterous and immediately the serious-minded peer phoned the editor of the London newspaper, demanding explanation. The English editor, no less puzzled, cabled

Williston in Toronto, and he in turn dispatched a telegram to the Mayor of Calgary.

Mayor Emerson was able to report the story as a hoax, that the Eye Opener's editor was a humorist, trying to provide a little fun for frontier consumption, and the best thing for all concerned was to forget it. But Strathcona, his lordly dignity terribly upset, didn't wait for the explanation before cabling his lawyer friend in Calgary, Senator Lougheed, instructing legal action against the author who made him so disgustingly friendly with a ruffian like Peter McGonigle.

Senator Lougheed, along with other western people had read the story as it appeared in the Eye Opener and laughed at it, but to explain to an infuriated Lord beyond the Atlantic that it was not to be taken seriously, was almost impossible. It wasn't for some time that the noble Lord was persuaded to withdraw the charge and let Peter McGonigle and Bob Edwards have their fun.

* * *

Returning to freedom, McGonigle went about his nefarious business and continued to make news, until 1911, at least, when Eye Opener readers received the sad news that he was dead. The great editor was buried in the garden patch behind the Gazette office at Midnapore. Death can be cruel but nobody should have expected it to strike McGonigle in any ordinary sort of way. His loving widow, obsessed with a premonition that Peter might not have been really dead when they buried him—perhaps only in a coma—pestered the authorities until they granted permission to exhume the body, buried for several months. After medical tests for signs of life proved negative and the doctors confirmed death, the stubborn widow resorted to a final test of her own contriving; with the cold body supported in a sitting position, she held a glass of whiskey at the lifeless nostrils and when the fumes passed upward, the great editor opened his eyes and raised his right hand to take the glass.

For a few more years, Peter McGonigle was back on the pages of the Eye Opener but in 1920, it was announced that he was really dead. While examining an ivory-handled revolver belonging to the bartender at the Nevermore Hotel in Midnapore, the weapon went off and the bullet lodged in Peter's stomach. The injured man was removed to a hospital in Calgary where an emergency operation was performed. The operation was "highly successful" but "Mr. McGonigle's heart, storm-beaten by many a howling gale, failed to rise to the supreme call." According to Bob Edwards, the physicians were of the opinion that the rather unfortunate circumstances of his heart stopping had more than a little to do with his death.

People mourned for Peter J. McGonigle whose name was one of the most familiar in all the west, even though no more than a fictional character springing from the fertile imagination of that fascinating fellow, Bob Edwards, editor of the Calgary Eye Opener.

CHAPTER XXVII

TOO SHORT FOR THE NAVY:
SEAGER WHEELER

WHEN a prairie exhibitor won the world wheat
championship in 1956 it was the 34th time since
1911 for Western Canada to claim the high honor.
With good nature in his voice, a citizen from south of the
border remarked that the way these western provinces have
been winning international wheat crowns "is becoming
monotonous."

When the news came through about the 1911 championship which started the long series of successes, Western
Canada was jubilant. The variety to win at the New York
Land Show that year was the new one—Marquis—and the
grower was a little man farming at Rosthern, Saskatchewan.

Needless to say, he could hardly believe it when the report reached him. His name was Wheeler—Seager Wheeler—and up to that time, hardly anybody except near neighbors had heard about him. But after he repeatedly won the world wheat championship for Saskatchewan five times, the names of Rosthern and Wheeler became known to everybody in the West and many people beyond.

The new variety, Marquis, destined to replace its parent, Red Fife, because it was earlier, was officially approved and released in 1909. At that time Seager Wheeler had been on his Rosthern farm for almost 12 years and was already studying his fields in the hope of finding better types and varieties of grains. Searching for better kinds was his chief form of recreation. In 1910 he discovered a head with promising superiority in his field of Bobs wheat and from it came Wheeler's Red Bobs. And from a selection made in 1911, came Kitchener.

* * *

But back to Marquis, the variety that did inestimable things for Western Canada. In the spring of 1911 the secretary of the Canadian Seed Growers' Association sent Wheeler a sample of the new wheat and Wheeler planted it with characteristic attention to details. The Marquis did well and in the fall, he sent a bag of the new crop to the provincial seed fair at Regina and won the championship. It wasn't his idea to send an entry of the same wheat to the international show at New York later in the same season but he was persuaded to do it and in due course word came back that Seager Wheeler's wheat was judged the world's best. People in many parts of the country pulled out their maps to see where Rosthern was located, while the little man living there and now wearing the mythical crown marking him the Wheat King, went about his farm chores as usual.

One thing certain, the $1000 in gold coins received as a world championship prize, came in very handy. It was the special award offered by the Canadian Pacific Railway. United States railway magnate James J. Hill had offered a gold cup valued at $1000 for the best sample of wheat "grown in the United States." Sir Thomas Shaughnessy of the CPR, knew Jim Hill and chided him about restricting the fine prize to United States growers, challenged him to revise the conditions of competition and allow entries from other parts of the continent to compete. Hill, however, stood firm, repeating in unmistakable terms, "grown in the United States."

At this point, the Canadian said, "All right, if you will not do it, my company will give $1000 in gold for the best hard spring wheat grown anywhere." That was the prize for which Wheeler qualified and the gold coins in a stylish leather case were presented at a banquet in Calgary shortly after the New York show. Then, having received the $1000 in the most dependable currency, the Rosthern man was able to make his last payment to the CPR for the quarter section he bought from the railroad company a few years before.

* * *

For Wheeler, the international championship was the beginning of things rather than a climax, and he went about the tasks of seed production with new vigor. In 1914 and 1915 he won the world championships for the second and third times with Marquis wheat, the variety sweeping across the prairie country like a grass fire. In 1916, he was hailed out but in spite of the misfortune, he won the world championship for the fourth time, won it with some Kitchener wheat he developed and carried over from the previous crop season. Nor did his run of international honors end there; his fifth wheat championship was achieved in 1918 with Red Bobs, another strain of his own perfecting.

After bringing the international wheat honors to Canada for the fifth time, Queens University confered an honorary degree of Doctor of Laws upon the Rosthern farmer and, quite clearly, nothing done by a Canadian University up to that time was more popular with the public.

* * *

But from whence came Wheeler and how did he happen to be in Saskatchewan? It seems the fates had more to do with it than any man-made plans. If Seager Wheeler had been an inch taller, he'd have joined the British navy and realized his boyhood ambition. Had the navy been willing to accept him as a sailor, he would certainly have accepted the navy and never seen the farm lands of Western Canada. Moreover, the new country would have been measurably poorer in wheat and coarse grains and even fruit. It he had been an inch taller, the Rosthern community would have missed some good advertising and missed a good citizen. The fates do strange things for people and communities.

Wheeler's birthplace was the Isle of Wight, where most folk with whom the boy associated were fishermen. He grew up knowing all about boats and fishing gear and ship-wrecks. He gathered strange treasures washed ashore and he listened to weird tales about the Blackgang pirates who were supposed to operate from caves in the cliffs not far from the boy's home. In such an environment it could not be wondered that his boyish heart was set upon joining the navy and riding the ocean waves to world parts holding the charm of mystery.

The disappointment of being rejected by the navy was a big one, of course. Even by stretching his muscles and trying to walk and stand "big," he was still too short. What would be the alternative? About this time, there came a letter from an uncle who had gone to the Canadian north-west, hinting about opportunities in the new land. Sig Wheeler was only 17 years of age but he was sufficiently disgusted at being blocked in the desire to be a sailor that he announced he was going to Canada. He suggested that his mother and sister go too.

The uncle's homestead was beside the Saskatchewan river, at Clark's Crossing. It was 180 miles by poor trail from Moose Jaw and about 20 miles from the village of Saskatoon. There the immigrant lad arrived in the spring of 1885. It was Rebellion year and Clark's Crossing was on the route taken by General Middleton and his troops as they travelled from Qu'Appelle station to the scene of fighting. But the shooting excitement was over when this young fellow arrived and there was nothing to do except the drab work of the homestead.

Because the uncle's farm was beside the river, somebody was always having to cross to get supplies. There was
no difficulty about that when Clark's ferry was operating
or when the river was firmly frozen over. But there were
the in-between seasons when there was no way of crossing
except by boat or swimming. Raised by the sea, Wheeler
wasn't frightened by water but when the river was running
full of break-up ice, it could be extremely dangerous.

There was that time when the young fellow thought
he could carry an armful of groceries and cross on broken
ice. But when he was at some mid-point, the ice shifted and
he had no choice but to swim. Being submerged in ice-cold
water was bad enough but trying to keep the sugar bought
with precious dollars, over his head so it would not get
wet when he swam and waded, was doubly trying. He made
the crossing, however, and nothing changed his determination to follow his uncle's example—homestead right there
beside the South Saskatchewan river.

* * *

But a young man starting to farm needed money. Accordingly, Wheeler went to Moose Jaw to earn some wages.
There he painted houses, dug ditches, snared rabbits and
worked for the CPR at anything capable of returning the
dollars he needed. By 1890 he was ready. He bought a
wagon and pair of oxen and with his mother travelling with
him, started northward. It was a rough trip and Seager and
his mother were glad to be at journey's end, north of Saskatoon. But no luxury was awaiting them. Their first house
on the homestead was a riverbank dugout, lined with poplar
poles. It wasn't elegant but at least it was an improvement
on the camps beside the trail and nobody complained.

By this time, Wheeler was out of money again and it
would be a year before he could harvest a crop. The river
furnished fresh fish, however, and to get flour and tea, he
worked as a repair man on the telegraph line to Humboldt
and in spare time gathered buffalo bones on the prairies.
When hauled to Saskatoon, white old bones were worth $8
a ton in trade and helped a lot. Selling bones was about

as good as selling frozen wheat anyway and bone-money bought most of the groceries in the community for a time.

In the second fall, Wheeler had a little wheat to sell and hauled a load to Saskatoon when the temperature was 35 below zero and sold it for 25 cents a bushel. That was why bones continued to be popular.

The Clark's Crossing homestead was all right for a while but Wheeler was not satisfied and in 1898, he bought the farm east of Rosthern from the CPR and moved there. He was happier at once and began to plant trees and experiment with grains. After a day's work, his relaxation was in sorting and selecting seeds and before long, neighbors were talking about him under their breath. Some thought he was "queer" and others were sure he'd never succeed as a farmer. As a matter of fact, he did come close to failure; after several years when his Red Fife wheat was frozen before it matured, the mortgage company threatened to take his farm. But a Rosthern friend came to the rescue and unknowingly did the whole of Western Canada a fine service.

Throughout his entire years on Saskatchewan soil, Wheeler was conscious of the challenge of crop improvement but it was after winning the world wheat championship in 1911 that his enthusiasm knew no bounds. In the summer, he wished the long evenings were longer so he could continue the search for promising new plants. Sometimes, as darkness fell, the little man got lost in the tall crop but what better place could there be for one of his tastes to be lost?

* * *

Certainly, Wheeler didn't restrict himself to wheat. He won championships with oats and barley and peas and potatoes and then he directed his interest to fruit. On a 16-acre orchard beside the highway leading to Prince Albert, he proved for all to know that the soil of his adopted Saskatchewan would grow almost anything, certainly most kinds of fruit.

In the course of casual conversation, one day in 1935 when Saskatchewan was in the grip of drought and depression, Wheeler reminded his wife he had been in Canada exactly 50 years. In all those years he had not seen the old home on the Isle of Wight. Somebody mentioned the matter to Sir Edward Beatty and before many weeks, Seager and Mrs. Wheeler were on their way to England, making the trip "with the compliments of the CPR."

What were the two prettiest sights on the long trip to England and back? According to Doctor Wheeler's telling, one was the Isle of Wight where he was born and the other was the home farm at Rosthern when he returned.

Finally, he retired to live at the west coast, close to the sea, and there he continued to work in the soil, grow flowers and fruits and other things. There in 1957, at the age of 89, he was still growing things, just a little sorry he didn't have the space for a plot of wheat.

CHAPTER XXVIII

WHEAT POOL PILOT:
ALEXANDER JAMES McPHAIL

WITH satisfaction born of triumph, Alexander James McPhail, Saskatchewan farmer-crusader, wrote in his diary on June 16, 1924: "Wheat Pool over the top today."

Achieved was the objective of 50 percent of the provincial wheat acreage signed to five-year pooling contracts by 46,500 farmers determined to serve themselves when denied the government wheat board they sought. With McPhail as first president of the Saskatchewan Co-operative Wheat Producers, Limited, better known as the Saskatchewan Wheat Pool, the farmers were on the march, determined "to improve methods and reduce costs of marketing grain; to reduce speculation, manipulation and waste of all unnecessary transactions in such marketing . . . and to preserve for the growers and the public their proper profits and economies."

They were rough waters on which the untried Pool Ship was launched and beyond the horizon were unforeseen reefs and angry gales storming to destroy the farmers' hope. Skipper McPhail, the first president of the Saskatchewan

189

organization, was also the first president of the Canadian Co-operative Wheat Producers or Central Selling Agency, and retained both offices until his death in 1931. He didn't live to see his good ship ride out the most turbulent weather of all, re-establish its position as the most impressive thing afloat on the sea of agricultural co-operation, and enjoy more pleasant sailing.

* * *

The McPhail who left his farming operations at Elfros and the office of secretary of the Saskatchewan Grain Growers' Association to become the Pool leader was a 40-year-old bachelor, studious but practical, determined but not reckless, and so intent upon the tasks ahead that he had no time for bridge and golf. For all that co-operation offered, McPhail was imbued with a religious zeal.

Nothing came easy for him. Even boyhood years were difficult and the home farm in Bruce county where he was born on December 23, 1883, afforded more of hard work than opportunity for education. Among the family worries was the father's sickness and a local doctor advised seeking better health in the West. Accordingly, on March 17, 1899, twelve McPhails—grandmother, mother, ailing father and nine children of whom Alexander James was oldest—arrived as landseekers in Winnipeg. They were travelling with money from sale of the Ontario farm and the journey was not in the luxury category. For years the boys believed they could identify marks on their impressionable buttocks made by the slats of colonist car seats, and at Winnipeg they didn't know which way to turn.

The father's trouble was tuberculosis and the hope for cure from Manitoba's clean, dry air proved empty. In the very next year he died on the farm selected for residence a couple of miles south of Minnedosa. By this time, the mother had the disease and in 1903, she passed away.

That the orphaned family would be kept together was the dying mother's wish and the burden in carrying it out fell upon the eldest boys, daughter Annie and Grandmother McPhail. Some of them could now take homesteads. Alex took one near Newdale, proved up, sold it in 1907 and went to the Elfros district in Saskatchewan where two brothers and the grandmother had already filed on quarter section farms. There Alex experienced the usual frontier adventures—falling to sleep on a load of lumber being hauled from Sheho by ox-team and awakening to find the wagon stationary and stuck in a slough, the sultry oxen waiting for the young driver to unload and carry the lumber through the water to dry ground.

Time, inevitably, produced family separations. With inherited fondness for education, younger members seized opportunities the older ones were denied but Alex, anxious to make up for earlier handicaps, enrolled in the fall of 1908 for a year at Manitoba Agricultural College. After that there were places in public service for him—a job as weed inspector and, after the outbreak of war in 1914, the responsibility of a shipment of western horses for England. Following that he enlisted but was discharged and went with the Saskatchewan department of agriculture, becoming assistant livestock commissioner. In 1918, he left government employment to resume farming at Elfros and took to buying and shipping livestock as a sideline.

Farm life at that period was something to bring out the best qualities of versatility. When McPhail wasn't working on his place, he was shipping cattle or hunting stray horses, conducting an auction sale, organizing a debating society, cutting hair for a neighbor's hired man, or reading a good book. The only people who were disappointed in his performance were those admiring mothers who had marriageable daughters. * * *

By 1919, McPhail was thoroughly interested in political action as a means of overcoming some of the farmer's problems. Nor was he alone in his views. In October of that year, the farmers' party was elected in Ontario and in the months following, the new Progressive party was gaining support. The need for direct and positive action of some kind was brought into sharp focus in 1920 when growers were annoyed about wheat marketing. A Wheat Board had been created by an act of July 31, 1919, but after a year of operation it was being discontinued and the open market restored in the face of strong farmer opposition.

191

Too often, McPhail and thousands of others sold their wheat at depressed autumn prices when they needed cash and then saw prices rise to give speculators a bigger profit than growers received. Now, with post-war depression gripping the country and the Wheat Board withdrawn, farmers were seething with dissatisfaction. In July, 1921, the United Farmers of Alberta carried the provincial election and in December, 39 Progressives from the three mid-western provinces were elected to the House of Commons. In '22, the farmers' group carried Manitoba's election and farmers, sensing new strength, were saying: "If we can't have a Canadian Wheat Board, we'll have provincial boards or we'll set up our own grower boards."

Came 1923 and exasperated producers across the three provinces were in a mood for bold action. But what action? In May of that year, McPhail stated his convicition that the solution was in "farmers organizing a co-operative association, owned and controlled by themselves," and based on the pooling principle. Conference followed conference in rapid-fire order, with United Grain Growers, Saskatchewan Co-operative Elevator Company, Farm unions and other sympathetic bodies participating.

Interest was aroused in the co-operative marketing experiences in California and decision was made to invite the man who could best tell the story, Aaron Sapiro, to address meetings in Western Canada. Spell-binder Sapiro very soon became a controversial figure and many times there were threats that directors and executives would resign if he were invited or not invited to return. But regardless of the controversy, Sapiro was convincing as he counselled farmers in eloquent and high-priced terms to "stop dumping and start merchandising."

* * *

It was midsummer, 1923, when the Saskatchewan decision was made to organize a contract pool backed by an inter-provincial selling agency. The aim in the short time remaining before wheat delivery would begin was a sign-up of 50 percent of the Saskatchewan acreage. McPhail and those around him were ready to give the campaign every minute of their time but it was too late in the season and, although Alberta operated that fall with a 45 percent acreage sign-up gained in a two-weeks campaign, Saskatchewan carried the drive for signatures into the next year and, on July 25, 1924, McPhail was elected president of the newborn and wobbly Saskatchewan Wheat Pool.

Later that year, representatives of the Alberta, Saskatchewan and Manitoba pools, ready for operation, met at Regina and organized the Central Selling Agency, with A. J. McPhail the president. As things turned out, it was a successful year and farmers were happy. Elevators were acquired and in 1926 the Pool bought the Saskatchewan Co-operative Elevator Company, even though McPhail had some early doubts about the wisdom of such a huge transaction and the burden of debt it entailed. But purchase was the will of the majority of delegates and McPhail accepted the idea.

Troubles? Of course there were new ones every day and powerful interests sought to embarrass the co-operative. But as the first contract period of five years ended with total marketings of over half a billion bushels of wheat and many millions of coarse grains, a new sign-up was undertaken. Farmers had confidence and the campaign went well enough — 77,404 contracts representing 10,735,000 acres signed at the end of October, 1928—but there were breakers ahead.

* * *

The fall of 1929 marked the beginning of world depression and the Pools were caught in a painful squeeze. At the beginning of the crop year when market prices for wheat were about $1.50 a bushel, the Pools declared an initial payment of a dollar a bushel, as they had done before. It was a mistake but who could know?

October brought the memorable stock market "crash" and prices for farm products fell faster than those for other goods. Wheat, before long, was selling at less than the initial payment. The Pools, chief victims of the misfortune, were in a bad position and provincial governments were called upon to guarantee advances made by banks to the respective provincial pools. Then, with market conditions becoming worse instead of better, the governments were obliged to implement the guarantees, thus placing the Pools in debt to the provinces. In the case of Saskatchewan, the debt was in the magnitude of $13,572,000.

Opponents of co-operation became loud in their criticism. Banks made exacting demands and through the appointment of a general manager acceptable to them, matters were temporarily taken out of the hands of the elected executive. A new selling policy was adopted.

While some people were urging liquidation of the Pools, a growing number of farmers and farm organizations were demanding legislation to provide a 100 percent compulsory pool. To McPhail, both ideas were repulsive. His faith in co-operation persisted but not in an enforced form. "In my opinion," he wrote, "when you introduce compulsion, you eliminate co-operation and I feel for many reasons that if this organization attempts to secure legislation, it will give the co-operative movement a setback for many years."

But in November, 1930, "Everything is tottering." Banks were proposing to close out the Pool and it was then that John I. MacFarland, approved by the banks, became general manager of the Central Selling Agency. "It is gall and wormwood to have to do as you are told by a bunch of bankers who are quite ignorant of the biz," McPhail wrote, but that was the way it had to be. To the president's displeasure, MacFarland ruled to close the London office and McPhail considered discontinuing executive meetings because authority was shifted. The banks and the grain trade seemed to be running the farmers' co-operative and it was humiliating. But he never relented in his effort to preserve unity in farm ranks and uphold the principles of co-operation. Firmly, he believed farmers should do things for themselves.

One of his last notations before his death on October 21, 1931, followed a Chamber of Commerce discussion concerning the ills of agriculture: "A good deal of rubbish . . . from men who have no interest in the question other than personal gain. Farmers are the only men who will remedy farm conditions."

For one like McPhail, it was a heart-breaking experience. His ship seemed to be sinking. Critics and foes radiated satisfaction—this would mark the end of foolish notions about co-operation in marketing wheat. But from a meeting in July, 1931, a new policy emerged; the Central Selling Agency was dropped and, when nothing better than a 35-cent initial payment, basis One Northern, Fort William, could be offered, contract obligations were relaxed with farmers granted permission to pool their grain or sell on the open market as they choose. Added were McPhail's words: "Whichever way you sell, please use Pool Elevator facilities."

* * *

With his beloved Pool still steeped in crisis, A. J. McPhail died following an appendix operation, at age 47, leaving a widow and one son. He had been married only four years. By early death, he was denied the satisfaction it would have brought to see his Pool completely rehabilitated, its debts to the government paid, its expanding elevator system making it the biggest grain handler in the world and its course less hazardous and trying for the pilot.

Having prepared the way for a Canadian Wheat Board accepted by governments as well as growers, the part played by the big co-operative changed a good deal but, nevertheless, upon the foundation of orderly marketing laid by McPhail's Pool—shaken though it was at the time of his death—was built the present far-reaching system of marketing with its excellent record of service to growers across the West. McPhail's was a lasting legacy.

CHAPTER XXIX

STATESMAN ON THE FRONTIER:

IT'S a common view that cultural and political greatness
will not be found in a new country. In early Manitoba
and the country beyond, one would expect to find rugged citizens but not poets and artists. In the same sense, the
primitive West might have politicians but not statesmen;
nobody expected the land from which the fur traders had
recently retired to have anybody resembling a Gladstone, a
Macdonald or a Lincoln.

To surprise those with a false humility about the fresh
soil and its people, however, it may be pointed out that
Manitoba's Premier John Norquay had unmistakable qualities of political greatness, as did British Columbia's Amor
de Cosmos and others who might be named—men with
integrity, vision and vigor. The student can only speculate
about now history would rate them had their political

destinies been in London, Ottawa or Washington. In any case, the John A. Macdonald of Western Canada, meriting well the name of statesman, was Frederick Haultain, known also as Premier Haultain, Chief Justice Haultain, Chancellor Haultain, Doctor Haultain and Sir Frederick Haultain.

"He stands to this day head and shoulders over any man who has taken part in political life in the West," wrote Saskatchewan's James Clinkskill who sat with Haultain in the legislative assembly of the North West Territories. "The fact is that he was too much the statesman and too little the politician to suit Canadian ideas in that period."

Who was the most ardent fighter for responsible government in the Territories? The answer is Haultain. It was he who drew the best plans for the new provinces of Saskatchewan and Alberta and it was he more than any other who ensured that the provincial universities in the prairie country would be founded with independence from politics and freedom from the controversies that embarrassed many of the educational institutions in Eastern Canada. In creating the new provinces in 1905, the federal government didn't follow the Haultain blueprint closely and history is likely to see that as the senior government's mistake.

* * *

Certainly there appeared to be nothing of world-shaking importance about Haultain's arrival at Fort Macleod. A couple of lines in the Macleod Gazette of September 26, 1884, told merely that, "the coach on Friday last brought in Mr. F. W. G. Haultain who intends opening an office and practicing law."

Frederick was born in England in 1857 but his family migrated to Canada and settled at Peterboro. After completing primary school in that Ontario community, he went on to Montreal and the University of Toronto, and now, in stepping off the stage coach at Fort Macleod, he was 27 years of age with material assets totalling $40. But he had a wealth of ambition and courage and after renting a log shack for an office, he hung his shingle to remind local people that he was there to practice law.

At first, the law office attracted no business and the $40 were soon exhausted. The young lawyer was practically

197

unnoticed in the town dominated by Mounted Police and cowboys. But Haultain was exactly what that frontier community needed and gradually, the folk of that southwestern area realized a scholar and a leader had moved in with them. Cattlemen in trouble about rustling and cowboys unable to collect their wages began to seek his guidance.

For a few years he helped to edit local papers at Fort Macleod and Lethbridge; he joined in a bit of fun and mischief with cattlemen and mounties; he sang in the church choir and was not above going early to church and pasting the parson's notes together to cause an ecclesiastical crisis about mid-way through the morning service.

* * *

Fort Macleod old-timers have some unrecorded stories about the man and his resolute stands when he believed wrongs were being committed; they've told about him going to visit a local minister who refused to conduct funeral services for a girl whose reputation was considered somewhat sinful. Haultain, who could not tolerate bigotry, appeared at the minister's door demanding a reconsideration and according to the most convincing version of the story, carried a switch in his hand. There is no record of discussions but evidently the young fellow came away with assurance that the funeral service would be conducted in the best church manner.

Frederick Haultain was a member of the first legislative assembly for the North West Territories, elected in 1888. But the assembly of that time was an impotent body, completely subservient to the rule of Lieutenant-Governor Royal who assumed that in the spending of federal grants, he was responsible to Ottawa rather than the territorial assembly.

When the Lieutenant-Governor invited Haultain and three others to serve as an advisory committee on matters of finance, western people were jubilant at the prospect of better government. But when the advice of the new committee was not heeded, Chairman Haultain and his associates, refusing to be "rubber stamps" for Royal, resigned.

* * *

Immediately there was a new wave of dissatisfaction, a new demand for government that would be completely

responsible to the people. Haultain knew what was wanted
and needed and readily accepted the challenge to fight for
a better deal in administration, just as Willian Lyon Mackenzie and Louis Papineau in Old Canada had fought
for responsible government half a century earlier.

Something was achieved in 1891. The Ottawa government authorized that the territories should have an executive committee responsible to the legislative assembly, rather
than to the Lieutenant-Governor. Haultain became the head
or chairman of that executive which resembled a cabinet
and in that office, he was considered as premier of the North
West Territories.

The newly formed governing body had much to do but
little money with which to do it. The Territories were still
being treated as though they were a colony of Canada.
Revenues were quite inadequate and Haultain took the
stand that nothing less than full provincial autonomy would
be satisfactory. In 1901, he formally presented his request
for provincial status but Ottawa refused. His proposal called
for setting up one big province rather than two small ones.

Federal indifference to the needs of the West was dis-
couraging but it was not defeat and Haultain pressed the
fight with renewed vigor. He understood what was needed.
He could see no sound reason for cutting the Territories
to make two provinces, requiring "two sets of legislative
machinery." He insisted that the new province or provinces
should have control of education and he was opposed to
the principle of separate schools. The new provincial government, he contended, should be permitted to tax CPR
land; and it should certainly hold the ownership of public
lands and natural resources.

In seeking to get provincial ownership of lands and
resources, one of his concerns was the danger of homesteaders and settlers being permitted, sooner or later, to
go into the dry areas of the present southwestern Saskatchewan and southeastern Alberta and convert good grassland
to poor wheat land.

When provision was finally made for the creation of the
provinces of Alberta and Saskatchewan, Ottawa's terms were
not in line with Haultain's demands and his opposition to

the conditions may have explained why he was not asked to become the first premier of one of the provinces. As it was, the man who had waged the most unrelenting fight to win provincial status and provincial rights and been the dominant political figure in the Territories for 15 years, chose to remain with Saskatchewan and became leader of the opposition in the new provincial legislature.

* * *

Haultain's friends were visibly disappointed but he accepted the responsibilities of his new office with neither bitterness nor lessening of enthusiasm. But the wisdom in the conditions to which he had adhered tenaciously during negotiations became increasingly clear. Sure enough, homesteaders were allowed to settle on land unsuited to ordinary grain farming and Haultain's warnings were heeded too late. And after a quarter of a century elapsed, the national resources were turned over to the provinces, where Haultain said they belonged.

The statesman continued as leader of the opposition in Saskatchewan until 1912 when he was appointed Chief Justice in that province. In 1916 he was knighted, and for 22 years after 1917, he was Chancellor of the University of Saskatchewan. Hundreds of scholars in successive graduating classes heard him say, "I admit you," and found the tension of the moment eased by the light of friendly mischief in his eyes.

Then there were honorary degrees from the universities closest to his heart, the University of Toronto and the University of Saskatchewan. Even the Cree Indians of southern Saskatchewan added their bit—made him honorary chief with more than the customary rights and privileges to shoot on the reserve; after death, his spirit could return from the Happy Hunting Ground and pursue the hunt on the same Indian land. The Crees said he would be a good Indian.

* * *

Quite clearly, the nation's highest honors came to him while he lived but people forget quickly, and in the course of some jubilee year discussions, a number of prairie high school pupils and a few teachers were heard to confess they knew nothing about that man whose leadership was so masterly. At the mention of his name, one grade 12 boy asked, "What team does he play on?" What the boy should have been told was that Haultain was the captain of a team of nation builders, a captain on whose record there should be at least a chapter of required reading in the western curriculum.

Without his leadership in Territorial years, western progress would have been retarded and without his ardent and sensible campaigning for provincial rights, the creation of the provinces of Alberta and Saskatchewan would have been delayed, almost certainly. If he had his way, there would have been a single province instead of the present two and it is everybody's right to speculate about which political party would be in power in the big province extending from the Manitoba boundary to British Columbia. Perhaps Haultain was right; perhaps the present Saskatchewan and Alberta should have been set up as a single unit —with the name, "Province of Haultain."

Bob Edwards of Eye Opener fame discovered what it is that makes a statesman. "A statesman," said he, "is a dead politician," and what the country needed was "more of them." But the same cynical Bob Edwards did not wait for death to remove the man he admired, before declaring: "Frederick Haultain is a very great statesman."

Said a Saskatchewan man, "I'm glad I knew that quiet, scholarly gentleman with unsurpassed record of public service—and the mischievous glint in his big eyes."

CHAPTER XXX

FRONTIER DOCTOR:
ALFRED SCHMITZ SHADD

PIONEERS in Saskatchewan's Carrot River Valley still
talk in terms of affection about Alfred Schmitz Shadd,
doctor combining many of the qualities of a Grenfell
and a Robin Hood. "I wouldn't be here if it wasn't for Old
Doc," said one of the elder citizens attending the jubilee
gathering at Melfort fair in 1955; "I was just a baby but
that good soul drove his bronchos nearly all night in the
rain when everybody thought I was dying. And he never
left our farm house till he knew the kid was recovering."

"Old Doc Shadd"—first medical doctor in that section
of the West—was a Negro whose people came out of slavery
in the South but nothing about his race or color made
people who knew him love him less. Somebody called him
"God's right hand man," and his funeral in 1915 was the
best testimony of the admiration and respect he enjoyed.

The MacEwans went to a Melfort farm in the spring
of that year, just at the time of Shadd's death and the
funeral held in the town on a March day was one never to
be forgotten by those who witnessed it. The service was arranged for All Saints Anglican church where the doctor

202

had been a warden for many years. But as the hour fixed for the funeral drew near and wagons, buggies and other means of conveyance converged upon the town of Melfort, it was quite apparent the little church would not accomodate all those who wanted to pay a tribute.

At the last minute, friends of the departed doctor arranged for an overflow service to be conducted simultaneously in the town hall, with a minister of another denomination in charge. The services were a little late in starting but the church was full; the town hall was full and hundreds of people of all races and creeds whose hearts the great unselfish doctor had ruled, stood outside.

The funeral procession over poor spring roads was a mile long. The most concise explanation for the events of that day was presented in an editorial of the Melfort Moon, (March 17, 1915) : "No drive was too long; no night too dark; no trail too rough to deter the doctor when the call for assistance came . . . Rich or poor, he made no distinction and nobly he performed his duty."

* * *

Though the father had grown up in slavery, the son was born at Chatham, Ontario, (in 1870). There the Shadds were farmers having a difficult time to make a living. When Alfred was through with public school, he was required to undertake a man's work. But within him was a longing for more education—his hope was to study medicine but for a long time that was a secret he kept entirely to himself because people would laugh at a poor Negro boy having such ambitions.

Young Shadd was serious, however, and he was determined. By dint of hard work he obtained matriculation, took normal training and then some college classes. The great test was still ahead—medicine. The medical course was costly and he had no money reserves. But he registered in the medical school at Toronto and sometimes had to work all night to obtain the money he had to have for tuition and books and food. For days at a time he ate nothing but bananas because they offered the cheapest means of satisfying his hunger.

In spite of economies, there came a time when this medical student was obliged to interrupt his studies in order to obtain additional funds. He turned to teaching and learned of an opening in the North West Territories—a place called Kinistino, 500 miles beyond Winnipeg. Shadd applied, more or less in the spirit of adventure, and the settlers at far-away Kinistino, hard pressed to find a teacher to venture so far into the wilderness, offered him the job. Packing all his belongings in a paper bag, young Shadd started on the long train journey to Prince Albert, from which place he'd have to drive to Kinistino.

A rumor that the new teacher coming from Toronto was a Negro reached Kinistino ahead of him and the local people were mildly shocked. A new problem arose about who would board the teacher and well-meaning parents wondered if they should send their children to school. The rumor was confirmed on a spring day in 1896 when J. M. Campbell who drove the mail stage from Prince Albert, delivered the new teacher.

Sure enough, the newcomer had a dark skin and local women whispered while children manoeuvred into position to peek at this unusual person. One wee girl bolder than others, climbed on the teacher's knee and after moistening a finger in her mouth, tried to rub some of the color off the man's face.

The problem of the boarding house for the teacher was solved when Charlie Lowrie, postmaster, volunteered to take him. Incidentally, it marked the beginning of a long friendship. And for all the residents, there was the discovery that this handsome young fellow had a laughing personality —that he was altogether magnetic.

* * *

The Agricultural Hall used for general meetings, political gatherings and socials in the evenings, and church services on Sundays, was to serve as the school at other times. There Shadd settled into the routine of teaching but nobody seemed willing to accept the story about this young fellow being a medical student, expecting to become a doctor—at least, not until a day when a man up the way of Birch Hills suffered an accident and had his head split open.

The victim's case looked hopeless but the teacher asked permission to dismiss school for the day and made his way to the injured man. Shadd worked patiently, managed to close the wound and the man lived. Everybody in the area heard about the achievement and from that time forward, school pupils had a holiday once or twice a week while their teacher was absent on some medical mission in the homestead country.

The teaching year expired and Shadd returned to the University of Toronto to complete the medical course. In the new class with which he enrolled, there was racial trouble, a group of the students refusing to sit with a Negro. It hurt, terribly, but he decided to talk plainly to his classmates and when the students were together, he made a short speech. He told them he was not a member of a travelling minstrel show and the struggle to get an education had not been easy. Moreover, he wanted to be friendly but if the other students really wanted to be unfriendly and rough, he figured he could better anyone in the University who considered himself a better man and chose to fight it out. Instead of accepting a fight challenge, the students accepted Shadd and grew to like him.

In the spring of 1898, Shadd graduated with honors and more friends than anyone else in the class. When asked where he was going, he replied, "Kinistino." A few weeks later he repeated the stage trip from Prince Albert to the scene of his former teaching activities. The news spread like a grass fire: "Shadd's back— a full fledged doctor, if you please!" Again he moved in with his friends, the Lowries, and in their farmyard erected a two-roomed log structure. One room became his bedroom, the "chamber of silence"; and the other his surgery, the "chamber of horrors." When he had an operation to perform, Mrs. Lowrie assisted, even to the extent of administering the anaesthetic.

Yes, he was the first medical doctor in the Carrot River Valley and calls came from far and near. There were those times when, on arrival at destination he discovered the reason for the call was a cow with milk fever or a horse with colic but in any case, he tried to relieve the trouble.

There were countless stories about exposure and long

nights on the trail. He'd have a case at Birch Hills and a rider would reach him to report a run-away accident at Fort a la Corne and then a tired and sweaty team might overtake him to bring word that a baby was expected in the Melfort district. But nobody ever heard him complain, regardless of the roads, the temperature or the poor prospect of payment "He was never dull, never tired and never sick," according to Francis T. Graves who knew him intimately in those years.

* * *

In 1902, the doctor bought a farm on the Carrot River, a short distance south of Kinistino and there in the next spring, he set out the first crab apple trees that anybody had shown the nerve to plant "so far north" The fruit trees, too, liked that black soil and did well. Then the farm became the doctor's headquarters, from where he drove a single-seated democrat and team of wild and fast ponies. Before long, he acquired a second team and one pair would be resting from a long journey while the other was in service. Driving himself, he always sat exactly in the middle of the seat and travelled fast enough that everybody knew he was coming.

* * *

Nor was this man with some Robin Hood characteristics above a little mischief. When on the Kinistino farm, a young Mounted Policeman lived with him. On one occasion, the Mountie came upon some local boys shooting prairie chickens out of season. It was a serious offence and the officer was obliged to seize the birds as evidence, and place a charge. The doctor learned about it and was saddened because the boys were really good fellows, even though they had made a mistake. He knew also that the bag containing the incriminatory evidence was hanging in his cellar. Nobody ever explained what happened but when that bag was untied at the trial, three old barnyard hens rolled out on the court table. Of course, the case was dismissed and the boys who were the doctor's friends were spared further embarrassment.

In 1904, "The Doc" moved to Melfort to practice. Before long, he bought another farm, 16 miles east of Melfort and north of Star City, and called it Craigbog. To it he brought some of the best Shorthorn cattle he could buy. His special pride was a white bull called Bandsman's Choice, a prize winner at the Toronto Exhibition, for which he paid $1000.

He loved the soil and when his big practice would permit, he'd steal away to the farm, plant trees and work among the cattle and sheep. He wanted to tend to his fields the way a good doctor would care for patients. He seeded tame grass when nobody else was thinking about it and followed a progressive rotation. He hated to see native trees being cut with no thought to the day when the community would need more shelter. Shadd was in almost everything in the district, started the Farmers' Elevator Company and had a lot to do with the organization of the Melfort Agricultural Society, of which he was the first president.

* * *

Along about 1907, the doctor went to the Old Country for post graduate studies. But his year at Edinburgh and London was costly, especially when he saw so much poverty inviting his help. The result was that he had to borrow money to come home.

At Melfort, they were glad to see him back, bankrupt or not. His big practice was waiting for him. But he had time for other things—many other things. He operated a drug store, engaged in journalism, served for periods on the Melfort school board and town council. He tried politics but not with success. In the provincial election in 1905, he was a provincial rights candidate supporting Frederick Haultain who had been premier of the North West Territories up to that time. The election went against him but in the course of the campaign Dr. Shadd expressed some of the finest views about schools and education.

And all the while, this man was making long and tiring drives to relieve the sick. He drove through floods when everything except himself floated out of the democrat, crawled across the Saskatchewan river on his belly to reach a sick man when the ice was too thin to hold him on his feet. And as another Melfort pioneer could tell, there was one wild drive in the course of which the driver didn't stop for either ditches or barbed wire fences—but the doctor arrived before it was too late.

* * *

It was an important day in the Melfort community when the "Doc" bought his first car—first automobile in that part. It was a red Reo and he drove it to the limit of its speed. Horses took fright when they saw or heard it coming and there were some accidents but, at least, the medical man was always on hand when the run-away horses threw the driver out of a buggy. And, according to its owner, the little red car "saved far more people than it killed."

He never gave up until appendicitis struck him early in 1915. Friends took him to Winnipeg but it was too late. He died on March 9, 1915, and a shadow fell over all the homes in the Carrot River Valley. The northern frontier had lost one of its most lovable personalities, a good doctor, a poor collector, a progressive farmer and a great and loyal friend.

"God's right hand man," they said.

CHAPTER XXXI

THE LORD MAYOR OF CANNINGTON:

THE early West had its islands of distinctiveness like the Doukhobor settlement about the village of Veregin, the Barr Colony at Lloydminster, the Temperance Colony at Saskatoon and that transplanted bit of Old England called Cannington Manor. Strange and exaggerated tales have been told about them all and one who grew up at "The Manor" had cause to proclaim that "at least half the lies told about the place are not true." Still, there was no more colorful community of settlers on all the fresh soil of the northwest than the group of Englishmen who settled some 40 miles south and west of Moosomin. Author of the idea and leader in the settlement was Captain Edward Michell Pierce—Ogema Chimogoni, meaning Soldier Chief, the Indians on Chief White Bear's reserve close by, called him.

The Pierces, with four sons and four daughters, were

well-to-do in England, at least well-to-do until a bank failure weakened their financial position. The Captain was not ruined by the circumstances but he was financially humbled and embarrassed. He resolved to take his family to Canada. That he did in the summer of 1882, making a temporary home in Toronto while he learned all possible about farming opportunities, especially in Manitoba and the North West Territories.

The Canadian Pacific Railroad was being built westward at a feverish rate that year, and a siding called Moosomin, marked mainly by four tents and a box-car for a station, saw its first train. To that point came Duncan Pierce, eldest son of the Captain, and as he explored north and south of the new railroad, he was attracted by park land just east of Moose Mountain. He sent word to his father that he had made a discovery. The Captain who was searching elsewhere came at once and liked the land as much as his son had done.

One of the four tents at the CPR siding which was to become Moosomin, housed a Dominion Land Office but when Captain Pierce arrived there to file on homesteads for himself and four sons, he learned that all that land south of the railway line had been withdrawn by the government.

Being told that he couldn't have the land of his choice, wasn't well received by this strong-willed Englishman and by the very next train he was on the way to Ottawa. At the capital he refused to talk with subordinates and secured an appointment with Prime Minister Sir John A. Macdonald. As a result of that visit, so we are told, the land in question was thrown open for one day but that was long enough to let the Pierces make their homestead entries. Before leaving Ottawa, the Captain told Sir John about his dream to establish a colony of English folk having some means—a place where English settlers would live as Englishmen like to live. He was sure he could transfer a bit of Old England to the North West Territories.

Pierce returned to the West and confirmed the location of his land. About the first of November, a basement was dug for the homestead home and construction of the building pressed to completion. Actually, it was a double house with large rooms—quite English in architectural style. Two teams of oxen hauled the materials from Moosomin. Then when the building was completed, Mrs. Pierce and the young ones came on from Winnipeg where they had been waiting—arrived at Moosomin on January 25, 1883, when the winter weather was at 40 below zero. The 40-mile drive from Moosomin to the homestead with both weather and winter roads in an unfriendly mood made a rough introduction to farm life. It took them three days to make that last lap of the journey.

Came spring. The Pierces broke some sod land and planted grains. The cereals did poorly on that spring breaking but the Captain lost none of his enthusiasm and went ahead with plans for his townsite, to be called Cannington after his native village in Somerset. Later, to avoid confusion with the Ontario village by the same name, the western Cannington became Cannington Manor.

Yes, Pierce was a dreamer, but he was also a man of energy and determination and after the spring work was completed, he hastened to England to invite the "gentlefolk" of his choosing to join him. The idea appealed to adventurous Englishmen and the response was instantaneous.

* * *

Community planning went forward. The Captain promised a church and the very first building erected on the townsite of Cannington was the place for Anglicans to worship. The Pierce boys hauled logs from Moose Mountain in the winter and on June 16, 1884, all the people in the new community turned out for a "church raising." There must have been some good ax-men about because four days later Bishop Anson opened the church. There wasn't much wrong with construction either, because that little church, called All Saints, was still in good condition 50 years later. From its beginning it was equipped as Captain Pierce ordered, with alter, bell, organ and surpliced choir. Lily Pierce was the organist.

Settlement expanded rapidly. The Captain announced his plan to accept student workers who wished to learn Canadian agriculture. Tuition was £100 per year, board included. Quite a few sons from wealthy English families came, some of them slightly wayward. And entire families came to start life anew.

But notwithstanding the elaborate blueprint which Captain Pierce had drawn, life in the colony was shockingly different from what settlers expected. Mistakes were many and often amusing. A newcomer seeded oats and observed their failure to grow. According to story, he went out and plowed the field to turn the seeds over after being told that he had probably planted the oats "wrong side up." The result, however, was no better.

One of the prospective settlers with the preliminary status of "pupil" was instructed to give the milk cow some of the green grass growing on the sod roof of the homestead stable in which she was quartered. Later he was seen standing on the sod roof, with the cow's halter shank in hand, trying for all he was worth to draw the animal up or, at least, make her stand on her hind legs to reach the grass.

There were those unscrupulous people who took advantage of the newcomers. A breezy gent arrived carrying an elaborate-appearing camera, and asked Captain Pierce's permission to take photographs which settlers might buy for friends in England. There didn't seem to be a reason why permission should not be granted because the local people welcomed the opportunity of securing some good pictures. Consequently, the photographer was kept busy for weeks. On each photographic exposure, the expert collected a dollar deposit, announcing that he would require the balance of payment when the pictures were finished and delivered. He left "to finish the pictures," but, sad to say, never returned. It was finally concluded that while the fellow had what resembled a camera, nobody had ever seen either film or plates for it. Presumably, the camera had no "insides." The man's interest was in the dollar deposit and he prospered.

* * *

The stage coach which operated between Moosomin and Cannington and carried incoming "pupils" and settlers might have told some good stories. It was not uncommon for an incoming "pupil" to have six or seven trunks. As a result of rough trail and nervousness in the bronchos hitched to the stage, a trunk belonging to one of the young Englishmen bounced off, unnoticed. The lost trunk was never recovered, but, months later, an Indian and his squaw appeared, wearing new clothes. The buck was decked out with Prince Albert coat and ribboned monocle, while his squaw wore an oversized white flannel gown which a recently arrived young man recognized as one of the nightgowns from his lost trunk.

There were tragedies, too. K. A. Price, whose land was west of the mill, recalled the sad fate of Settler Blagden. Early in the winter of 1887-88, Blagden went with oxen for a load of wood. He called at Price's place on the return. A storm was developing but Blagden was sure he could get home before it became severe. But the wind came up quickly and Blagden never arrived home. The load of wood was located when the storm subsided next day; it was stuck in a snowdrift about a stone's throw from Blagden's stable. The oxen had been released and Blagden had wandered away and perished. His body was found several miles away.

There was endless work to be done but Pierce's people found time to play and homesteaders beyond the settlement looked at Cannington with some astonishment. Socially, the community was half a century ahead of its time. The Cannington Englishmen played tennis, soccer and cricket; they rode to hounds and enjoyed billiards in baronial halls. Periodically, they dressed for dinner in the best London style, and partook of refreshments served by butlers who knew exactly how it should be done.

But the race course was in many respects the center of community activity. For a time, the annual Cannington Manor sports, offering prizes as high as $5000, featured horse racing. The oval track was southeast of the mill. At the first race meet in 1887, most of the horses were from local farms but some were brought from Birtle and Binscarth. The first steeple chase was in the same year, celebrating the jubilee of Queen Victoria, and was won by The Dude, with the Mr. Price to whom reference has been made, in the saddle.

Invitations to the races and to the hunt club parties went far. Two French aristocrats from Whitewood, Count Rouffignac and Count Jumiac, attended regularly. And what a picture their arrival presented in the village—a gorgeous carriage drawn by four horses and driven by a groom in full livery, top hat and all. But not even the Frenchmen could outclass Captain Pierce's Englishmen.

The acknowledged leaders in Cannington sports were the Becktons, the fabulous Becktons. Their lavish entertainment and varied sporting interests set a prairie record not soon to be challenged. William and Ernest Beckton were among those who came as farm pupils. Later they were joined by a third brother, Herbert or "Bertie" and, in a short time they learned that some ill-regarded iron-mine shares at the bottom of a trunk had soared in value. It marked the dawn of a new day about Cannington. The boys drew plans for a gigantic residence for their Didsbury Farm—10 bedrooms, billiard hall, drawing room 25 feet long and everything in proportion. When that 25-room house was completed and occupied by the three bachelor brothers, two hired men spent most of each winter cutting wood for fuel and hauling it from Moose Mountain.

* * *

In 1889, the Becktons imported eight of the best English Thoroughbreds available and brought a famous stallion called Jase Phillips from Kentucky. Cannington was on the racing map, with "the best appointed stable west of Winnipeg." (Macleod Gazette, Sept. 3, 1891) Jack Daw, Miss Tax, Piccaninny, Imogene and Cloe Martin were Thoroughbred names every racing fan recognized. Imogene won the Queen's Plate in Winnipeg one year.

The Beckton racing barn was 120 feet long, with separate quarters for the fox hounds, bull dogs and fighting cocks. Three of the famous Bull Terriers, Flesh, Fury and Devil, bred for badger-baiting, got loose one night and, unable to locate badgers, attacked and killed one of the Beckton cows.

There were no dull moments at Cannington. If it wasn't riding to hounds or cock-fighting, it was cricket or tennis or soccer or sailing on Kenosee Lake. And boxing—lots of it. 'Tis said that when an honest grudge fight started somewhere, there was so much fussing about Queensbury rules that they could scarcely get on with the combat.

Cannington may have had the first agricultural fair in what is today south-eastern Saskatchewan. It was Pierce's idea but the result was disappointing. A fair ground was marked and adequately fenced and on show day, cattle and horses were assembled. There being no stables, the animals were tied to the fence. Now, as everybody knows, music is an essential part of an exhibition and with no band available, a Scotsman living some miles away was induced for the consideration of a bottle of whiskey to come with his bagpipes. But when the Scot began to play, the ungrateful English cattle and horses took fright, pulled up the fence to which they were tied and departed for home. The fair was over for that year.

It was all a great adventure in farming, one which adds lustre to the story of the West. Captain Pierce, in whose fertile mind the idea was formulated, did not see his colony really mature. He died on June 20, 1888, but the spirit of the Captain lived on and the refined ideas of the Cannington Manor people went far beyond the boundaries of the colony.

KING OF THE CATTLE TRAILS

LONG, lean Tom Lynch, acknowledged King of the Cattle Trails leading to the early Canadian range, sat on a horse as if he were part of it. Said one of those with whom he rode: "Instead of burying Tom in a coffin, they should've done it with his seat on a saddle."

Not only did Lynch drive some of the first cattle into what is now Southern Alberta but he brought some of the biggest herds. He'd tackle any trailing job whether it was a 300-mile drive requiring a month or a 1000-mile drive calling for three months on the trail. If a river like the Missouri had to be crossed, Tom Lynch had the experience and skill needed to induce a thousand ornery southern cattle to take to the water and swim to the other shore. If a stampede started, he knew how to check it and when Indians or outlaw white men tried to steal part of his herd, Lynch could deal with them too.

But when Fred Stimson of the Bar U ranch asked Lynch if he would undertake to cut poles with which to construct a corral, the old cattleman replied that he would undertake the job if the ax-work could be done from horse-

216

back. With a horse under him, nobody was more versatile than Tom Lynch, a man who should be remembered as one of the greatest cattlemen of the old range.

* * *

Missouri was Tom's birthplace but when he was a small boy, his family moved to the Montana frontier where men carried their ideas about law enforcement on their hips. When still in his teens, he rode out with the northern cowboys and helped drive cattle from Oregon to Montana mining camps.

Curiosity took the young fellow as far north as Fort Edmonton where he made the acquaintance of another two-fisted adventurer, George Emerson. Together they decided to drive Montana cattle to communities on the Canadian side and sell them to settlers or whoever wanted breeding stock. The first herd, a small one, was driven to Fort Macleod where the Mounted Police had established so recently, and there the cattle met ready sale.

On their next drive, Emerson and Lynch took their cattle—wild critters, only a generation or two removed from the longhorns of Texas—right through to Fort Edmonton. Again there was ready sale but at this point in operations, the two men resolved to try ranching on the good grass they observed along the Highwood river, west of Spitzie Crossing where the town of High River emerged later. It was a bold decision because nobody had ever released a ranch herd to graze as far north. But Lynch and Emerson were determined men and in 1879 they brought 1000 southern cattle to that foothills grass and turned them loose to feed in any direction.

The Emerson and Lynch ranch headquarters were just a short distance west of the present High River townsite, on the north side of the stream. The bold experiment in untried country was a success and both men declared their intention to remain in that general area. After a time, the partnership was dissolved, however, with Emerson moving a little more deeply into the foothills and Lynch merely crossing to the other side of the river and branding his cattle with the now famous TL brand.

217

Emerson became a conventional rancher but Lynch continued to have sidelines and was a cattle driver more than a producer. When anyone was confronted with the problem of a difficult drive, he turned instinctively to Lynch. The man's biggest assignment was in 1882 when Fred Stimson of the newly formed North West Cattle Company—better known as the Bar U—instructed Lynch to bring 3000 cattle from Idaho. The same Tom Lynch drove the first herd northward for the Military Colonization ranch started by General Strange; be brought a lot of herds for Pincher Creek ranchers and he delivered the first horses for the High River Horse ranch, bringing these from the Snake river in the State of Washington in 1887.

And to Lynch belongs the credit for bringing some of the West's great cattlemen, among them, one of the most famous cowboys of his time, Negro John Ware. When in Idaho with Stimson to secure 3000 cattle for the new Bar U ranch, Lynch was trying to hire experienced riders for the long drive to the Canadian foothills. He wanted Bill Moodie, a cowboy with a well proven record, but Moodie's reply was: "If you want to hire me, you'll have to take my partner too." Lynch agreed but was surprised and somewhat disturbed when he discovered the partner to be a negro. Negros, Lynch reasoned, had never shown much aptitude for cattle and this might be a mistake. But as time was to show, Ware had the qualities to become one of the greatest riders in Alberta range history, as well as a successful cattleman and a loyal and greatly loved pioneer. Had Tom Lynch done nothing more than bring John Ware to Canada, he'd have earned the right to be remembered.

* * *

A man directing trail herds and exposed to all the dangers of new and lawless country needed the best cowboys he could get. If cattle were to be delivered in good condition, the benefits of experience and skill were needed on every mile of the journey. On that trip from Idaho to the Highwood river, Tom Lynch and his men averaged 13 miles a day. It was considered a good rate of travel for a long drive.

To begin the day, a trail herd would be grazed for a

couple of hours, being eased along lazily in the proper direction. Then the cattle were driven along at reasonable walking speed until noon when there was a two or three-hour rest. Again there was grazing and again a period of driving before halting for the night. And at night, there was no corral in which the cattle could be held securely and conveniently; instead, riders had to remain on duty through all the long and dark hours preceding sunrise, to guard the herd.

Although he performed some of the essential services in founding the cattle industry, it was as a horseman that many of the pioneers remembered Tom Lynch. On his TL ranch, west of High River, he ultimately ran horses more than cattle. When he herded the big band of horses from Washington for the High River Horse ranch, he brought along a hundred head for himself. He was a judge of quality in horses and for a long time he furnished the Mounted Police with most of the horse stock needed for their purposes. And like all true horsemen, Lynch was ever ready for a trade. William Henry of High River recalled Lynch giving J. D. McGregor of Brandon 250 range horses in exchange for 300 Manitoba-bred "dogie" heifers. That was in 1889 and McGregor took the horses to Manitoba and sold them to farmers.

* * *

Oh yes, Lynch always had a few race horses around him. Grey Eagle was a well known flier brought in with the High River ranch stock and Satan was another famous racer with which Lynch on one occasion drove to Blackfoot Crossing to be ready for some matched races the day treaty money was paid. This Satan was an ugly-appearing blue roan and nobody was impressed by him—not until the horse was seen in action, anyway. Whether by coincidence or design, Satan was hitched in Lynch's buckboard with an attractive chestnut that looked as if he could run—even though he couldn't. The Indians and others offered even money for a race between a local horse and the chestnut but eagerly came forward with big odds that they could beat the dejected-looking blue roan. But Satan was a snare and a delusion and the rate at which he sped over the course at Blackfoot Crossing served as a lesson to all who lost money that beauty and speed are not necessarily related.

In one of his strange horse deals, Tom Lynch contributed in a bigger way to Thoroughbred history on this continent. Billy Henry told the story. It was about 1889 and an American horse fancier—Reynolds by name—breezed into Calgary, with four racers in his possession. Before long he ran out of money—a state of affairs not uncommon among horsemen. To obtain a loan, Reynolds offered his good horses for security and then faced the ugly prospect of having them seized.

In a moment of desperation, the visitor resolved to whisk his beloved horses away before the Canadian sheriff caught up with him. But how was he to get them back across the border without being seen on the trail? A Calgary friend who felt some sympathy for the fellow, whispered: "You go and talk with Tom Lynch; nobody can move cattle and horses like that man."

Lynch was consulted and, believing the American was the victim of some sharp Calgary horsemen, he agreed to help. The understanding was that if he could deliver the four Thoroughbreds across the United States boundary, he could claim his choice of the mares, as payment for his time and trouble.

With Lynch in charge, the Montana race horses were removed from a Calgary corral at a midnight hour, driven south a few miles, then west along Fish creek and south through valleys skirting the mountains, to reach the Montana border at a point rarely seen by white men. The mare Tom Lynch chose for himself was one called Froila although she had gone by the name Sangaroo when in Calgary. Anyway, she was returned to make her home at the TL Ranch, just west of High River.

Lynch made no mistake in his choice of mares. This Froila had good breeding, refined type and a great store of Thoroughbred metal. After being sold to Duncan Cameron in 1894, she produced a filly foal by Eagle Plume, a stallion imported by the Quorn Ranch. The foal was given the name May W, one that many horsemen will recognize, and after being trained at Calgary, the filly raced extensively in the United States and was rated the fastest two-year-old on western American tracks in her time. The late James Speers said he considered May W to be the best mare ever bred in Canada. Ultimately, she was sent to England where she added to an already great reputation.

* * *

Tom Lynch was a shrewd dealer but, in the words of Billy Henry, "everybody was his friend." Anyone needing food or a place to stay received a welcome at the TL ranch, even though he had the appearance of a criminal. When a heavily armed man wanted for a shooting at Fort Macleod rode to the Lynch cabin and told his story, Lynch reacted as usual and said: "Sure, tie your horse in the stable and stay as long as you like."

The hunted man accepted the invitation and unsaddled. Billy Henry was breaking horses there at the time and when he went to the stable early in the morning, a day or two later, both the guest and his horse were missing. Nothing more was heard about the gun-man for several weeks and then came word of another shooting, this one at Deer Lodge, Montana, in the course of which, the same travelling man had an argument with the local bartender. But this time, the bartender was the first to draw and the man who had enjoyed Lynch's hospitality was killed.

When Tom Lynch sold his place near High River, he moved back in the hills, and started another TL ranch, on the north side of the Highwood, where large scale ranching operations are still being conducted. But in 1892, after living at the upper place for only three years, Lynch died suddenly. For a long time, he had a cough and friends suspected tuberculosis. A respiratory hemhorrage took him away.

Tom Lynch was married but had no children. He made money but didn't believe in hoarding. Anybody in need could get a loan or a donation and what he left behind was mostly his influence upon the cattle range. In seeding the Canadian ranch land with breeding stock, this man who was at home anywhere that chinook winds blew and could do marvelous things with a saddle horse and rope, was unquestionably the biggest single factor.

When the stirring events of the early trail days are dramatized, the hero in the play must be a wiry and unshaven fellow with a crust of dust on his brow, a good-natured and kindly fellow, Tom Lynch by name.

Chapter XXXIII

SIR JOHN OF THE BIG SPREAD

SIR John Lister Kaye, founder of the Canadian Agricultural, Coal and Colonization Company—better known as the "76"—struck the prairie country like a March storm, spectacular for a time but with no great lasting effects, either good or bad. Had big ideas about farming and ranching been convertible to real money, however, Sir John would have been a millionaire and his company would have paid handsome dividends. As it was, errors in judgment cost the company a good deal and the chief rewards were in experience and entertainment for those who watched Sir John and the big show he directed.

He was the dynamic and rather tempestuous little Englishman, possessing the optimism of an oil promoter and the courage of a she-bear with a new cub. If the old range cows with long horns and short tempers didn't like the idea of being milked to support Sir John's dairy undertaking, he'd see that they were milked anyway. If the rains didn't come during the growing season, he'd raise wheat without rain. But this energetic newcomer was short on dry land experience as he was short in stature and growing wheat and grass without rain wasn't simple and Sir John had troubles.

Men in the homestead country saw him for the first time in the vicinity of Balgonie, east of Regina. There, in 1885, he was associated with Lord Queensbury in a 7000-acre farming project. But it was only 7000 acres—not big enough for the man, even though he sent 30 ploughs to the field at one time in the summer of 1887 when 1100 acres were broken for cropping in the next year.

* * *

Carried away by the program of that year, he secured English capital and organized the Canadian Agricultural, Coal and Colonization Company. Acting for that new organization, he secured 10 blocks of land at points along the main line of the Canadian Pacific Railway, the locations extending from Balgonie on the east to Langdon. on the west and each block consisting of 10,000 acres. About half the land was bought from the government and half from the CPR.

The plan was to raise livestock, grow grains and promote immigration. English and other Old Country people desiring to farm in the North West Territories could work for Sir John for a while and ultimately settle on a half section of land with buildings provided, a team of horses, other livestock and 20 acres under cultivation. The arrangement was attractive but most of the land was in the driest section of the prairies—excellent for grazing but alarmingly uncertain for cropping.

Sir John, it seemed, could only count in hundreds, thousands and millions, and under date of October 6, 1888, the Edmonton Bulletin reported him as giving a contract for two million feet of lumber for the construction of his farm buildings. To bring the prairie sod under cultivation, he was buying 500 Clydesdale mares in Ontario, planning to send 50 to each of the new farm units. In that same year he bought 7000 cattle from the Powder River Ranch Company which had recently moved its big herd from Wyoming to Mosquito creek in the Canadian Foothills.

That number would divide nicely into lots of 700 per farm or ranch. And with those Powder River cattle came the brand "76" and thereafter, the company ranches were known accordingly.

* * *

Sir John had no intention to limit his livestock breeding to cattle and horses. Pigs were to have a place. It was a time when there were comparatively few porkers on the prairies but before long, the 76 ranches could report 700 of them, with three breeds represented—Yorkshire, Suffolk and Berkshire. But it was about sheep that Sir John's enthusiasm reached the highest pitch. He had confidence in sheep as a profitable investment and his plan, so he told the press of that time, was to buy 50,000 in Washington and Oregon.

He didn't actually buy that many but in 1889, a flock of 10,000 head was driven overland from Idaho and Montana to Maple Creek where it was turned over to the company's sheep manager, William Rutherford. At that point, the sheep were loaded on freight cars to be distributed to the various farm and ranch locations, east and west. The idea was to place 1000 ewes on each place as a foundation for bigger things but this was seen as an error and in the next year, the flocks were brought together at Swift Current, Kincorth and Gull Lake.

The sheep multiplied as they were supposed to do and John Oman who came into the company's service as an experienced Scottish shepherd in 1892, found 30,000 head including all ages. During the ensuing grazing season, the sheep were divided into 15 flocks of 2000 each and distributed with the sheep camps extending for 50 miles.

It was a big operation but there were big disappointments. Depression struck the sheep industry in 1893 and it took a good wether to bring two cents a pound. Sir John believed he could do better by exporting surplus sheep to England and on his instructions, some 25,000 head were sent from the 76 ranches to the English markets.

In spite of difficulties, the sheep were more profitable than most other farm and ranch ventures, certainly better than wheat. Had Sir John not been in such a big hurry, he might have learned of the uncertainty of wheat in some of the areas in which he selected his properties. But he couldn't wait. When the rains failed, he decided to draw water in wooden tanks to irrigate the thirsty fields. That was one of the prize errors in the southwest.

* * *

To carry out the plan to beat the drought, 44 pine water tanks were ordered from wagon-makers, Ryan and McArthur in Winnipeg. Each tank, to be carried on wagon wheels, was 11 feet 4 inches long; 3 feet 7 inches wide, and 2 feet high. Each would have a capacity of roughly 575 gallons. But the woeful ineffectiveness of trying to meet normal water needs of crops on Sir John's fields by this means, didn't occur to him. He didn't stop to figure it out that to furnish an inch of water over a single acre would require 110 tons of water or about 40 trips with one of his water tanks.

It must be said for him, however, that he was never afraid to experiment. Some of the farm implements he introduced seemed strange mechanical monstrosities to the experienced people round about. Among the new machines introduced from Scotland were the two-furrow walking plows called Aberdeens. They did seem to offer something in improvement but like the pine water tanks for irrigating the huge fields, they didn't survive for long.

* * *

Some of Sir John's ideas about cattle were progressive. He believed in good breeding and when the 7000 Powder River ranch cattle were purchased, he announced that 99 Aberdeen Angus and Galloway bulls had been purchased in Scotland and were already on the way to Canada. Moreover, he decided it would help his cattle business if he had his own abattoir and retail stores. Accordingly, a big slaughtering plant was constructed at Calgary and retail shops were started at several points, including Lethbridge. Cattle, sheep and pigs from the company's ranches furnished most of the meat handled in the stores.

Sir John's decision to develop dairying on the ranches was a major source of amusement for cattlemen who observed the result. Perhaps the dividend-hungry directors back in London were prodding him to increase company revenue. At any rate, when wheat production proved disappointing, the order went forward to milk the wild ranch cows wearing the 76 brand, as a means of improving the company's financial security. Sir John would build a creamery at Swift Current to handle the cream from the ranches and offer a silver trophy to the ranch manager who would have "the largest number of cows milking by October, (1889) ."

No self respecting cowboy fancied milking cows and Sir John's workers were not exceptions. As for the ranch cows with quite a bit of Texas Longhorn strain still showing, they had very strong views about the propriety of it all. They made it very clear that they'd be glad to fight it out with anybody who tried to become familiar with their mammary departments.

Long chutes were constructed into which the wild cows were driven at milking times. Once in the chute, a cow was made secure by means of ropes and while one cowboy handled the ropes, another would attempt the humiliating task of extracting some milk. Sir John, never one to admit defeat, reported the project to be going well but no ranch worker would admit as much. As expected by observers, the scheme was soon abandoned, much to the relief of ranch hands and ranch cows.

* * *

If determination could have achieved it, the 76 outfit would have succeeded. As it was, one mistake after another proved costly to directors and shareholders and, finally, a couple of severe winters with heavy cattle losses led to an admission of failure. Sir John retired.

Ranch Manager D. H. Andrews went to England in 1895 and promoted a new company known as the Canadian Land and Ranch Company, to take over the holdings of the old one. Andrews who came to Sir John with the Powder River cattle, was an able fellow and had his counsel been followed, the original venture might have succeeded. Certainly the original failure wasn't due to any extravagance on his part, as the early correspondence would show. Writing to his Crane Lake foreman about a steer threatening to die, he advised: "If the steer . . . does not look like getting better, you had better kill him and corn the beef that you cannot use fresh."

In another letter, Andrews commented about the ranch

inventory that had just come to his desk and pointed out that the list of equipment was not complete. There should be added, observed this man with a complete grasp of the big business, "one drawing knife, one screw driver, one cold chisel, two hammers and a hay knife."

The new company, retaining both the 76 brand and name, did quite well. But in 1906, Andrews died and three years later, the Crane Lake ranch which had become the headquarters ranch a couple of miles east of the town of Piapot, and the famous brand, were bought by the firm of Gordon, Ironside and Fares. And it was indeed a famous brand, still capable of commanding a cattleman's best attention. It was registered in the Brand Book of the North West Territories in 1886 and thereafter, placed on the left ribs of thousands and thousands of prairie cattle, it was about as familiar as a Stetson hat. When Andrews reported his cattle count on a June date in 1890, he listed 6446 head, and could have added for sheep, some 25,000 or 30,000 head.

But however much folk laughed at Sir John Lister Kaye and his grandiose schemes, he left an impression on western agriculture, indirectly if not directly. His experiences helped to confirm the folly of some practices and people who followed were spared the necessity of repeating his mistakes. Many of the immigrants he directed to the prairies remained to become successful farmers and ranchers and influential citizens. And though it was in a costly and rather clumsy way, Sir John helped to enrich the story of agriculture.

Chapter XXXIV

PARSON WITH A WHEAT CROWN

IT WILL come as a double surprise that the wheat to win the first recognized world championship for Canada was grown beside the Peace river and exhibited by a Church of England parson, Rev. John Gough Brick. To commemorate the life and work of that enthusiastic farmer-missionary, a bronze tablet was unveiled at Peace River town on September 12, 1954.

The championship was at the World's Columbia exposition in Chicago in 1893 and interested people in most parts of the world heard the news a full month before it reached the man who grew it at far-off Peace river.

* * *

Brick was one of the first to sense the agricultural resources and charm of the new and allegedly frosty North, beside the mighty Peace. It wasn't that he had been out seeking charm for his surroundings; on the contrary, his ideals in service to fellows were such as to take him wherever he could be most useful, but it was one of the rewards for unselfishness that the remote northern area to which he travelled in 1881, brought rich satisfaction.

His early years at Upton-On-Severn in England, where

he was born in 1836, proved he could have been a successful business man. But being interested in church and social work, the ministry became his goal. By going to Canada for his theological studies, he could save time. Brick, no longer a young man, was in a hurry.

He and wife and four children said farewell to England and crossed the Atlantic. In Eastern Canada he studied and graduated and his first charge from the church was beside the St. Lawrence river where he listened to stories from men who had paddled fur-trade canoes to the far northwest and back. What those old voyageur fellows told brought new ideas to the energetic parson and he sought permission from his church superiors to start a mission at Dunvegan, far back on the Peace river.

Permission was granted and early in 1881, after settling his family in Toronto, the middle-aged missionary was on his way to the northwest. The first part of the journey was easy enough but after leaving the rails at Winnipeg, travel was by the most primitive means, across Lake Winnipeg and up the Saskatchewan River to Prince Albert by Hudson's Bay Company boat, overland by wagon to Clearwater river, across Lake Athabasca and finally, river boat on the Peace to Dunvegan where the Hudson's Bay Company had a trading post for many years. It was a rough initiation for a minister having no experience with rough trails, the traditional vocabulary of western ox-drivers and the merciless appetites of northern mosquitoes. And for a man who was instinctively in a hurry, the slow pace by water and trail was very trying.

From Winnipeg, the journey was one of 1500 miles and primitive all the way. There was some farming at Prince Albert and some garden plots at Lake Athabasca where Peter Pond of early fur-trading fame grew vegetables a hundred years before.

At Dunvegan where Brick was a total stranger, there was no reason to anticipate a welcome but there was a pleasant surprise. Awaiting Anglican Brick was a friendly hand-shake from Roman Catholic Father Hudson who was in charge of the local mission supported by his church. It marked the beginning of a long and splendid friendship and when Brick was building his Protestant church, his most helpful assistant was the Roman Catholic priest. It is unfortunate that no pictures were obtained of the two missionaries of different faiths working together, whip-sawing spruce boards for the construction of an Anglican church. But it was the spirit of the North.

* * *

The building spot Brick fixed upon after weeks of searching was beside the river, about midway between Dunvegan and Peace River Crossing. He bought an ox to "snake" the logs from the forest but all other construction work had to be done by hand and the soft ministerial hands became so hard that not even a spruce splinter would penetrate.

He was now determined there would be a farm in conjunction with his mission but the building of the church had to come first. Before the end of the year, the chapel was ready for services and in the spring of the following year, the missionary planted the first seeds in soil which was to be his Shaftsbury farm, called after his home town in England.

Brick could see so much to do; either a mission or a farm could utilize a man's time fully. It helped, however, when his two sons, Allan and Bertie, came from the East in 1883 to assist in preparation for agriculture at the mission and to start farming on their own account at a point known as Old Wives lake, about four miles west of the present Berwyn.

Five years after arrival beside the Peace, Rev. Brick returned to the East to visit his wife who was ill at that time, and, perchance, secure some additional financial support for both mission and farm. Bishop R. J. Pierce of Peace River reports that Brick's annual stipend was $750, from which he sent $400 to his wife. Thus there wasn't much left with which to develop a farm that might be an inspiration to the northern natives and others. But in Eastern Canada and later in England he found people eager to hear about his work in the far reaches of the West, and willing to help. His absence from farm and mission

231

lasted two years but throughout that time he was making plans for the return trip with stock and equipment.

Having obtained money for the purpose, Brick bought what he considered to be most needed on the farm and his shipment to the Peace river in 1888 was much more imposing than that of seven years before. Moreover, the missionary was now taking his wife to the new home.

The new and history-making shipment was moved by CPR from Toronto to Calgary. Every item of goods showed that Brick was serious about his farm plan. At Calgary, the freight was transferred to carts; 23 ox-carts in regular freight service, two wagons and a democrat for Mrs. Brick's riding comfort, were included in the cavalcade starting northward.

Brick was making news as well as agricultural history, as the Edmonton Bulletin of August 25, 1888, indicated by its report:

"Rev. Mr. Brick, the Church of England missionary, is now on his way to Peace river. He is bringing up a large outfit, including a portable grist mill, agricultural and carpenters' tools. Also a thoroughbred Durham bull, two Holstein heifers and an Ayrshire cow, Berkshire and Yorkshire pigs and some poultry. The freight amounts to about 17,000 pounds. The rates are: Calgary to the Landing 4½ cents, Landing to Slave lake 2½ cents, Slave lake to Dunvegan, two cents. Mr. Brick has raised $5000 for the purpose of his mission, including $2000 contributed by the federal government, in his two years absence. He is bringing his family with him."

That was the Edmonton Bulletin's report and it might have been added that the pure bred animals were probably the first of their respective breeds to set foot on soil now Northern Alberta. Moreover, the loaded carts were on the Calgary-Edmonton trail for 20 days and another six in making their way to Athabaska Landing. At the latter point, the machinery was transferred to York boats for the trip across Lesser Slave lake, while horses and cattle were driven overland to a place at the west end of the lake, now marked by Grouard. From there to Shaftsbury mission and farm, the freight was again carried on carts and wagons.

How the wife and mother, recovering from a recent illness, withstood the weeks of hardship on the trail, is not recorded but it is fairly evident that she, like her husband, possessed the fibre of a true pioneer.

* * *

During Brick's absence from Peace river, the mission herd increased to 30 head of cattle, probably the biggest herd in the North, and the missionary's son, Allan, had hay stacked and ready for the additional animals his father was bringing. Shaftsbury farm was becoming a reality. Trappers and traders who had scoffed at the idea now looked with interest. With more than a little surprise they admitted that a parson can be resourceful. They saw horses and oxen hitched together to break new land and they saw tree trunks with short pieces of branches protruding, being dragged over the new breaking to cultivate in the absence of a disc-harrow.

There is no record of crop yields in the first years but they must have been satisfactory to the man who was seeing a dream being fulfilled. This much is known, that for the spring planting in 1892, Brick had a bushel of seed wheat of a new variety, at least new to that area. Red Fife was its name and it had the reputation of superiority for milling purposes. From the new seed, the crop stand was excellent, and the kernels were heavy and plump. The yield seemed to reach the unbelievable record of 72 bushels to the acre. And even an acre represented a lot of work because the crop had to be cut by means of sickle and threshed with flail on the floor of the church. The final operation in threshing consisted of tossing forkfuls of the beaten crop into the air to let the northern breezes separate the straw and chaff from the grain.

But there was unsuspected reward in store. There was the World's Fair at Chicago and somebody suggested to Brick that he enter a sample of his wheat. The missionary agreed to make entry, reasoning that even though his wheat didn't win anything, it would at least bring the name of Peace river to Chicago.

There was no such thing as hand picking at that time and Shaftsbury didn't have as much as a fanning mill to aid in the preparation. But the Peace river wind had done a good job in blowing away all but the heavy kernels and a bushel of the plump and richly colored wheat was sacked for shipment. Then there was the problem of taking the sample out to Edmonton and it fell to Allan Brick to make the journey over winter roads. It took him 10 days to reach Edmonton and temperatures dipped to 50 and 60 below zero along the way.

The wheat arrived in Chicago, barely in time for the judging, and then what had seemed impossible, happened. Men in conversation around the show were exclaiming in their astonishment, "Wheat from Peace river won the championship; where is Peace river?" Newspapers carried the story about a sample grown north of latitude 56 winning the world championship for wheat but the papers were weeks old before they reached the settlement at Peace river and Rev. Brick on whose head the "Wheat Crown" was to rest, was one of the last of interested people to receive the great news.

* * *

John Gough Brick's faith in the North was at least partly vindicated. The Chicago triumph was a well deserved reward. But in 1895, Brick's health was worrying him and he felt obliged to return to Eastern Canada. He accepted a church call in New York State but illness forced his retirement and he died there in 1896.

For today's traveller in the North, there is the memorial tablet at Peace River, erected by the Department of Northern Affairs and National Resources on recommendation of the Historic Sites and Monuments Board of Canada; and eight miles west of Peace River are the log buildings of Shaftsbury Farm, ancient but dignified and sturdy, memorializing the courageous work of Missionary-Farmer Brick.

CHAPTER XXXV

MEDICINE MAN WITH MESSAGE

NAMES can be misleading. Not all the McLeans belong to the Scottish clan claimed by some followers to be so ancient its clansmen had their own ark at the time of the Old Testament flood. George McLean of the Alberta foothills was not a true clansman, his other name, Tatunga Mani meaning Walking Buffalo, being a better indication of his background. This Medicine Man and, for a time, chief of his tribe at Morley, was an Indian of purest Stoney breeding. As thousands of people saw him at Calgary stampedes and Banff Indian days, watched him in parades and dances, he was a noble and colorful representative of his race. Tourists delighted to have pictures taken beside him as he posed in native dress topped off with distinctive head-piece carrying the finely pointed horns of a buffalo bull.

To his credit, George McLean was one of the founders of the Indian Society but long before that organization existed, he was recognized by Stoney tribesmen and others as a man of wisdom, a seeker after truth and a person who knew where to find it. Throughout his life he was a student and Nature was his teacher. He became one of the best authorities on Indian legends and had a message he wanted to share with the white man. Trouble was, the white man wanted to be the teacher and wouldn't listen.

* * *

But how did a full-blood Stoney Indian come by the two names, one of them Scottish? Back of both names were stories. As one of those stories goes, the subject of this sketch had something in common with Remus and Romulus, founders of ancient Rome who were supposed to have been mothered by a she-wolf. When still a small papoose, this Stoney's mother died and nobody had any interest in the child. Hungry, he toddled away from the lodges of the tribesmen and his absence was unnoticed.

Months passed and then, one evening after the sun had set, members of a Stoney family squatting in their tent, heard the trample of heavy feet above the noise made by wind in the trees. The Indians listened carefully and the squaw said, "I hear a papoose whimpering." Going out into the chilly night, the woman was startled at seeing a small child being nursed by a buffalo cow.

As the story goes, the cow spoke to the squaw, told how she found this small child wandering in the hills, searching for food; out of pity for the helpless thing, she allowed it to nurse and follow her and had saved its life. "Now," said the cow, "I turn the care of this papoose back to you." At that, the buffalo walked away into the darkness of the night and the youngster was taken into the Indian family and given the name, "Walking Buffalo."

The circumstances leading to the Indian's Scottish name were more than legend. Some time after being left an orphan, the boy was placed in Rev. John McDougall's orphanage and school at Morley and at the age of seven he was adopted after a fashion by prairie missionary Reverend John McLean. It was then that the Indian boy was given the name George McLean.

The missionary's interest resulted in the young fellow getting something better than an ordinary education at Morley. Partly with the idea that he'd continue to university and study medicine, he was sent to school at Winnipeg. But as preparations were being made for his entry to university, objections came from the reservation; his Indian foster-father and Chief Jacob Bearspaw, (one of the signatories to the Treaty of 1877) made protest to the plan. They demanded that the young fellow be returned to live the life of a good Indian on the reserve. The Indian wishes prevailed and George McLean went back to Morley, to adopt again the life of his own people.

* * *

But regardless of education, this Indian was progressive and destined to be a leader. He took to ranching and raised both cattle and sheep. He worked to improve the position of his fellows and though he had lived with people of the two races, he was satisfied and proud to spend the rest of his life as an Indian. At the age of 23, George McLean became a counsellor and interpreter to his uncle, the great Chief Jacob Bearspaw. In time, following Moses Bearspaw, McLean became the Stoney Chief and filled that office for 15 years.

Naturally, too, he was a hunter, always. His foster-father was a great buffalo hunter but when McLean was still a small boy the huge herds of buffalo were destroyed; the white man with guns, whiskey and a lust for exploit had arrived. Bow and arrow hunting demanding the maximum of skill was George McLean's boyhood experience. Then he graduated to the flint-lock type of gun and admitted it was a wonderful invention. But hunting to him meant more than killing. It afforded opportunity to study the wild creatures and their surroundings. He never indulged in "mass slaughter" but he knew what it was like to walk 50 miles on a day's hunt and stalk a single animal for a full half day, studying its every turn, to ultimately outguess it. Yes, and he knew what it was to go hungry when the population of game animals dwindled and his people were reduced to the necessity of living on herbs.

"So much to learn about Nature's laws," McLean said when in his 83rd year. "Nature," he added, "is a Bible to me— not written by human hands, but by the Great Spirit himself. Too bad the white man doesn't know more about it. He's a smart fellow but he can't boss Nature all the time. He took the country that didn't belong to him and pushed the Indians into some corners. Then he killed off the buffalo. Pretty soon he'll destroy the rest of the game and then the trees and the good grass and soil. And he thinks he should teach the Indian how to live. He's a smart fellow but he forgets the Indian could teach him a few things about living. The white man will not listen." They are the words of the Indian wise man, the Indian philosopher.

*　*　*

George McLean was not one to consider any particular color or race as superior to another but in defence of his own people he recited or composed an Indian story about creation. The Great Spirit, according to the telling, saw this part of His world without people and said, "I will make men." Accordingly, a man was fashioned out of mud and placed far in the North where the weather was cold. There the man became a living thing with a pale and sickly white color of skin and the Great Spirit, looking at this creature of His invention, exclaimed, "That won't do; I'll try again."

And so, He fashioned another man of mud, this time placing him under the hot sun of the far South until the skin was burned to the color of charcoal. Still not satisfied with what He had created, the Great Spirit resolved to try once more, and compromise. On this, the third trial, the mud figure was placed to bake and mature in the sun, midway between north and south. The result was good. When this one became a living thing, he was observed to be "neither too light nor too dark." Here was the intermediate "color of the Indian and the Great Spirit was satisfied."

Men of science may contend that the original Indians migrated from the Old World by way of Bering strait and Alaska but George McLean chose to believe they were placed here, just like the North American buffalo, to be part of Nature's community of plants and animals.

Perhaps the Great Spirit had a special purpose in placing Indians here. Perchance the Great Spirit knew the white people would come and the Indians might teach them something about sensible living, even though they don't want to be taught. If the Indian had a chance, he'd shout that the thing called civilization is weighted with folly, people hurrying to make money, using up the natural resources, talking about a better world and making bombs with which to destroy it.

* * *

When George McLean ceased to be serious, he could be good entertainment. As there was logic in his reasoning, there was charm in the legends of his telling. Nobody was required to believe the story about the child being nursed by a buffalo cow but it would have been misfortune if that and other Indian legends were lost. George McLean not only helped to perpetuate them but created some, like the one about how the fox acquired a silver fur.

An Indian went alone on a hunt and killed a goose. After preparing the bird for his meal beside a lake, a fox came by and Indian and fox held a conversation. Naturally, the fox was interested in having a meal from the goose being roasted over the fire and the hunter proposed that he and the fox race around the lake, travelling in opposite directions, the winner to have the roasted goose.

"But I am lame," said the scheming fox. The hunter, being a sporting fellow, replied, "All right, to offset your handicap, I'll tie a stone to my ankle."

And so the race started, the fox limping away in one direction and the Indian making slow progress in the other. At the opposite side of the lake they passed each other and then the sagacious fox, with no further reason to play lame, dashed on to the goal and consumed the goose. Leaving nothing but the bones, he went to have a sleep in the tall grass on a neck of land extending out into the lake. The hunter arrived, concluding that he was back first, but when he found only the bones where he expected the roast goose, he realized he had been tricked and was very angry.

Finding the fox asleep and wishing to have revenge, the hunter set fire to the grass and the animal was trapped behind the flames. The well-fed fox awakened in fright and in jumping through the flames to escape death, he singed his fur, making it appear dark and silvery. And so, there were silver foxes thereafter.

*   *   *

George McLean had ideas and convictions and legends —too good to be wasted. But Indian wisdom has been wasted. "The white man wouldn't listen."

But George McLean wasn't bitter. As he remarked, his experiences with "Indian savages and white savages," convinced him there were mistakes on both sides and both sides had something to offer. Sitting on a buffalo robe spread over the floor of his teepee, the Old Man of the Stoney tribe gazed at his moccasins and then, looking up, said, "Why don't we try to understand each other?"

CHAPTER XXXVI

CRANK ABOUT CONSERVATION

L ET'S save all the water possible. It's liquid gold where we have fertile but dry soil, you know." So said George Spence, homesteader, legislator and man with dedicated determination about conservation. "It's a crime," Saskatchewan people heard him say again and again, "to allow water to run across this dry land, down to the sea, without making an effort to conserve and use it to augment the scanty supplies nature has given us."

Born on an Orkney Island farm, George Spence had no objection to the bonny name of Orkney for his village in southwestern Saskatchewan, and no doubt, he had some·thing to do with the choice. A secret pride burns in Orkadian breasts and it may have been George's father who, saying farewell to his son, had a parting word of admonition: "Don't ask strangers where they're from; if they're from the Orkneys you'll soon know and if they're not, no good will come by embarrassing them."

The Spence boy's travels took him to Edinburgh for studies in electrical engineering and then work with the North British Railway. In 1900, when he was 21 years of age, he came to Canada, not sure what he wanted to do. The choice was between digging for gold in the Klondike, engineering and farming and, as things turned out, he did them all, in that order. In 1912, he took a homestead in dry southwestern Saskatchewan, 100 statutory miles from a railroad. It was the country of buckbrush, cactus and antelope—and had some rattlesnakes, too. It had handicaps but the soil was good and Spence said there must be some way of reducing the ravages of drought.

* * *

The first thing he did on the homestead was break two acres for trees. Though he was far removed from a railroad and it wasn't easy to get mail and groceries, Spence packed 200 young trees on his back over the 100-mile trail from Swift Current. And to further astonish the neighbors, he planted fruit trees, plums, apples and cherries. He was situated 3000 feet above sea level and the precipitation was only about 12 inches a year, but he was determined to grow fruit, even if he had to cross apples with native cactus plants to do it. He did have success and his dry land surprised everybody. But he wasn't letting any water escape from his farm—even had a dug-out reservoir to solve his stock watering problem, long before the idea was popularized.

* * *

The entry of Dry-Farmer Spence into politics marked the beginning of a long period of public service. He ran in eight provincial and federal election contests during his 21 years in politics and won them all. His first election was to the Saskatchewan Legislature in 1917 and after being re-elected twice, he resigned to enter federal politics and sat in the House of Commons until persuaded to return to take a cabinet post in the government of Saskatchewan. Successively, he was minister of highways, labor and industry, and finally, public works, from which he resigned in 1937 to accept the directorship of the Prairie Farm Rehabilitation Act.

Government efforts to rehabilitate the prairie area devastated by drought and wind in the 30s, fascinated him. Having homesteaded in the driest section, he knew the problems, studied them and slept with them. As early as 1920 he was serving on a better farming commission and studying conservation of water and organization of community pastures. A preliminary conference was held at Swift Current to discuss drought and, as Spence recalled vividly, just as the meeting was called to order, rain started and as it fell in torrents on the metal roof, it made so much noise that the meeting could not continue. Farmers who hadn't seen rain in months, rushed out to refresh their memories and feel it. Nature was just reminding the planners how unpredictable she can be.

The Prairie Farm Rehabilitation Act, passed in 1935 and expanding rapidly, needed a director and George Spence seemed a logical choice to carry out that work, so close to his heart. His appointment coincided with Saskatchewan's darkest year of drought, 1937, when the dwarfed and desiccated wheat in the province averaged two and one-half bushels per acre and some discouraged people in the Palliser Triangle said, "Write it off as wheat land; turn it back to grass for cattle and buffalo."

Mother Nature and Father Depression seemed to be "ganging up" on rural Saskatchewan but tall, lean George Spence with the soft Scottish accent and Orkadian determination was not capitulating. "Patience lads," he was heard to say, "we're only beginning. God didn't give us all that fertile soil for nothing." With new vigor he preached conservation of water, community pastures, feed reserves and better cultural practices.

Under his direction, PFRA changed many things on the prairies while Nature was relenting somewhat. Dams to service large and small irrigation projects were constructed; sub-marginal areas were regrassed; better methods of cultivation were demonstrated and when Spence resigned in 1947, the midwest had 75 community pastures embracing a million and a half acres of grassland and carrying 80,000 head of livestock in the grazing season. No fewer than 35,000 small water conservation projects, mostly dug-outs and dams, had been completed with PFRA assistance. Small dams were irrigating over a hundred thousand acres and large undertakings like the St. Mary and Milk river scheme and a still bigger one with a 210-foot dam on the South Saskatchewan were being studied. Gradually, water-saving projects, big and small, were doing something for farm

security in a big area of the West. And back of the planning was that man, repeating rather monotonously, "Patience lads, we're only beginning; and remember, those soils
are the greatest of our natural resources."

* * *

When he concluded that the big job in PFRA was for
a younger man, he resigned, but another task was awaiting
him—another responsibility with water. He was appointed
a member on the Canadian section of the International
Joint Commission and continued to study the distribution
and use of water at the international level.

But throughout his years, George Spence had time for
many other activities and the Ford car his constituents
gave him in 1925 should have known its own way on every
Saskatchewan highway. With special sentiment for it, he
drove that car until its outdated lines were as conspicuous
on the roads as pantalettes would be at a Firemans' Ball in
Winnipeg. After using it for 16 years, the famous Ford was
raffled off with the proceeds going to the Red Cross.

Among the "other activities," the events of 1938 would
have a high rating—when Lord Tweedsmuir, then Governor
General, was touring the country and George Spence was
in charge of arrangements in the southwest. On the itiner-
ary were a stop at the Gilchrist ranch, another at Bill Martin's sheep ranch and an inspection of the new irrigation
project at Val Marie. George Spence was a good story teller
and the Val Marie experience was an excellent subject. He
notified the town overseer: "The Governor General will visit
Val Marie on May 11th," and was able to comment later,
"Wars have been declared in fewer words but never in
history did ten words create as great a commotion in such a
small place, in such a short time."

The tempo of the town mounted; nothing to rival the
excitement had occured in 20 years. School children dramatized a John Buchan story; weeds were uprooted; paint
brushes were put to use and where there was neither time,
money nor paint for all sides of a house or building, only
its front was painted. A bulldozer was requisitioned to push
scrap machinery and a few abandoned outdoor toilets into
the river. In the scramble, errors occured and some of the

outdoor fixtures still an essential part of the town's sanitary system, were pushed away too. Cows which normally roamed the peaceful streets were haltered or sent away to distant pastures; chickens were confined to pens and mothers took to pressing clothes.

Of course, there'd have to be music, good music, appropriate music. George Spence said so and suggested bagpipes. Fortunately, there was a set of pipes in the district but not a good Highland uniform, without which a piper might appear ugly indeed. An appeal was made publicly and in response, bits and pieces of Scottish dress were sent in until a completed outfit resulted—one that would have done credit to the proudest MacCrimmon.

It was May 11, 1938, and the vice-regal party toured the irrigation project, lunched at the PFRA tent where Tweedsmuir insisted upon washing "with the men" rather than in special quarters provided especially for him, and then moved on to the outdoor meeting to which people had come from far and near, some by wagon, some on bicycles, some on horseback and others by car. It was Val Marie's great moment and George Spence said that "drought and relief, even death and taxes were forgotten."

The piper for the day did a masterly performance, getting in his last blow with "Cock o' the North." The Governor was delighted and insisted upon speaking to him. "Congratulations, my man," he began, "and what tartan do you claim?"

It was the awful moment George Spence had feared because, as he related, the piper didn't know one tartan from another and simply replied, "My name's Olson and I come from Minnesota." The Spence heart beat wildly but the Governor set everybody at ease by commenting that congratulations were all the more in order because of the fine judgment in the choice of instrument and music.

George Spence became a part of everything in the big community described as southwestern Saskatchewan, ranching country and farming country that had not lost its frontier characters—the "Dad" Gaff type and the "Windy" Simpson kind. Gaff, once a buffalo hunter in Kansas, claimed a record of 5200 buffalo in one summer, more than

Buffalo Bill's biggest one-season kill, and it was he who, when faced with what he considered an exorbitant price for a hotel room at Govanlock one night, became annoyed and bought the hotel.

He was Spence's friend, as was Simpson, keeper of the post office at Battle Creek, who, before his death in 1934, instructed that neither the officiating minister nor pall-bearers were to be sober when they buried him. Carrying out a friend's last requests may present difficulties but George Spence believed the departed would have been reasonably well satisfied with the efforts. That's all he would say.

* * *

But it will be as an Apostle of Conservation that Spence will be remembered. His words of warning should be repeated again and again: "The practices commonly followed to conserve moisture under the one-crop system will in time deplete the native fertility of even our best soils and break down the granular structure. That would cause soil drifting . . . abandonment of large areas and national disaster . . . We have been exporting our soil fertility, selling it by the pound. This system of drawing on Nature's bank account without putting anything back is not conducive to stable agriculture, nor does it add permanent strength to the national economy."

On Dominion Day, 1942, Conservationist Spence became a Civil Commander of the British Empire and in 1948, the University of Saskatchewan conferred upon him the degree of Doctor of Laws (honoris causa), "for outstanding public service."

On a public school examination in Saskatchewan's dry belt, there was this question: "To what do the Orkney Islands owe their importance?"

A pupil answered: "George Spence," and to the teacher's credit, was given full marks.

CHAPTER XXXVII

UNCLE GABRIEL

A TOURIST crossing the South Saskatchewan river north of Saskatoon a few years ago, asked the ferryman for his name. "Dumont," was the answer and at once the traveller enquired if the riverman could claim any relationship to Gabriel Dumont who was Louis Riel's strongman in what people still call the North West Rebellion.

"Ah, you know something about Uncle Gabriel?" the ferryman replied. "He was one great man; every kid around Batoche wants to be like Uncle Gabriel Dumont. He was the strongest man along the river and nobody could shoot buffalo as well."

The ferry languished in midstream as the native son waxed more and more eloquent. "I tell you something," he went on; "if Louis Riel followed Uncle Gabriel's advice and our half-breeds didn't run out of ammunition, not one of Middleton's damned soldiers would ever have seen Toronto again. Sure, that old half-breed Dumont knew how to fight."

The slow-moving ferry hit the shoreline on the west side and the tourist though anxious to complete his journey to Saskatoon that evening, felt a compulsion to linger and learn more about that superman, Gabriel Dumont, from

247

a member of his race and family. The stranger parked his car beside the river and rode back across the stream while the ferryman chatted on about the man who was his hero, telling convincingly that if it had not been for the restraining influence of Louis Riel, the whole of Western Canada might have been a bloody battle field in 1885.

* * *

Riel was not a fighter by nature. He was an idealist and when the first major clash between Metis and Mounted Police occurred a few miles out of Duck Lake, Riel appeared, unarmed and holding a crucifix aloft. But the rum-drinking, hard-fighting Dumont would have been happy to completely annihilate the troublesome white imposters who were threatening to uproot his Metis society for the second time in 15 years. The idea of settlement and the thing they called civilization, he could not contemplate without feelings of anger. He and his Metis followers wanted none of it. They were buffalo hunters while the buffalo lasted; they loved the free, wild life with which they grew up. Civilization? Ba! If the whites wanted civilization, all right, they could have it but why try to force it upon people who wanted most of all to be left alone to live the lazy, care-free life beyond the frontier?

At the time of the Red River Insurrection in 1869-70, Gabriel Dumont was a young member of the Manitoba Metis community. He was one of a family of 11 with a Cree mother and French father. As a Metis, he belonged to the biggest single group in that area which was about to become a province. That was part of the trouble; too many people were overlooking the fact that Metis far outnumbered the whites when the province of Manitoba was formed. In spite of numbers, they were the forgotten people. The new form of government was being set up without consultation with the majority group; it was enough to fill any self-respecting half-breed with wrath. Adding further insult, government surveyors appeared unheralded in the half-breed settlements, giving the impression that residents would lose their claims to land. Such were the circumstances leading to the militant stand by Riel and his people.

When Riel's provisional government finally collapsed, many discouraged and disgruntled Metis moved west to begin again. Some moved to Wood Mountain, some to the South Saskatchewan river. Gabriel Dumont led a party of nearly 40 families to settle at Batoche on the South Saskatchewan. Surely, the Metis reasoned, those civilizing whites would never reach far-away Batoche!

For a few years, life on the South Saskatchewan was quite satisfactory. Men could hunt buffalo to their hearts' content; they could get enough furs to pay for their needs in sugar and tea and rum; and the two-fisted Gabriel Dumont was their acknowledged leader. Community laws, such as existed, were of his making. On organized hunts, he was the captain and his famous Winchester rifle was in capable hands. Not only was Dumont the best man in the community to make the home-spun laws by which people lived but he was the one most able to enforce them. He was broad-shouldered, had massive hands and a convincing stride. Nobody argued much with Uncle Gabriel.

* * *

For a few years the Metis were content but then there was a re-appearance of those circumstances which drove them from Manitoba. Settlers were coming again. Land was being surveyed and a government with a short memory was showing no willingness to grant titles for the land on which Dumont's people had squatted for years. On top of all that, the buffalo upon which they depended largely for food, had disappeared. The white man was being blamed for destroying the buffalo and threatening Metis security. Requests and demands sent to the Canadian government were ignored.

There would have to be a showdown but leadership of a different type would be needed and Dumont recognized the requirement clearly. He could cope with a buffalo hunt or a drunken brawl but he was no orator and not much at writing letters that government men would read. He believed the educated and religious Louis Riel should be brought back. He could make speeches that people would listen to and write letters with nice words such as the people in government used.

And so, in 1884, Gabriel Dumont and James Isbister and two others mounted on Indian ponies, rode the 600 miles to where Riel was teaching at a mission school in Montana. Riel was married now and had a family to consider but after some meditation he concluded it was God's will that he return with Dumont and see the Saskatchewan Metis out of their trouble.

Early in 1885, the people about Batoche and Duck Lake heard rumors about soldiers being sent to watch the Metis. The wild spirits of Dumont's people rebelled at the idea. They gathered up all the guns and ammunition within reach and even did some looting of stores nearby to increase their strength. Mounted Police Major Crozier at Fort Carlton heard about the plundering of stores and the rattling of guns and considered it wise to saunter toward Duck Lake with enough men to scare Dumont's Metis boys. But Dumont with 25 mounted men met the bigger troop of over a hundred police and volunteers. There was an attempt to parley but a shot was fired from a gun on the police side and Gabriel's brother Isidore was struck and killed. Instantly, the battle was on. The half-breeds were in the best position and their guns were taking the biggest toll. The soldiers and police began withdrawal and as they did, Dumont's men saw a tempting chance to cut off all escape. Dumont rushed forward, receiving a bullet on the top of his head. He fell to the ground and his followers thought him dead. Another brother, Edourd, took command and seemed to be in position to cut down many of the men in uniform but at this point in the conflict, Louis Riel appeared, unarmed, pleading for an end to the bloodshed. Five Metis and an Indian on Dumont's side were dead and 12 on the police side.

The police abandoned Fort Carlton and marched to Prince Albert. Dumont was for ambushing them at a place he knew very well and shoot them down as they retreated but Riel couldn't approve. Pretty soon an army was on its way from the East to put down those people called rebels.

* * *

At this point in the campaign there was more serious conflict between Riel and Dumont. They weren't the same sort of men in temperament. Riel wanted to win this war without bloodshed but Dumont was ready to do battle the rough way and if he had followed his inclinations, the cost in lives might have been multiplied a hundred times. When Metis scouts brought word that Middleton's army was marching from Qu'Appelle, Dumont, the gambler, had a proposal—one which might have led to annihilation of the eastern army. He was confident he could induce the Indians in every direction to rise and kill every white person they could reach, while he would lead his fighting men, 200 of them, to meet Middleton. By conducting a guerrilla type of warfare, especially at nights, he would cripple the Queen's soldiers. The eager Metis loved the prospect, as much as they would a buffalo hunt, but Riel vetoed the plan and Dumont who hadn't lost all his respect for Riel's judgment, faith and religious zeal, agreed to submit.

With Dumont's guerrilla plan blocked, the Metis fighters were obliged to wait for attack from the Middleton army. At the Battle of Fish Creek where they exchanged their first bullets with the easterners, the Metis had the best of things, and it took Middleton a few days to be ready to strike again. But when the soldiers did attack again, they had the advantage of adequate ammunition and won the encounter. Riel gave himself up, refusing to escape with Dumont who mounted a fast horse and rode south toward Montana. At Regina, Riel was tried for treason, convicted and sentenced to be hanged.

* * *

In the Montana half-breed communities, Dumont was received as a hero and while the Canadian authorities had warrants for his arrest they didn't try very hard to capture him or have him returned. The late Robert Sinton of Regina told about encountering Dumont in 1886. Mr. Sinton was buying Montana horses for sale to settlers around Regina and on one of his trips he stopped at the village of Choto on the Sun river. Striking up a conversation with a personable big half-breed who said he was from Canada —"from Batoche on the Saskatchewan River"—Sinton asked, "What's your name?"

"Gabriel Dumont," was the reply. "Did you ever hear that name?"

Mr. Sinton knew there was a reward posted for the capture of this man and he reported the incident to the police at Regina. But the police were not interested much; "Let Dumont stay there," they said, "we don't really want him."

As a matter of fact, Dumont wasn't trying to hide either his identity or his whereabouts and he didn't stay in Montana. Late in 1885 he let it be known he was willing to come to Regina and accept the blame for the killing and thus clear Riel who was under sentence of death. And just prior to the date set for the hanging of Riel, there was a plot to free him and whisk him away to the United States on a relay of fast horses. Was Gabriel Dumont in on the plot? Of course he was a big part of it—he was ready to lead a direct attack upon the jail at Regina if necessary. Dumont was loyal to the condemned man, even though the two had disagreed about the campaign of 1885. But none of the plots materialized and Riel went to the gallows.

Dumont didn't remain in Montana. He visited Batoche about any time he had the urge and he went as far east as Montreal, being received as a hero at both places. When he died in 1906, the people about Batoche mourned and placed a stone at his resting place. And in 1955, Saskatchewan's Jubilee Committee erected a stone marker there.

Man of muscle and courage and few words, he was the kind of man that folk of his race could admire. And the ferryman said again, "Uncle Gabriel—he was one great fellow."

Chapter XXXVIII

JOLLY OLD JOHN

A GROUP of men who habitually wear wide-brimmed hats, sat not long ago discussing the formation of a society to keep alive the character of the Old West. There was agreement about the need—to make western people conscious and proud of their traditions—and then the question came up: "By what name would the society be known?"

Several suggestions were presented but the one to meet with general favor was "The John Ware Society," because, as it was agreed, nobody portrayed the pioneer qualities of modesty, courage, resourcefulness and friendliness better than that great negro cowboy and rancher, John Ware. Although the society, conceived in enthusiasm, did not flourish long, it served to show with what admiration and affection those students of western character regarded John Ware.

Whether or not he is voted the ablest cowboy and broncho rider the West has known, will depend upon who does the balloting. It is obviously impossible to compare one like John Ware who did his best riding 60 years ago with champions of recent times but there are some oldtimers who insist that he was "the greatest of them all."

* * *

Nobody expected a Negro to be a good rider. A back-

ground in slavery and cotton plantations was scarcely conducive to cowboying and the cattleman Tom Lynch of High
River who was in Idaho in 1882 to take delivery of 3000
cattle for the recently-organized Bar U ranch, was not impressed. According to William Henry of High River, Lynch
was anxious to hire the experienced Bill Moodie for the
long and dangerous drive to Canada but Moodie was difficult, said, "I won't go unless you hire my friend Ware
to go too."

Lynch yielded against his own better judgment and
Ware, making no boasts about being a rider, was assigned
to a poor saddle and a decrepit old horse. After a few days
at the "drag" end of the cattle drive where both horse and
rider consumed pounds of dust, this hired man mustered
enough courage to speak to Lynch, said, "Boss, ah was just
awunderin' if you'd give me a little betta saddle and a
little waus hoss 'cause ah think ah can ride um."

With Lynch's helpers anxious for some entertainment,
John Ware was provided with all he requested—certainly
a "waus hoss." What he was given was an outlaw and cowboys gathered to see the fun, see the big fellow from the
South "tossed." Ware was raised amid cotton, sure enough,
and his people came out of slavery, but what none except
his friend Moodie knew, he had ridden north on the Chis-
holm Trail with some big Texas herds and he was not as
green as those around him suspected

Playing like a professional actor, Ware said, "What side
do a cowboy get on at?" and "What'll ah do if he bucks?"

No sooner did John Ware have his six-foot-three-inch
frame in the saddle than the wicked horse went vigorously
and violently into action, kicking, pitching and doing un-
named contortions in mid-air. The negro made some fiendish yells as though terribly in trouble but, to the astonishment of the spectators assembled for a laugh, the rider was
not unseated. Instead of hitting the ground, Ware staged
a finished exhibition of rough-riding and won the admiration of the seasoned cattlemen with whom he was now
travelling.

And with a rope or "six-shooter," the grinning big negro
was just as proficient. There is a story about rustlers cut-

ting out a group of Tom Lynch's cattle and John Ware being sent to locate the stolen animals. As he came upon the cattle in an out-of-the-way place, the thieves drew their guns. But evidently John's rope was even faster than the culprits' guns and the two cattle-stealers were escorted to camp at the end of the cowboy's lariat.

* * *

At the trail's end, as cattle were delivered on what was to be their home range beside the Highwood river, John Ware remained with the Bar U ranch, was still there when George Lane came to work on it.

From the very beginning, Ware was making friends and on June 23, 1885, the Macleod Gazette reported: "If there is a man on the round-up who keeps up the spirit of the boys more than another and provides amusement to break the monotony, this man is John Ware. John is not only one of the best natured and most obliging fellows in the country but he is one of the shrewdest cow men. . . . The horse is not running on the prairie which John cannot ride, sitting with his face either to the head or tail, or even if the animal chooses to stand on its head or lie on its back, John always appears to be on top when the horse gets up, and smiling as if he enjoyed it."

John Ware had been in the country less than three years when that note was written about him.

From the Bar U, he went to the Quorn ranch whose cattle grazed where Turner Valley oil wells sprouted later. The Quorn suited John's fancies well; the ranch had good horses and with a pronounced English influence, there were racing and riding to hounds and a good deal of entertainment for English aristocracy. One might have supposed that the monocle-wearing gentry visiting the West for the first time would not get to know John Ware. He never played rugger or cricket and had no Oxford accent; as a matter of fact, he could neither read nor write. But he could do unbelievable things with horses and he had a sunny disposition and very quickly he became a favorite with the Englishmen.

* * *

John Ware was in love with Alberta grass and made up his mind to ranch for himself. With accumulated savings, he bought a place on the North Fork of Sheep creek, west of the present Millarville, and began branding his own cattle with the hideous Four Nines (9999). Why he chose that brand is not clear but it has been told that Ware was nine years old when the slaves gained their freedom and he considered "nine" to be his lucky number.

The Sheep creek stockmen of later years never ceased to talk about Ware's feats in a saddle. Joe Fisher who lived seven miles from him, related the climax to a long day in which he and John rode together hunting for cattle. Ware shot a coyote that day and at about sundown the two riders arrived at Fisher's cabin with two very tired saddle horses. Said John, "I'd like to borrow a fresh hoss for the ride home, and leave this tired nag here to rest up."

Fisher explained, however, that he didn't have a fresh horse in the stable—except for a middle-aged stallion that had never had a saddle on his back. John said, "That's a' right; ah'll take him."

The stallion was roped and kept well snubbed until John tightened the saddle-straps. "Now, get on," Fisher instructed, "and I'll let him go."

But John wasn't ready to get on. "No, no," he exclaimed, "keep 'm down till ah gets that wolf on, too." And so the dead wolf whose hide John wanted was tied across the horse's back and then John mounted and called, "Let um go."

With a saddle, a man and a dead coyote on his back, the unbroken, range stallion practically exploded at the indignity of it all. But John had him headed in the proper direction and Fisher watched as the infuriated horse with its varied cargo plunged into the river, up the bank on the other side and finally disappeared beyond the hills—still bucking with all the fury in him. A couple of days later, John Ware returned, riding the stallion, now about as gentle as a school pony, and released him in Joe Fisher's corral.

* * *

As time went on, John Ware found himself in love with more than the Alberta grass. In Calgary, he met an attractive negro girl, Mildred Lewis, whose father was a carpenter in the new town. Thereafter, John ran short of groceries rather often and considered it necessary to go to Calgary just as often. Sometimes he took Miss Mildred for a drive behind his team of half-domesticated bronchos. On one of those drives in the country, there came a thunder storm and a bolt of lightning killed John's two horses outright, leaving the young rancher and his girl-friend sitting unharmed but helpless in the democrat, several miles from town. But John was not one to surrender to a bit of misfortune. He removed the harness from the dead horses, threw it in the back of the vehicle, seized the democrat pole and proceeded to pull the rig with Miss Mildred sitting in it, all the way back to Calgary. As those who knew John Ware would understand, he didn't stop until he was back in town. They say, he was still grinning when he arrived.

Before long there was a wedding and John Ware took his bride to live on the ranch beside Sheep creek. Mrs. Ware was new to ranch life but she was a good cook and a generous person and folk round about found John's home a fine place to visit. "They're good neighbors," the people nearby said.

*   *   *

John got along pretty well with the Indians, also, but there were strained relations at times, notably when a little dog belonging to the Wares was stolen and thought to be in the Indian encampment where preparations were being made for a feast. Single handed, John advanced on the camp. The earth fairly trembled as the big fellow strode in in anger. Sure enough, he found the little dog and recovered it. But before leaving camp, he had some advice for Indians; although but one facing a hundred reckless natives, he promised there would be serious trouble if one of them ever again laid a hand on his dog. And John was emphatic enough that the Indians were suitably impressed.

Children were born there on the Sheep creek ranch and the Wares were happy. But with settlers encroaching upon his grazing, John decided to move. About the year 1900, he loaded his family and belongings on wagons, rounded up his 300 cattle for a long drive and started for the Red Deer river, north of the site of Duchess. Tilley was the nearest post office. There the Wares settled to ranch on a larger scale.

John Ware was still a great horseman and continued to break numerous bronchos. Mrs. Ware, who never condescended to get on a horse, would come out to the corral and cheer when her husband was working an onery one. But tragedy visited the Ware home on the Red Deer in 1904; Mrs. Ware, a woman of charm and fine character, died in .that year and in the next, John's saddle horse stepped in a badger hole and fell, throwing the heavy rider. John's neck was broken in the fall and he died almost at once.

* * *

John Ware must have had the qualities of a great athlete. His versatility in the saddle would be partial evidence. He could out-sprint a three-year-old steer and he could leap into a saddle without benefit of stirrup. With a corral full of bulls, he was seen to walk nimbly over the backs of the irritated animals, stepping from one to the other.

He was powerful and when he undertook to throw three husky men into Sheep creek, he was successful with the first two but the third turned out to be a heavyweight boxer and the tussle ended in a draw, with both men rolling into the river. John Ware was frightened of nothing except a snake and if one of the slithering little green things crossed his path, he was likely to sprint in the opposite direction.

Negro John Ware was an athlete and a horseman but it was in spreading good cheer and friendliness, in sharing food and blankets, that he enshrined himself in the hearts of a generation of pioneers.

THE PIONEER PUBLISHER

AMONG the best records of frontier events after 1878, are the copies of the Saskatchewan Herald, published at Battleford by Patrick Gammie Laurie. From boyhood years it was the Scottish lad's ambition to publish a newspaper where no paper existed before. He considered Winnipeg while that place was still without printed news but two other men with similar ideas "beat him to it" and it remained for Laurie to start the first paper west of Winnipeg.

The North West Territories needed a spokesman urgently and he accepted the challenge, made homesteaders' problems his problems, pleaded for better transportation and, being close to the violence of 1885, he issued the clearest reports and warnings. Nor did the people around him fail to appreciate. As an expression of gratitude in 1887, the Battleford folk, though terribly short of money, collected a purse of $220 and presented it to him. On this gesture, the Edmonton Bulletin (Feb. 19, 1887), commented: "If any editor ever deserved such recognition, the editor of the Herald is the man. He has been engaged in the speculation of publishing a two-horse paper in a one-horse town for so many years that it is about time the latter tried to even up a little."

* * *

Patrick Gammie Laurie was born in Aberdeenshire, April 7, 1833. With his father, Rev. William Laurie, he came to Canada in 1842 and learned the printing trade at Cobourg, Ontario. When still in his early 20s, he was publishing the Owen Sound Times and dreaming about going west, starting a newspaper at Fort Garry. Indeed, his plans for the long and hazardous journey to Red River were almost complete when news reached him that William Buckingham and William Coldwell were already there getting ready to publish. These two young men, an Englishman and an Irishman, brought their printing press from the east, hauling it from St. Paul to Fort Garry by ox-drawn cart, and the first issue of their paper, "The Nor-Wester," came off the press on December 28, 1859.

Obviously there would not be room for two papers in that infant community so Laurie changed plans, temporarily. He went to Windsor, started the Essex Recorder, but lost none of his interest in the West. By 1869, unable to restrain the urge longer, he was on his way to Red River and its metropolis with population of 215. It was a crucial period in western history because the Hudson's Bay Company which had ruled for 200 years was about to relinquish its territorial claim and the half-breed population was agitated and ready to fight.

The Nor-Wester had changed hands and become the property of Dr. John Schultz, later Sir John. Laurie accepted work on that paper and was nicely established when Louis Riel and followers set up their unconstitutional government. Riel considered the Nor-Wester as an obstacle to his plans and publication was rudely disrupted; he took over and used the press to publish his "New Nation."

With some other paper employees, Laurie withdrew to Lower Fort Garry where he printed the proclamation defying Riel's authority. So effective was that printed opposition to the leader of the insurrection that Riel offered a handsome reward, something like $2000, for the capture of Patrick Gammie Laurie. But Laurie was not easy to catch and slipped past the sentries; he made his way to Pembina and from there back to Windsor, Ontario.

After Riel quit Fort Garry, Laurie returned to Red River. He returned to resume work with Dr. Schultz and very shortly, he bought the printing business and published the Manitoba Newsletter. His editorials, in 1881, led to the formation of the Manitoba Agricultural Society, the first organization of its kind in the West. But Laurie sold his business and when the Weekly Free Press was started in 1872, he took charge of the new printing department.

Lingering in Laurie's heart was the longing to start a paper where no paper had been published before. His plan to start the first paper at Fort Garry had been thwarted but now he had a better idea. Fellow journalists in Winnipeg tried to discourage him but he clung tenaciously to the scheme. And so, the biggest adventure of his life came on May 24, 1878, when he loaded a printing press and other equipment on four Red River carts, hitched an Indian pony to each of the primitive vehicles and started westward. It was 650 miles to Battleford which was, in that same year, named capital of the North West Territories. That was where Laurie was going.

As Columbus on his voyage of discovery repeated the journal entry: "This day we sailed on," so, in the same sense, day after day for two and one-half months, Laurie might have written about the same: "This day I drove on." But on August 11, his carts came to a stop at Battleford, shack-town of a few score inhabitants, existing mainly as a stopping place on the trail to Fort Edmonton.

Laurie may have had doubts from what he saw but if he did, he kept them to himself, tightened the bolts which rough trails had loosened on his press and prepared for operations. In less than two weeks after arrival, the first issue of the Saskatchewan Herald was published. The printing office was a log cabin with sod roof, situated on a flat south of the Battle river and what came from it that day was the first issue of the first paper west of Winnipeg.

The North West Territories were coming to life. From

that year of 1878, the Territories had a government and a paper, both with headquarters at Battleford. The first session of the council of the North West Territories was at Livingstone on the Swan River, not far from Fort Pelly, in the previous year. But it was at Battleford that the best legislative effort to domesticate the wild West was made. In that year of '78 there was a petition for a public school and a bill for the protection of the rapidly disappearing buffalo. Nobody could accuse the government of reckless spending because it had virtually nothing to spend. The practice of borrowing money which subsequent governments would have to repay, had not become popular, and revenue in that year of 1878-79 was made up by a fine of five dollars for setting a prairie fire, a ferry-license fee of four dollars, eight marriage licenses at two dollars and a few other items. The council's expenditures for the year totalled $237.37, some of which went to P. G. Laurie for printing services.

* * *

The Saskatchewan Herald was in the best position to tell the story about territorial legislation. The editor was both counsel and critic and in the years to follow there was no more ardent fighter for provincial autonomy. Indeed, it was he who proposed the name, Saskatchewan, for the central mid-western province.

In Winnipeg, the Daily Free Press of August 16, 1878, carried this news item: "The Saskatchewan Herald was born today at Battleford, N.W.T., as will be seen by our telegrams and the noteworthy event in the history of the Far West caused the greatest enthusiasm to prevail in the land of the setting sun." Battleford, it should be noted was in the "Far West," much as Singapore was in the Far East. Anyway, it was a notable date and thereafter, the Herald was published fortnightly, the annual subscription being $2.50.

From its beginning, the Herald was carried in Her Majesty's mail, slow though that might be, as far west as Fort Edmonton and as far east as Winnipeg. John Todd, who carried the mail to Edmonton, travelled by Red River cart and horse in the summer season and by dog team in winter. He would have the Saskatchewan Herald in Edmonton twelve days after it was published—considered pretty good service.

Two years elapsed and Laurie's paper was still the only one in the North West Territories. But along in the summer of 1880, Publisher Laurie had a visitor, an unshaven traveller who looked no better or worse than the rest of the weatherbeaten freighters on the Edmonton trail. His name was Oliver—Frank Oliver—the man who was to become Edmonton's first elected member in the North West Council, and minister of the interior in the Laurier government at Ottawa. He was no stranger on the Edmonton Trail because he had gone over it many times with freight. This trip, he made it a point to call on Laurie.

Oliver, too, had learned something about printing, in Ontario, and he too had worked with the Free Press in Winnipeg. But on this freighting trip, Oliver had an unusual load—a printing press. It was the second machine of its kind in the Territories; it was Oliver's personal property and he was taking it to Edmonton—had another 300 miles to go.

Laurie gave Oliver some good advice about publishing but it didn't help in getting that west-bound press across the Battle river, just outside the town. Frank Oliver and his helper constructed a raft on which to place the heavy equipment and then, one of the men had to swim across, carrying the end of a tow-rope. It proved to be a dangerous undertaking—dangerous for the man as well as the machine—but determination triumphed and the Edmonton-bound carts were on their way again.

* * *

It was nearly four years after Laurie set up for business at Battleford that he again saw Winnipeg, and then the trip was mainly for the purpose of bringing his two daughters, Mable (later Mrs. Ried) and Effie (later Mrs. Storer), to the new home. Leaving Winnipeg on February 10, 1882, father and daughters were at Battleford 52 days later. Mable and Effie may have been the first white girls to cross the prairies in the winter season. Travel was by horse-drawn wooden sleigh, the kind known as a jumper. And while they tried to be at a stopping place or Hudson's Bay post at nightfall, that was not always possible and there were nights when the Lauries had no choice but to pitch their tent in the snow beside the trail. On all that trip, strangely enough, nobody was frostbitten and nobody admitted that he or she wasn't enjoying it. Mrs. Laurie came on to Battleford in the summer of '83.

In addition to being a pioneer publisher, P. G. Laurie was a bona fide homesteader. He filed on the land of his choice in 1883 and by putting in three months of residence on the property in each of three years, breaking up a certain acreage and erecting a "habitable house," he received his title. That homestead was on the south side of the Battle river, about three miles upstream from the town of Battleford. He loved that little farm, refused to sell it, and had it until the time of his death.

That Laurie homestead attracted a good deal of attention during the period of the North West Rebellion. It was like this: Goodwin Marchand, a Manitoba man of mixed breeding, was freighting from Swift Current for Battleford merchants, Clinkskill and Mahaffy. In the months before the shooting started, Marchand was observed to be arriving at Battleford with only half-loads of freight. His explanation was, "bad roads," plausible enough at times. The truth was something quite different, however; Marchand's carts on the northward trips carried half freight and half loads of guns and ammunition. The latter he would cache in a bluff on Laurie's homestead where Poundmaker's Indians got them on March 29, 1885.

Evening and night of that date were grim ones in the community; the Indians came on to raid Battleford. Citizens took refuge at the Mounted Police Barracks and before morning, they saw the war-crazed Crees looting the town. But Battleford was organized; Laurie was serving in the Home Guards and most of the young men were with the Battleford Rifles or out on mounted patrol.

That night-attack by the Indians might have been more

serious but as things turned out, the only human casualty was Barney Tremont, a foreman on the telegraph line who was shot while greasing the axels of his wagon, on a farm south-west of town. Later, Goodwin Marchand who had the secret arsenal in the poplar bluff on Laurie's farm, was arrested and tried.

Laurie was of a retiring disposition but forceful. He demanded accuracy both in speaking and writing. He had a passion for justice and everybody knew his views about issues. He loved the out-doors and the homestead. Though not a typical homesteader, it was his choice to cultivate land and keep chickens and ducks and cows. And however one may rate his farming interests, he was certainly a leader in the agricultural community which became Saskatchewan. He, the homesteaders' mouth-piece, died "in harness" in 1902 and was buried there at Battleford. And on the wall of the little Anglican church he helped to build and in which he held office as Peoples' Warden for many years, there hangs a tablet to his memory, placed there by the people who lived with him on the frontier.

CHAPTER XL

"HONOURABLE JOHN"

MANITOBA'S "man of the hour," in the 80s of last century was John Norquay, school teacher, trader, farmer and ultimately, premier of his province. Not to be overlooked was the fact that this man with qualities and gifts of statesmanship was a native son. He was Manitoba's first native-born premier and for half a century, the only one.

Three hundred pounds of fighting Conservative was the way some people saw this man. Indeed, Sir John A. Macdonald at Ottawa and Honourable John Norquay in the new province of Manitoba, made a combination to awaken students to the importance of that period.

The Norquays were Orcadians in origin. The name stems from an Aberdeenshire man who went to the Orkney's, settling "north of quay" and, for reasons best known to himself, refused to reveal his name. The first Norquay in Rupert's Land, however, was Oman Norquay who came with the Hudson's Bay Company in 1791. He was the grandfather of John Norquay.

The boy who was to be premier was born in a log

house at St. Andrews, about midway between Upper and Lower Fort Garry, on May 8, 1841. Life there on the riverside was not without its moments of excitement. There was the annual buffalo hunt in which every able-bodied man and many of the women, children and Red River dogs took part; there was almost constant activity on the river highway; there were local contests of strength—wrestling and fighting. And when a barnstorming buffalo bull wandered into the settlement and locked horns with one of the domestic Ferdinands, men and boys turned out to witness the struggle. What spectators saw was a buffalo pitching the bellowing barnyard hero into the Red river and they watched helplessly while the paralyzed victim was carried to his death by drowning.

Young John was powerful and athletic. He played ball and he swam in the Red river. And when there was a dance in the community, John Norquay was almost sure to be present. It was his custom, in going to a dance, to carry something in his hip pocket—an extra pair of moccasins. He was light on his feet, notwithstanding his great size, but he was a man of unusual vigor and he knew that before a Red river dance broke up about the time of sunrise, he'd probably have worn out one pair of moccasins and a man wouldn't want to be caught at a dance in bare feet.

* * *

At an early age John Norquay was left an orphan. At that time he was taken and brought up by Mrs. James Spence and, as good fortune would have it, he came under the sympathetic and interested eye of Bishop Anderson. The result was a better than customary education for that time and place. He attended St. John's school and then St. John's academy where he struggled with French, Greek and Latin in large doses. At the age of 17 he began teaching at the parish school of St. James. They were short of readers for the pupils at the school so they used Bibles for reading exercises, there being no community shortage of the good books.

After a year, John Norquay accepted a teaching appointment at Parkdale and about that time, a young woman entered his life. She was Elizabeth Setter, whose family belonged to pre-Selkirk Orcadian stock. Her home was at High Bluff—not very handy—but now and then during his teaching career, John walked from Parkdale to High Bluff for a short week-end visit with his sweetheart. Hitch-hiking had nothing to offer, unless a person had so much time to spare that he could be attracted by a ride with some ox-driver on the trail. Under the circumstances a lover's devotion could not be questioned and in June, 1862, John Norquay married the young woman and discontinued the long weekend walks.

Teaching was all right for a while but Norquay wanted to farm. He went to High Bluff and settled on land of his choosing, determined to remain. But to augment revenue from his cultivation, he devoted some time to fur trading and called himself a mixed farmer.

He was getting along well. He loved that farm but it was increasingly apparent that he possessed the stuff from which politicians and leaders are made. Everybody knew the young province needed leadership—needed it urgently. John Norquay had a smiling personality; his honesty had never been questioned and he was an orator. More than that, he could speak the Cree language and Saulteaux and Sioux. And if there was good reason, he could carry on a semblence of conversation with other tribesmen. Gaelic was the only language heard about Red river in which he could not participate. With his qualifications for leadership, there wasn't a chance that he would be left to his farming.

* * *

In the first election for Manitoba's legislative assembly, in December, 1870, John Norquay was elected for High Bluff. Thus he was one of the 24 representatives, 12 English and 12 French, who met in the first Legislative Session, in a Winnipeg building owned by A. G. B. Bannatyne, in March, 1871.

In the legislature, his fine speech was soon recognized; his voice was clear and musical and his enunciation was fine. In December of 1871, he was invited to enter Premier

Henry J. Clarke's government as minister of public works and before long he was given the portfolio of agriculture also. He held one cabinet post after another until 1878 when he was asked to form a government and become Premier.

Although he never lost an election, he had one very narrow escape—when his majority consisted of a single vote. It was learned later that a certain citizen with loyalties to Norquay's opponent, was on his way to the polls when chased by a neighborhood bull and forced to take refuge in a tree. The bull, with what must be seen as a fine sense of public responsibility, took up guard at the base of the tree and when the settler was finally able to come down from the branches, it was either too late to vote or his interest in democracy had deserted him, because John Norquay was able to say later, "I owe my election to Scott's bull."

Norquay continued as Premier of Manitoba until December, 1887, only little more than a month before his death. As premier he saw the rails come to link Manitoba with the south and then with the east. He saw the tide of settlers rolling in and he saw troops moving westward to put down an uprising. Eventful years they were, when every new siding in the west country was a potential town and a railway siding supported by a post office and more than one store gave promise of nothing less than a city.

Eventful years and, in politics, stormy years! Manitoba, the newborn, was struggling for its rights. The young province wanted control of public lands; it wanted reduction of duty on agricultural implements and building materials; it wanted extension of provincial boundaries to Hudson's Bay, and it wanted the right to grant local railway charters.

"Disallowance" was a bitter issue. The dominion government contended that no province had the right to grant charters to railroads which would extend beyond local boundaries or connect with foreign rails. Naturally, the Canadian Pacific Railway with a monopoly clause in its charter and a huge investment, was opposed to competitive railways. There were those people who supposed that

CPR traffic would never "pay for the axel grease" it needed and sooner or later it would fail. Manitobans who wanted some further guarantees of transportation, asked noisily if the interests of the country were to become subservient to those of the monopolistic rail corporation.

Norquay and most Manitoba people at that time were opposed to monopoly in anything, furs, trade or rails. Citizens were mad. The crack of a pistol might have started rebellion. Norquay, at first, was inclined to defend federal policy but he grew impatient when he recognized Manitiba's urgent need for rails. He resolved to break the monopoly. He was determined to start something even though there was grave political danger in so doing. His government would undertake to build the Red River Valley Railway to the international border, build it without outside assistance if necessary. At the same time plans were being drawn for the Winnipeg and Hudson's Bay Railroad. But funds ran low and construction work was halted. Norquay's popularity waned and, faced with failure in completing the rail ventures, he was deserted by many from whom he might have expected loyalty. He resigned in December, 1887. Dr. Harrison was chosen as leader and formed a government which had but a short life.

* * *

During those years of Norquay's premiership, another strong man was gaining prominence in Manitoba. He was Thomas Greenway from Crystal City. He, too, was a farmer and he, too, an orator of note. Like Norquay, he was a huge man in phyiscal bearing. There is no record of Norquay and Greenway ever sleeping in the same bed although the result would have been roughly the same as when Norquay made his first campaign speech at Brandon and was obliged to share a bed with Sam Bower, reported to weigh close to Norquay's 300 pounds. The proprietor of the new Royal Hotel recognized the risk to his property, that close to one-third of a ton of Conservative man-power would be a test for any bed. But, so it is told, the bed suffered from nothing worse than a permanent bulge to the springs.

It could be said of Norquay and Greenway, however,

that though on opposite sides of the political street, they presented a united front when Manitoba's interests were threatened. There were many opportunities for the two political leviathons to work together.

Norquay had few betters in oratory. One of the pioneers remarked that he had listened to Sir John A. Macdonald and Sir Charles Tupper and the best of them and the only one who could rival John Norquay on the platform was D'Arcy McGee. One may try to envision the young Norquay making a maiden speech at High Bluff. There was the threat of Fenian raids. "We will be unworthy representatives of our forefathers if we allow the invaders to defile our soil with their rebel feet."

And as for stories, nobody could tell them better. When he was about to tell one, he'd have a good laugh at it first and all 300 pounds of him would shake. His laugh was contagious and everybody would laugh. Then he'd tell the story and all would laugh some more.

He was about to address a political meeting which opposition forces were determined to ruin. There was to be an organized evacuation when Norquay began to speak. As he mounted the platform, an opposition henchman shouted: "Clear the hall; the meeting's over." People began to move toward the entrance. But John Norquay was not asleep. His powerful voice filled the hall as he began to tell one of his famous stories. The people sat down to enjoy it and as the hall refilled, the speaker eased from story to his address and had a successful meeting. Those who came to jeer remained to cheer.

* * *

John Norquay, the man who worked to place politics on a high plane, man with whom Manitoba's welfare was above all else, man with a big heart, died at age 48. Death followed appendicitis and peritonitis and Manitoba was cheated because of so early a call. He was the father of five sons and three daughters; otherwise, he died a comparatively poor man. But what he left in example and tradition was better far than gold. He was buried at St. John's Cemetery where a monument bears this message:

271

"To the Memory of The Hon. John Norquay
Who was for many years Premier of Manitoba.
By his sudden and all too early death
His native land lost an eloquent speaker
An honest Statesman and a true friend.
Born May 8, 1841, Died July 5, 1889
This monument is a Public expression of his sterling
worth."

His roots were deep in the soil of the west, exactly how deep is not entirely clear. In the course of one heated debate in the legislature, a member of the opposition shouted, "Now you're showing your Indian."

The Premier bared his arm and raised it saying slowly, "I am proud of every drop of blood that flows in my veins." Whether that was intended as an acknowledgment or denial of some Indian ancestry has been debated. But it doesn't matter in the least. Far more important was the demonstration that western soil could produce the stuff from which great premiers and statesmen are made.

Chapter XLI

THE COWBOY SENATOR

A FTER walking west to the foothills in 1883 and living there for 65 years, rancher Dan Riley became a prominent part of southern Alberta, just like the Bow river and the Calgary stampede. Of that fabulous breed of men which opened the West, he was a worthy representative, and his pride in the land of his adoption grew steadily. In his years as a senator he said, "The more I see of Ottawa, the better I love High River."

A Thanksgiving week-end spent with him on the Flying U ranch in his enchanting foothills was an experience not soon to be gorgotten. It was an adventure in ranchland hospitality and a short course in frontier lore. The story about the Lost Lemon gold mine with a succession of deaths coming to those who discovered the secret of location, came from him readily but getting anything about himself was as difficult as pulling stumps. Modesty forbade discussion about himself and his achievements.

Here, however, was another son of Prince Edward Island, another to leave a valuable impression upon the West. He enjoyed the advantage of a little more schooling than most Island boys of his generation received and he took to teaching for a while. In the spring of 1882, however, the bonds holding him to the teaching profession on

273

his island, snapped and he journeyed to Winnipeg. It was a bold move because Winnipeg seemed terrifyingly far away to most residents. The booming Manitoba city wasn't really as distant as Timbuktu but in the eyes of most Islanders, it was almost as remote and only slightly more inviting.

Winnipeg afforded various jobs until such time as young Riley could advance his plans. On March 1, 1883, he was on his way, farther west. He went to Regina by Canadian Pacific Railway work train and from that point to Calgary, he walked behind a Red River cart.

Somewhere between Winnipeg and Regina, Dan Riley acquired a travelling companion. It was safer for strangers in the country to travel in pairs and certainly less monotonous. He was a nice chap, this fellow-traveller, and the two men got along like brothers—at least, until they reached Regina. At that point, the partner enquired of Riley, "Dan, what you got in that wooden box?"

If Dan Riley had replied, "dynamite" or "snakes," everything would have been satisfactory, but he made the mistake of telling the truth and said "books."

"Books?" was the horrified response. "What kind of books you packing out here?"

Continuing to speak honestly, Dan replied, "Oh, mostly poetry and some biography." That was too much for the partner. He would never, consciously at least, be caught sharing blankets with a man who read poetry and the partnership broke apart there and then.

Dan Riley medidated, decided to leave the box of culture in Regina and have it forwarded to Calgary at some later and safer time. There was no point in creating more frontier suspicion than necessary. But Dan Riley never saw those books again and for some time felt no regret. A clean break with poetry seemed the best thing at the time because, obviously, a man would get along better in the ranch country of the 80s if he didn't confess to an association with Tennyson and Shakespeare.

* * *

Arriving at Calgary, Riley's assets consisted of the

clothes on his back and $30 tucked in his shirt pocket. His first mistake upon arriving there at the Bow river, so he told, was in washing his shirt. Sleeping on some Indian robes, he had acquired a vigorous generation of those tormenting things called lice. At the river he was inspired to wash the shirt and at the same time drown some parasites. But the operation deserved more care than it received and proved costly; the shirt broke from the still water in which it was soaking in the river and floated away. When it was well beyond his reach, Dan remembered that his remaining money, all he had in the world, was still in the pocket of that shirt, now floating toward Hudson's Bay. Now he was without both shirt and money.

But the land against the hills was casting a spell upon him. He was being drawn to the grass, ankle deep, and fascinated by the whitened bones littering the ground and telling of countless buffalo which so recently disappeared. It was cattle country, any way one looked at it. Riley hired with French and Smith who ranched west of the present site of High River, then called "The Crossing." The wage was $20 per month with as much food as one could eat and as much sleep as one could get before the rising hour of 4.30 a.m. French and Smith were Americans who had been trading with the Indians in pre-Mounted Police days and their cattle brand, "OH", was taken from Smith's initials. That ranch has changed hands a few times through the years but it is still the "OH."

Dan Riley was in the foothills less than two years when the Riel trouble started on the South Saskatchewan river. Soldiers, freighters and others were needed and Dan Riley volunteered to do anything, go anywhere. Leaving his work as a cowboy, he was assigned to dispatch riding, keeping communications open from Edmonton south. He didn't see any open warfare in that area but the Indians on all sides were becoming bold and insolent; they brandished their guns and fingered the triggers more than ever and every white person had sleepless nights.

But there was no shooting near Dan Riley and when hostilities ceased, he went back to the range country west of High River. Anyone who rode in the years of open range, however, saw a lot of country. Frequently, he rode the 70 miles to Fort Macleod and when there, would sleep in Kamoose Taylor's celebrated Macleod Hotel where the rules were: "No more than five in a bunk; no spurs to be worn in bed; no horses allowed upstairs; no poker games in the kitchen; shooting irons to be checked with the bartender; no rustlers or vigilantes taken in." Of course, Kamoose Taylor varied his hotel rules from time to time and the above which was carried on the cover of Dan Riley's guest book, is slightly different from some versions which have been passed down.

* * *

In 1886, young Riley went with Hull and Trounce on the "25" ranch. That partnership had been furnishing beef for rail contractors in the mountains but with a slump in rail building, energies were directed at other things. A big band of horses was driven from the inter-mountain ranges to the foothills and Riley was hired to be manager of the horse ranch. The horse business flourished and Riley liked his work. He pronounced W. R. Hull, "the best business man of them all." But welling up within him was the urge to start ranching for himself, and in 1890, he made two courageous moves, married and bought his first cattle.

A year later, anticipating a big demand for farm horses, Riley bought 310 head in the state of Washington, shipped them to Baltic, Montana, and drove them overland to High River. Delivered at High River, the horses cost $30.30 per head and with homesteaders clamoring for power, Riley made a big profit. That horse deal marked the beginning of bigger horse dealing operations. He built a sales stable at High River and in a short time he was horse dealer, liveryman, hotel keeper and ferryman, as well as rancher and farmer.

While reminiscing about livery stable experiences, he recalled a stocky young Irishman driving in by democrat, late one night. He said his name was Burns, Pat Burns. He was in a hurry, enquired excitedly if Riley had seen an old man on a good horse.

"Yes," Riley replied, "I just bought the horse and gave the old man a bed for the night."

Said Burns, "The horse is mine and old John stole it."

A lantern was lighted and the two future senators sauntered to the barn to inspect the horse. Sure enough, it was Burns' horse, the explanation being that John had been working for Burns and when the latter refused to advance more money for whisky, old John took a horse and fled.

Next thing was to awaken old John and see what he had to say. The old man admitted the crime and returned all but five dollars of the seventy dollars Dan Riley had paid him for the horse. Burns made up the missing five dollars and ordered John to get into his pants; "we're going back to the camp tonight." With Burns and old John in the democrat and the stolen horse tied behind, Dan Riley watched his new acquaintances disappear into the night. After that, Pat Burns and Dan Riley met often.

* * *

Riley acquired ranch land on Willow creek in the Porcupines and grain land near High River. He agreed that cattlemen should be organized and was one of those who worked to start the Western Stock Growers' Association, an organization of which he was president for several years. Public life made increasing demands upon him and when High River was incorporated as a town in 1906, he became its first mayor.

He was chairman of the first school board, and when the first political meeting was held in the town, Dan Riley was the chairman. The speaker at that meeting was a young politician from Edmonton, Frank Oliver. The meeting was in the new school house and everybody for miles around attended. But a political meeting was a new experience for the local residents and Dan Riley said they didn't know what to do; they didn't cheer, didn't clap and didn't boo the speaker. Oliver was disappointed that there was no demonstration of emotions, even if it was to heckle him, but according to Dan, "every one of them voted for Oliver and elected him."

277

Those who knew Dan Riley will always associate his name with the Lost Lemon gold mine. Not that he found it or saw it but he was one who believed firmly that the mine was more than a myth, one who spent both time and money in the search for it. He knew the Stoney Indians as few men knew them and was in the best possible position to get their side of the story. As he related the events, the mine was discovered in the early 70s of last century by two prospectors, known only as Lemon and Blackjack.

It was late in the season, after these two soldiers of fortune were moving toward their home base in Montana. Somewhere up the Highwood River or one of its tributaries, they encountered good showings of gold and followed them upstream to a bed of unbelievable riches.

Gold makes men do strange things and in order to safeguard the secret of the mine's location and have it all to himself, Lemon arose in the night and murdered his partner. Then, at the thought of his dastardly act, Lemon became partly insane, but managed, nevertheless, to make his way back to Montana. At a mission in that state, he confessed his crime and told about the gold. During the winter, he was nursed back to sanity and in the spring, a party was organized to return with him to relocate the mine.

When the party neared the region of the mine and of the crime, Lemon again lapsed into insanity and had to be taken back. Several efforts to find the gold were launched from the mission. A man by the name of Mac-Dougall went into the hills and never returned. A Fort Benton whisky trader followed MacDougall and was never seen again. Lafayette French, friend of Dan Riley, was supposed to have obtained a map prepared by Lemon and made a series of expeditions, all fruitless in spite of overtures to Stoney Indians. The Stoneys, if they had the secret, were bound by oath to their chief never to share it with white man. After some years, French made a deal with a new chief but on the eve of the day they were to meet in the mountains, the chief died.

Riley believed that French ultimately found the mine, but on his way out following the presumed triumph, he stopped at George Emerson's cabin. That night the cabin burned down and French suffered burns which led to his death. Blackjack was dead; MacDougall was dead; a whisky trader was dead; a Stoney chief was dead; French was dead and Lemon was insane. To the Indians, nobody could know the secret of the mine and live, but that didn't stop Dan Riley from hunting for it.

* * *

In 1927, Cowboy Dan Riley was named to the Canadian Senate and there he sat for many years. He was not one of the noisy ones in the upper house; on the contrary, he was quiet but he missed no opportunity to speak for the agricultural industry, whose representative he considered himself.

On November 18, 1947, Senator Riley, surrounded by friends and family, celebrated his 87th birthday. "I'm getting old," he said at that time, "but I can still walk into the senate chamber without a crutch or a couple of canes, and that's more than a lot of my colleagues can do." About the same time, he reminded a friend that he had walked into southern Alberta and if it were necessary, he could travel out the same way. But it was his last birthday; the call to "the last roundup" came on April 27, 1948. His friends who were many were ready to judge him much as he judged his fellow-cowboys, of whom he wrote:

"To the memory of these men with whom I rode, stirrip to stirrup, for hundreds, nay thousands of miles, my tribute is that according to their lights, their environment and their limitations, they served well and filled well the place God gave them here."

CHAPTER XLII

WARDEN OF THE PLAINS—
CUTHBERT GRANT

C LAN Grant turned out its share of fighting men. Oatmeal with a selected beverage to wash it down produced a race of men with big knees, boney shoulders and hair on their chests. Half-breed Cuthbert Grant, Warden of the Plains, combined the fibre of the clansmen and the hardiness and courage of the Crees and carried name and title convincingly.

But he did not escape bitter controversy. Was this man who stood above his fellows on the soil of Rupert's Land, a villain or a hero? Was he a murderer or a good citizen worthy of the public offices ultimately thrust upon him? The Seven Oaks affair in which he played a conspicuous part was called a massacre. That brief and bloody battle in West Kildonan was indeed a tragedy but in the events which led up to it, unprejudiced observers are likely to see about as much provocation on one side as the other.

Ultimately, however, when peace came to the little settlement at Red River, this native son won the esteem of most people in Assiniboia and was employed by the Hudson's Bay Company. Recovery of public favor may be judged in part by the report that John Richard MacKay of the old Hudson's Bay Company, at Brandon House during the period of trouble, singled out Cuthbert Grant and bequeathed to him his most prized possession, his spy glass. Actually, Grant did not lack admirers at any time and it is unfortunate that historians failed to retrieve him from the alleged disgrace of massacre.

His father was Cuthbert Grant, senior, from the Scottish Highlands and his mother was a Cree. Like the wolf-dog cross which produces superior sleigh dogs, here was a biological union that produced superior buffalo hunters and voyageurs.

The Province of Saskatchewan might lay claim to young Cuthbert because he was born at one of the early trading posts on the upper Assiniboine river, about 12 miles southeast of where Kamsack stands. The post, known as Grant's House was started by still another Grant, Peter Grant of the North West Company, in 1791. Two years later, the elder Cuthbert Grant who was with the same company in its Athabasca division, arrived to take it over and there young Cuthbert was born later in the year. The site beside the Assiniboine was an attractive one and there the elder Cuthbert Grant remained until 1798, a year before his death.

* * *

The Grant boy was strong and agile. He could run fast enough to worry a fox and he could outguess a coyote. There was no school between Lake Superior and the Pacific ocean but officers of the North West Company recognized talent in the lad and when his father died, they sent him to Montreal to get an education. He hated it in the East and the prettiest thing he saw all the time he was away was the canoe brigade which would bring him back to the buffalo country. But he did learn to read and write and at the age of 19 he accepted employment as a clerk with the North-Westers at Red River and the Qu'Appelle.

Competition between the Hudson's Bay Company and the North West Company was verging on hostility much of the time and to make matters worse, the English company was experimenting with colonization. Lord Selkirk's farm colony at Red River was like a sword pointing at the heart of the fur trade. Quarrels and threats were numerous and in June of 1815, many of the settlers agreed to quit Red River and accept the other company's offer of free transportation to Upper Canada. The remaining colonists took refuge at the north end of Lake Winnipeg and Fort Douglas at Red River was burned. Wishful thinkers said the colony was dead.

But the colony was only stunned; more settlers, 80 of them travelling with Governor Semple, were on their way from the Old Country. Fort Douglas was rebuilt and Colin Robertson with 20 men arrived from Montreal. Thirteen families came back from Lake Winnipeg and the colony revived.

But the peace was brief and in the spring, trouble broke afresh. Governor Semple's judgment was not good and he added fuel to the smouldering fire. Seizure of the North-Wester's Fort Gibraltar at the forks, invited retaliation. Equally annoying was the interception of North West Company freight from Fort William. A freight blockade would produce a company crisis and reprisals could be expected.

Alex Macdonell of the North-Westers' post on the Qu'Appelle authorized 23-year-old Cuthbert Grant, now the acknowledged leader of the half-breeds, to muster a force of sufficient strength to ensure that the company's canoes from Fort William got past the forks. Instructions were to by-pass Fort Douglas and molest no one unless assaulted—simply protect the brigade. Sixty mounted men, mostly half-breeds, followed Cuthbert Grant out of Portage la Prairie. As they came within view of Red River and veered northward, panic seized the people at Fort Douglas.

Governor Semple called for 30 men to follow him in a display of resistance. He and his nervous followers marched north, probably along the trail that became Winnipeg's Main street. But he was ill-prepared to meet a force like Grant's and when the inadequacy of his party was realized, he sent back for reinforcements and a cannon but time was short and they never reached him.

As the two groups came together a short distance north, one of Grant's men rode forward to meet the governor and was asked what he wanted. "We want our fort," the fellow replied. Angry words were exchanged and a gun-shot rang out. Who fired it and from which side it came will never be proven but from scanty evidence, most writers have assumed it was from a half-breed's gun. There is no doubt that Cuthbert Grant sought to restrain his men but it was too late. There could be no stopping until one side had gained victory. In the end, Semple and 20 of his men were dead, the rest wounded or prisoners. It was needless slaughter. A stone beside Winnipeg's Main street marks the place.

* * *

With men fighting for their lives, it was a wild melee and nobody was concerned about keeping the record straight for students of history. In the view of the settlers, Grant was a murderer, notwithstanding his mid-battle instructions to have the wounded Semple conveyed to the fort—an order, incidentally, which was thwarted when a battle-crazed Indian shot the wounded governor in the chest. All in all, it was a story which could have a pronounced bias, depending upon who told it.

Acting on behalf of the North West Company, Cuthbert Grant accepted the surrender of Fort Douglas, as settlers who sought refuge there fled again to the shores of Lake Winnipeg. By this time, Lord Selkirk, with a miniature army of hired soldiers, was on his way from Montreal. Word of the slaughter reached him at Sault Ste. Marie. He changed his course, took possession of the North-Westers' Fort William post, charged the occupants with complicity in the Red River affair, sent some of the Fort William officers east as prisoners and seized various bits of property, including some cattle he found there. In due course, Selkirk's men arrived at Red River, captured Fort Douglas and set about to re-establish the discouraged settlers.

Cuthbert Grant was placed under arrest and required to appear for trial in the east. The charges were murder and theft but nothing came of them and he returned to Red River.

Nobody realized more than Grant that the Battle of

Seven Oaks was a colossal tragedy, and he succeeded in convincing Governor Simpson that he tried to prevent the bloodshed. Actually, Grant did a good deal to reduce the hardships and losses of settlers who fled. He itemized the belongings of each, 7000 items, and turned the record over to colony leaders so that owners might recover property later. He did more, sent some of his men to protect the settlers as they retreated to Lake Winnipeg.

When the two companies were united in 1821, Grant was not acceptable for employment but in little more than a year, Governor Simpson admitted that this young man, popular with a majority group, athletic and unsurpassed as a buffalo hunter, should be in service for the company. Having in mind the Indians and half-breeds, Simpson said, "There is not a man in the country that possesses half the influence over them." And so, Simpson sent Grant westward to work as a clerk and then placed him in charge of freighting to Norway House and made him his personal constable. A Governor would feel safer with a man like Grant ready to act for him.

But it was still too close in time and distance to Seven Oaks and when Grant received money from his father's estate in 1824, Simpson helped him secure a tract of land at White Horse plains, about 12 miles west of Fort Douglas. Friends followed him to locate in his district and the farming community he founded and called Grantown in honor of his father's home in Scotland, became the second of its kind in Rupert's Land. By 1832, the new settlement had 298 acres of cultivated ground and in 1838, it had 800 acres. To supplement the colony, Grant built a dam and grist mill at nearby Sturgeon creek.

* * *

Ironical as it seemed, Grant was now a farmer but he was still a leader among his people. When Indians threatened attack upon the Red River Settlement, Grant with his followers sprang to the defence. Folk in trouble sought Cuthbert Grant. His counsel was good and he was the handiman, of which every pioneer district had one. He was a good horseman; he could make carts of superior strength and he had a bag of remedies which would cure the disorders commonly occuring among men, women and cattle in the colony.

Grant's chief local fame was as a buffalo hunter, however, and one may try to picture the sturdy frontiersman leading the annual hunt for some years after 1830. He wore a leather coat, rode a fast horse sired by Fireaway and treated the buffalo-hunt with the seriousness it deserved. As the source of meat for much of the year, the hunt was a community effort, meticulously organized, with rules rigidly enforced. To be elected captain of the hunt was the highest of local honors because it meant the ultimate in public confidence. As everybody knew, Captain Grant demanded good discipline and could enforce it when necessary with two good half-breed fists. Field Marshal might have been a better title.

The organized buffalo hunts began about the time of union between the two companies but not until the bloody affair of 1816 was blunted by time did the settlers generally seek Grant's leadership. The hunt started late in June each year and usually the course was in a south-westerly direction. Red Hiver Historian Ross tells that in 1830, no fewer than 820 carts, close to a thousand men, women and children, most of the colony's horses and all the dogs, went out for the hunt.

What a cavalcade it would be, what creaking of dry cart wheels, what dust, what dog-fights and what problems in administration! At six o'clock in the evening, the flag was lowered as a signal to make camp. Carts were arranged in a big circle and tents erected in the enclosure. At an early morning hour, the flag went up and half an hour later, Captain Grant would ride away at the head of the column.

Scouts sent ahead reported the location of a herd and when the last camp prior to an attack was made, all was excitement. The rules of the hunt were restated: nobody to go off by himself or shoot before the general order; an offender might see his coat or saddle cut to shreds as punishment or he might be flogged.

285

Several hundred mounted men with the chief captain at the lead, would line up for the attack. Moving away slowly at first to avoid giving alarm to the drowsy herd, the horses would go into a trot and, when the signal was issued, the hunters dashed forward at a hard gallop.

There was confusion and dust as shots rang out and hunters reloaded while travelling at full speed over rough ground. The extra balls were carried in a hunter's mouth and in his excitement, he could easily swallow a few. But there were even more dangerous ways of getting lead bullets in the stomach and it was no place for a man who was not popular in the community because stray bullets went in unpredictable directions.

When the shooting was over, the hunters brought the tongues into camp for a banquet while the women and children undertook the skinning of 500 or 800 carcasses and cutting in preparation for drying.

It was the institution of the Buffalo Hunt, with at least as much appeal as the baseball tournament to emerge much later. And Cuthbert Grant ruled; finally they gave him the more dignified title: "Magistrate of the Buffalo Hunt." More honors came; he was named Warden of the Plains and thus he became a roving magistrate who carried a good deal of law enforcement inside his mitts. This post paid a salary of £200 annually. Then he was Justice of the Peace at his Grantown center with its thousand people; and finally, he was made a member of the Council of Assiniboia.

To the end of his life, Cuthbert Grant remained active, practicing his brand of medicine, enforcing order and stimulating industry in and around Grantown. He died July 15, 1854 and in accordance with the church's appraisal of his worth, he was buried beneath the chapel of the mission there at his Grantown, now St. Francois Xavier. He was Cuthbert Grant, Warden of the Plains.

CHAPTER XLIII

SLIPPERY DAVE COCHRANE

THE Cochrane name was well known in the southwest. Senator H. M. Cochrane brought the first big herd of cattle to the Chinook Belt in 1881—3000 head whose ancestors came over the trail from Texas to Montana —and made the initial ranch headquarters west of Calgary where the village of Cochrane stands today. Another Cochrane brought the first automobile to southern Alberta and frightened many of the High River horses out of their driving harness. But as for Dave Cochrane, his fame was such that nobody of similar name sought to establish a relationship. He was a breed apart.

Dave came as one of the "originals" with the North West Mounted Police, Regimental Number 22, in 1874, and found Fort Macleod society very much to his liking. Pardonable mischief claimed rather much of his time but in the conduct of police duties, Dave Cochrane was courageous and moderately efficient. About 1877, however, he retired from the service and took to farming and ranching, with variations. It was then the fun started—at least, it was fun for those who were not Dave's victims.

287

Dave, it should be understood, had "lifting tendencies," and whether he indulged in his nefarious activities for fun or for profit, neighboring farmers and ranchers didn't sleep as peacefully after he squatted near them. The rate at which his herd grew defied the laws of normal reproduction and spectators with cattle roaming at large on the open range, had premonitions of fear as well as suspicion. Neighbors might wonder how this man managed to stay out of jail but for those who had nothing to lose as a result of his escapades, the good-natured and big-hearted Dave furnished the best in outdoor entertainment.

Dave Cochrane became something of a legend in that country where plains and foothills meet and not all the stories related about him need be accepted as truth. A person may justifiably hesitate on the tale about Dave stealing the roof from a settler's shack while the settler was cooking some eggs for this controversial fellow who had just dropped in for lunch. But Dave's nonchalance in any situation was hypnotic and if he did steal a homesteader's roof, the victim would probably not realize the loss until the culprit departed. It did happen now and then that a settler returned home at noon or night to find Dave frying some bacon and with typical good nature inviting the proprietor of the premises to stop for dinner.

* * *

Following his retirement from the force, the ex-policeman squatted on land being considered for Blood Indian reserve. When the government officials asked him to move, he refused. He'd move if they made it worth his while, and it was only when an arbitration board awarded him $3500 and another homestead that he quit the reservation. The new homestead didn't hold him long either; having discovered what would now be termed a racket, he took residence where John Hollis had squatted on or beside the Walrond ranch lease, about 10 miles north of the northwest corner of the Piegan reserve. There the cunning Dave became "a thorn in the side" of Walrond manager, Dr. Duncan McEachern.

Everybody enjoyed the jovial and reckless Dave but

288

nobody wanted him living nearby. Dr. McEachern was no exception but Dave's price for leaving the Walrond range was $5000 or the award of a board of arbitration. The ranch manager realized very well that he couldn't afford to have Cochrane living beside his cattle but he hesitated at the terms until there was a "gentle hint" of consequences if the squatter "accidentally" dropped a lighted match in the dry grass there on the Porcupine Hills range. Arbitration was agreed upon and this time, Dave Cochrane left with an award of $2700.

To Dave Cochrane, the sin in stealing depended entirely upon circumstances. There could be no wrong whatever in stealing cattle from a cattle rustler. Ex-Mounted Policeman Neal "Nick" Nicholson recalled Dave's observation of two rustlers gathering mavericks and driving them along Beaver creek to a secluded branding corral. He knew the men would plan to brand the animals in the ill-gotten herd next morning and so, during the night, Dave released the cattle and drove them to his own corral. When morning came, the original rustlers went in search of the cattle and when they found them, were shocked to discover Dave Cochrane's brand freshly burned in every hide. Certainly they were in no position to make more than a very private protest.

* * *

Dave's years with the police imparted some big ideas and not all good ones. Vigorously he pursued the whisky smugglers and traders and made life miserable for them, but when he left the force, there was the temptation to indulge in a bit of trading on his own account. Moreover, he wasn't easy to catch; he was "Slippery Dave." It seemed that any time he allowed his wagons or ponies to be intercepted by police officers on whisky patrol, the suspicious-appearing containers were found to be carrying kerosene or water or nothing at all. It is told that an officer was given the special assignment of watching Dave Cochrane's pack ponies returning from Montana. The young policeman was very confident that he could end the illegal business and when he spotted a train of ponies plodding northward under heavy packs, he felt certain that his moment of success had come. At last the law would deal with this troublesome fellow bringing disgrace to all who at any time wore the police uniform.

Dave and the string of ponies were brought to headquarters but only then was it learned that Dave had two strings of pack ponies—one serving as a decoy was taken to police headquarters with neither whisky or convicting evidence while the other, loaded with contraband, had passed safely to an undisclosed destination.

It was while Dave was squatting near Fort Macleod that he acquired a kitchen stove which has gained increasing fame with passing years. The splendid new stove came to the fort in a shipment of supplies for the police. While still outside, awaiting police attention, it attracted the envious eyes of Dave Cochrane. At once he had a vision of that good stove standing in his cabin and his own squaw preparing his meals on it. To remove it in one piece would be impossible but in the days following, he removed a convenient part or two each time he was in town. A stove leg disappeared, then a lid, a door or something else. When nothing remained but the heavy frame, somebody must have poured a pail of water over it because the glistening metal became ugly with rust.

Dave then presented himself, in usual innocent way, before the commanding officer and wondered if he might take away a load of junk, including "what's left of a rusty old stove." The officer, captivated as most people were by Dave's friendliness and fortuitous manner, said: "Sure, take it away."

Without delay, the prize stove was loaded and taken to the Cochrane cabin where all the parts were re-assembled and polished to become the most up-to-date thing of its kind in the country—the envy of every homesteader.

When a police officer, making one of his regular patrols, called at Dave's shack to exchange some stories, his eyes fell upon the shining stove and he shouted: "Where in the world did you get that?" With childlike innocence, the proud owner replied: "Oh, the stove; it was in that load of junk the commanding officer gave me permission to haul away."

Ed Maunsell told of a typical Dave Cochrane trick that occured at Fort Macleod. Maunsell was buying an old buckboard from J. B. Smith, in anticipation of moving out to his ranch, but hesitated because, as he observed, one nut required to hold the wheel on the axle was missing. In the face of the dilemma, Smith suggested that Dave Cochrane, always ready to help a friend in trouble, might be able to find a solution. Moreover, Dave was resourceful and he was the best authority in the North West on the subject of junk-pile resources. Dave might know where a spare nut to make a buckboard serviceable could be found.

Maunsell set out to find Dave Cochrane and, having located him, recited the problem. Dave said he would "take a look." A search of the legitimate junk piles failed to reveal the part so badly needed but Dave wasn't one to admit defeat. He asked Maunsell to excuse him for a few minutes while he extended the search elsewhere.

Sure enough, Dave reappeared in a matter of minutes, gleefully fingering a nut of the exact size and shape required by Maunsell. The rancher was delighted and while still marvelling at the Cochrane resourcefulness, set out to meet Smith and complete the purchase of the democrat.

Before going far, however, Maunsell overtook the Fort Macleod-Fort Benton mailman, just starting southward on his long journey, but in great distress. The driver of the Queen's mail complained that when only a few yards from his starting point, one wheel of the democrat had fallen off. What explanation could there be? The only one possible was that the nut holding the wheel in place had become loose and fallen off when the vehicle was crossing a pool of water on the trail.

Maunsell offered sympathy and agreed to stop and help in the hunt for the lost nut. No pioneer would do less than offer help in such a situation. But almost immediately, he sensed a possible connection between the democrat nut he received from Dave Cochrane and was carrying at that instant, and the piece which was supposed to have dropped from the mailman's wagon, to allow a wheel to fall.

Maunsell walked back to find Cochrane. Having
located him, the axle nut was returned with the comment
that it wasn't the right size. Then going back to see the
distressed mail-carrier again, Maunsell said: "Why not see
Dave Cochrane? He may know where you can get a spare
axle nut. Dave's never stuck in a case of this kind."

It was an excellent suggestion, better than the mailman
could have realized. Together, he and Maunsell set out to
find Dave Cochrane. Patiently and with cherubic expression
Dave listened to an account of the problem. Finally he
nodded, said: "Sure thing; I'll find you something—but
it'll cost the Queen a dollar."

Before many minutes passed, Dave had an axle nut—
found it in his pocket, strangely enough—and as soon as
the missing piece was fixed to the wagon, the mail was on
its way to Fort Benton.

* * *

Of the latter part of Dave Cochrane's life, very little is
known. With the gold rush to the Klondike in 1898, the
distinctive ex-police sergeant left the range country—became more or less lost except for some reports coming back
about a jovial fellow encountered now and then on Yukon
trails—helping some folk, worrying others and amusing most
of them.

He wasn't at any time a big rancher and nobody would
argue that he possessed the usually accepted marks of greatness. But Dave Cochrane left stories assured of living as
long as cowboys ride horses.

Said one who remembered him: "It was funny about
Dave. You could suspect him of stealing your best heifer
but you couldn't help liking the rogue."

Chapter XLIV

PRESIDENT OF THE PRAIRIE REPUBLIC

IF THE name of Thomas Spence is to be inscribed upon the pages of history, it will not be for reasons of lofty and lasting contribution to Canadian life but rather, because of the unlawful and unholy Republican Monarchy set up on the western prairies in 1868. The nefarious scheme of which Spence was the author brought him only temporary glory and no admiration but, at least, such a brazen adventure in government should not be overlooked by those who find pleasure in Canadian story. Moreover, Spence gave Portage la Prairie the distinction of being the only republican capital in Canadian history.

It happened just one year after confederation of the eastern provinces. The West was still Rupert's Land and not even the Province of Manitoba was created. Such government as existed in Rupert's Land was pretty well dominated by the Hudson's Bay Company and some change was needed. Nobody really doubted that but the abortive government set up at Portage la Prairie offered no solution;

compared with anything that went before, it was worse rather than better.

Thomas Spence, as principal actor in this strange bit of prairie drama, came to Fort Garry in 1866. His purpose was not clear and he seemed to have little interest in furs which constituted the only industry in the country. He was one of those fellows who yearned for authority and public attention. Perhaps under other circumstances he'd have been identified as a revolutionary. Soon after his arrival at Fort Garry he attracted public notice by calling a general meeting to discuss federation of all the British colonies between the Atlantic and Pacific. It was an imposing purpose but there was suspicion that the cunning fellow had an undisclosed motive, possibly the annexation of the northwest to the United States.

That scheme came to nothing but in a short time Spence reappeared before the public as the author of a letter, written on birch bark and addressed to the Prince of Wales in London, inviting him to be the guest of the Indians of Red River and go hunting with them. The letter promised the best in buffalo and bear hunting for the Prince's pleasure. But as those who were coming to know Spence could well understand, the Indians who were supposed to have authorized the letter, knew nothing about it. It was the irrepressible Spence's idea, entirely, but he had the satisfaction of receiving a reply from the colonial secretary, conveying to the Honorable Indian Chiefs, the Prince's profound regret that he would find it impossible to accept the generous invitation to go bear hunting with them.

* * *

As one might expect, the Spence popularity about Fort Garry deteriorated and in 1867, Confederation year for Canada, he moved to Portage la Prairie which was to become the scene of his wildest adventure, the setting up of the Republic of Caledonia.

Portage la Prairie was a small and unimposing settlement, founded a short time before when Archdeacon Cochrane started a mission in 1853. It was far enough from the center of Rupert's Land government at Fort Garry that a man with bold ideas could do about as he pleased. And so the effervescent Spence decided to create a republic. Why not? Nobody had a better idea and there was very little chance of organized opposition to it. Moreover, he couldn't think of anyone better suited to the post of president of the republic than himself.

There was really no need to confer or consult with others thereabout because the Indians and whites didn't seem to be concerned—not at that stage anyway. And so, without preliminaries or formalities, Spence announced to the local inhabitants that they were now living under the laws of the Republic of Caledonia, that Portage la Prairie was the capital of the republic and that he, Thomas Spence, was president. Spence's friend, Findlay Ray, was made secretary of state, or something like that, and other friends, after taking an oath of allegiance to the republic, were accepted into President Spence's council or cabinet.

In founding a republic, there must be many matters requiring diplomatic attention but Spence faced up to a president's duties like a seasoned statesman. First of all, the boundaries of the republic would have to be determined and that could have been time-consuming. As Spence demonstrated, however, it was no problem at all; without bothering to confer with his cabinet or with sovereign neighbors, he announced that his domain would extend southward to the United States, westward almost to the Rockies, northward indefinitely and eastward toward Fort Garry as far as it was safe and comfortable to go.

Then there was the matter of law enforcement. Rulers must not neglect security. Among Spence's first needs, therefore, was a jail. But even more urgent was the assurance of revenue. A republican president needed money, needed it quickly, and so taxation by a system of customs tariffs on incoming goods was decided upon and instituted. All those who were engaged in local trade were advised of their new taxation obligations. There were objections but people can be expected to protest any new tax and Spence wasn't worried. When the Hudson's Bay Company trader replied to a demand for tax money, that he would refuse to pay until told to do so by the council of Assiniboia, Spence reminded the unco-operative fellow that the new jail was almost completed and when it was ready for use, the tax order would be repeated.

Things seemed to go rather well for a while and Spence managed to achieve something in which many an eager administrator since that time has failed; the Republic's budget was balanced, constantly balanced. Not as impressive is the explanation, however, that revenue from taxation and expenditure for whisky consumed by Spence and fellow members of the cabinet were always equal—neither surplus nor deficit to worry about.

But it seems to be the tate of rulers and potentates that sooner or later they make a costly blunder and the edifice of their making falls upon them. Spence's experience was no exception. He should have known better. He might get away with laws of his own making and he might successfully extort taxes from traders but, in picking a quarrel with a member of Clan MacPherson, he should have known better.

* * *

The MacPherson was a shoemaker, living at High Bluff, not far on the east side of Portage la Prairie. He objected to Spence's taxes and was quite undiplomatic in shouting his protest that the main purpose of the tax money was to buy whisky for the members of an illegal government. MacPherson was warned to be quiet but that only made such a Scot talk all the louder. Spence concluded that he could not let this sort of thing go unnoticed and unpunished and placed a charge of treason against the shoemaker. Two of Spence's constables, William Hudson and Henery Anderson, who functioned as cabinet ministers in their spare time, were ordered to drive out and arrest this terrible fellow.

"Bring him in, dead or alive," the constables were told, but that proved a bigger assignment than anybody had anticipated. When they arrived at High Bluff after driving over the winter trail, they found MacPherson cleaning his gun. Now, to prepare themselves for any eventuality that might be ahead, the Republic's two policemen had taken a few snifters of government whisky and were feeling good but not really reckless. One of them entered MacPherson's house and invited him to be arrested, the other remaining on guard outside. MacPherson was in no mood to accept arrest and a struggle ensued. The second policeman rushed to the aid of the first but MacPherson was able to beat off both officers and started eastward on foot. The constables could not afford to return to Portage without their prisoner and with the aid of their horse-drawn outfit, they overtook their man. There was another tussel, this time in deep snow; the Scot was overpowered and bundled into the sleigh to be taken to Portage la Prairie to face trial.

On the way to town, the police cutter overtook a sleigh driven by John McLean, the first farmer in the Portage district. MacPherson took hope and called out for help. McLean was not one to see a fellow-Scot being persecuted and seizing the only weapon in his sleigh, a two-inch auger, he advanced and commanded the police officers of the Republic to "stand back or I'll rin the auger through ye."

The officers were wise enough to stand back and McLean enquired about the reason for it all. MacPherson told his side of the story and the constables told theirs. It was like a preliminary hearing and after standing firm with auger in hand, McLean advised MacPherson to go along peaceably, adding that when the trial was called in Portage that night, he, McLean, would be on hand to see justice carried out and everything would be all right.

McLean rushed to his farm home to milk his cows and prepare for the trip to town. By good fortune, he found three friends waiting to see him; they were hard-muscled miners with nothing to do and they welcomed the prospect of some excitement that night. There is no record of their names but such as Fraser and MacTavish and Robertson could not be considered improbable.

Anyway, supper over, McLean and his three friends made their way to town and discovered that the trial for treason had already started. The dejected-looking prisoner was surrounded by servants of the Republic but brightened when he saw McLean enter. From the center of the long table a kerosene lamp threw just enough light to make faces distinguishable. MacPherson sat at one end of the table and President Spence at the other. There was an exchange of hostile glances as MacPherson's friends entered the "court" and McLean at once asked what charge had been laid against the accused. Spence answered, "Treason to the laws of the Republic."

With scorn in his voice, McLean shouted, "What ye mean? We hae no laws." He kept on talking. "And who is prosecuting?" he demanded. The reply was "President Spence." At that, McLean turned to the head of the government and gave him a pungent piece of his mind: "Come oot o' that, ye whited sepulchure," he called; "ye canna be baith judge and accuser."

McLean's bold speech sounded like more treason and one of the policemen arose to either arrest him or throw him out. McLean and his friends were quite willing to leave peacefully, provided they could take MacPherson with them but they were in no mood to be arrested or thrown out.

One of the miners caught MacPherson's coat and proceeded to drag him away from the prisoner's end of the table and when that action was resisted, fists began to fly. One of the policemen was heaved across the room and in the course of his flight through space, he upset the stove, the lamp, table and president. The court room was now in darkness but the fighting continued until one of the miners drew his revolver and fired a shot into the ceiling.

At this point, the noble leaders of the Republic seemed to disappear and it was possible to re-light the lamp. The President, acting more like a mouse than a monarch, was found hiding behind the upset table, pleading for mercy because he had a wife and family who needed him. He promised to behave and to buy MacPherson a new suit of clothes to replace the one which became torn in the course of his arrest.

At any rate, it marked the inglorious end to the Republic, originally called the Republic of Caledonia and later Republic of Manitoba. But whatever they called it, thanks to the MacPherson and a few of his friends, its back was broken. About this time there was another rebuke for Spence—a letter received from the secretary of state for foreign affairs in London, reminding him of what he already knew, that he was acting illegally. But it didn't matter because the Republic was dead. One is entitled to speculate, however, about how much longer the Republic would have survived if a MacPherson and a McLean hadn't rebelled. Spence left Portage and when last reported was in the business of making salt on the shores of Lake Manitoba.

Back of every city, town and community in Western Canada there are gems of romantic sentiment, some unnoticed. Portage la Prairie, in the heart of one of the best farming communities in the world, has lots of them and must, indeed, be the only city in Canada that can boast of having been the capital of a republic.

As for Spence, perhaps he wasn't mighty in good works but, at least, his mighty scheming served to further enrich the story of the West.

CHAPTER XLV

A STOCK SADDLE WAS HIS THRONE

IN THE summer of 1956 Lieutenant-Governor J. J. Bowlen of Alberta was invited to fly over the North Pole to Europe. "I'll go on one condition," he told his secretary, "that they'll guarantee to have me back in time to attend the Rangemens' Dinner at Calgary." Prompt return was assured; the lieutenant-governor made the historic trip, visited with old world royalty and was back in time to fraternize with the folk closest to his heart, the old rangemen who gather once a year to drink a toast to the cowboy's saddlehorse and swap stories about the early years when a man could ride across country for 50 miles without opening a gate.

From a little farm on "Spud Island," (Prince Edward Island for those who must be technical) to the office of lieutenant-governor of the proud province of Alberta is quite a great distance any way one looks at it. And for Jack Bowlen it was not a straight trail by any means. It had twists and detours and rough places that would discourage less persistent people. But as the First Citizen of the province noted, one must travel over the rough roads to fully appreciate the smooth ones.

Albertans knew Jack Bowlen as a rancher and politician. But as one of the western pioneers who had to fight for every nickle he acquired, his early experiences embraced many other activities, even a job as street-car conductor in the city of Boston and a stint in army service wearing the United States uniform at the time of the Spanish-American War. In the course of early adventure he travelled extensively and so, when he finally pronounced his adopted Alberta as the "best place in the world," he spoke with some authority.

* * *

The home farm on Prince Edward Island to which the Irish Bowlens went several generations back and where Jack Bowlen was born on July 21, 1876, was a small one, just like all the other farms in that section of Canada. There the boy attended school, milked cows, hoed potatoes and did the usual farm chores. Thereabout, at the age of 12, he earned his first money, having hired with an Island neighbor to pick potatoes at a wage of 40 cents a day. The work lasted 10 days and on a rainy afternoon some time later, young Jack skipped school to collect his pay. That, however, wasn't easy; the farmer had no money and could do nothing better than give the boy an order on the local storekeeper who was buying the potatoes. The order was passed to Jack's mother who needed groceries and all he got out of 10 days of hard labor in the potato field were a thorough wetting in the rain, a whipping from his father for leaving school and another from his teacher for the same misdemeanor.

At the age of 16 years, Jack Bowlen considered himself as a grown man and set out to make his own way in the world. There were five brothers and five sisters and things were a little crowded about home. Boston was the place to go; it was the city that attracted young Maritimers and when a neighbor returned from there with savings totalling $60, Jack Bowlen borrowed $15 and set out to make his fortune. In big and bewildering Boston the young fellow's

301

first job was as a teamster on city streets and then he was promoted to the high post of street-car conductor at $2.25 for every 12-hour day. That was a great job—so much easier than milking cows and more profitable.

The desire for adventure burns in every young heart and with the Spanish-American War in progress, the street-car conductor joined the United States Army. From army service he acquired new experience and malaria and when the war was over, he and his new Boston wife decided to return to Canada with the $1000 they had succeeded in saving. The freedom offered by farm life appeared more attractive after being away from it for a time and the Bow-lens settled on a small place on the Island.

But the fact was that Jack Bowlen didn't feel entirely settled. He hadn't seen the west of Canada and what he was hearing about it sounded as inviting as a strawberry festival. Manitoba seemed a long way from the Island but there he went in 1902 and was directed to a job as a farm hand at Carievale in the North West Territories. The stay was brief; before the end of the first day on the Carievale farm the boss called the new hand to the house and Jack Bowlen was sure he was going to be fired. Instead, the farmer reported that a friend living at Elva in Manitoba had been called to the east because of his wife's illness and a good man was wanted to take over his farm for the summer. The young Easterner admitted lack of experience in western farming but said, "sure, I'll tackle it." And so Jack Bowlen resigned from his $15 a month summer employment and took over the Manitoba farm. Evidently it was a good move and when the owner returned in the following autumn, his crop was in the elevator, summerfallow was in good shape and everything about the place was spic and span. Jack Bowlen's share of the returns amounted to $2000, more than he had been able to save in all the eight years in Boston.

With so much money he would start for himself and it was then that he went to Muenster, close to Humboldt in Saskatchewan, and bought a quarter section of land for $1600. But troubles were not over by any means. For three seasons in succession his crops were frozen and if that wasn't enough to drive a young fellow back to the Maritimes, his five horses died from swamp fever. But Bowlen wasn't quitting and he reported with pride that he was able to make a few necessary dollars in other ways and didn't have to mortgage the land. He fed his frozen grain to pigs and sold the dressed pork for five cents a pound. When the horses died, he acquired a team of oxen; they were cheaper and immune to swamp fever. With these sulky brutes he hauled fire wood and sold it at $2.50 a load. He hauled hay and hauled anything that would give him a dollar or two.

In that struggle to "keep the wolf from the door," Jack Bowlen began buying and selling horses and in the winter of 1906-07 he decided upon a mighty gamble; he borrowed money from the bank with which to buy a carload of Manitoba horses around Gladstone. The horses were sold in the Humboldt district, mostly "on time" but settlers were honest and debts were paid. The venture must have been profitable because Bowlen went back for more horses and during the next 20 years, horse dealing was a major enterprise.

Happening to be at Fort Macleod one day in 1908, waiting for a train, Bowlen saw a band of horses being driven through town. He learned the horses were for sale and instead of catching the train he offered $7500 for the 150 head. The owner said "sold" and Bowlen made out a cheque for the total amount, forgetting that he had neither that much money nor that much credit. Realizing what he had done, he had visions of dire consequences but happily the Humboldt banker had confidence in this young fellow and the cheque was honored.

Those horses were driven to High River and wintered at straw piles. In the spring, four riders equipped with a cook wagon began driving the horses over the 600-mile route to Humboldt. All went well until the outfit reached the Red Deer river. It was in flood—fairly boiling in its evident anger. It posed a problem. Would Bowlen's party wait for lower water or swim the dangerous river? The decision was to swim it without delay and with some extra help, the big band of undisciplined horses was induced to enter the water. Even then the troubles were not over because nine horses were lost by drowning.

At a Mounted Police Veterans' Association reunion in Calgary many years later, (Feb. 25, 1956) ex-Mounty Whiteoak was reminiscing about his police work in running down horse thieves. A gang of rustlers had been stealing from the Bar U Ranch and when a band of good-looking horses was driven northward through the Town of Brooks, travelling very fast, the police were notified and the constable took up the pursuit. He arrived at the Red Deer river just in time to see the big band of horses making its way out of the river on the opposite side. Looking at the wild current, the policeman considered it unwise to follow and telegraphed ahead to have a policeman on the north side intercept the horses and the suspected horse thief. But the reply to the communication was not what Whiteoak expected: "No horse thief; just Jack Bowlen on his way to Humboldt."

In spite of the loss of nine horses which failed to navigate the swollen Red Deer, that venture was completed successfully and the horses sold at a profit of about $10,000. Needless to say, the horseman went back to Alberta for more horses and for some time to come he was selling about a 1000 Alberta horses a year in Saskatchewan.

* * *

He moved to Macklin, Saskatchewan, where the horse market was fresher, but Alberta was increasingly attractive. In 1910 he bought an Alberta ranch at Rosebud Creek and after a few years sold it and bought the 90,000-acre Tony Day ranch, south of Medicine Hat. Day had suffered a severe set-back in the bad winter of 1906-07, when most of his huge herd of "Turkey Track" cattle perished. Then he built up a big band of horses on his Q Ranch, north of Wildhorse. But Day's ranch was for sale and Mr. Bowlen told that in buying it, the negotiations lasted exactly five minutes. Five cents an acre was the price for the leased land and $70 a head for Day's 1700 horses. When the purchaser offered to pay for the haying equipment and milk cows, Day said, "No, I'll give you all that and hope you can make it go."

The winter of 1919-20 was another tough one for ranchers and everybody in the country. Mr. Bowlen was living in Calgary at the time but had a premonition that things were not well at the ranch. There being no telephone, he went by train to Govenlock on the Saskatchewan side of the border and started from there to go to the ranch by saddle horse. It was a mistake; the trails were hidden under drifts of snow and the horseman became lost. Had he not come upon the ranch of George Griffiths where he was taken in for the night and thawed out, he'd have frozen in the saddle.

On his own ranch the situation was desperate; the horses were starving. Bowlen got back in the saddle, rode another 50 miles to consult his cattleman friend Jim Wallace. Said Wallace, "I don't like horses on my range but you're in a bad spot, Jack. You feed the hay you've got to your mares and foals and bring the rest over here where the chinooks have cleared the range." The instructions were followed and 1600 horses were trailed to the distant ranch and the whole band was brought through without loss. And Wallace would accept no settlement.

Next year Jack Bowlen reduced his horse herd and decided to go into cattle. But before long he sold his Q Ranch to Jim Wallace. According to Mr. Bowlen, the sale agreement was recorded on the back of an old envelope after a few crisp enquiries and answers that went something like this:

"How much you want for your spread, Jack?"

"Fifty cents an acre for the lease."

"I'll give you 40; now, how much for the cattle?"

"$72.50 a head."

"I'll give you $70," Wallace replied. "How many cattle you got?"

The answer was, "808 head," and Wallace said, "Call 'em 800 and we won't need to count 'em. I'll give you

$25,000 cash and the balance when the lease is transferred."
Thus was the big deal completed and confirmed, ranch style.
Now, Jack Bowlen was out of ranching but not for
long. He bought land at Alderson and bred up a horse
band of 3000 head. One of the horses foaled there was
Bouncing Buster, the game old jumper known to everyone
who attended horse shows for years. But by 1929, the horse
business was failing and Mr. Bowlen disposed of his horses
and went into sheep. The change was profitable and as
many as 5000 breeding ewes were carried at a time on the
Alderson ranch.

There were other ranch deals and there were big grain
growing operations at Carseland. The floor of the rumpus
room of the lieutenant-governor's Edmonton residence bore
testimony with 19 different Bowlen ranch brands, used at
one time or another, inlaid in it. Then there was politics—
fourteen years (1931-1944) in the Alberta Legislature—and
honors, lots of them. In 1947, he was appointed to the
Board of Governors of the Canadian Broadcasting Corporation; he was Honorary President of the Western Stock
Growers' Association; an Honorary Doctor's degree was conferred by the University of Alberta; he received the Order
of St. John of Jeruselem, Knights of Grace; and in 1950, he
became the lieutenant-governor of his adopted province
of Alberta and filled the high office with friendly dignity
which came so easily to him.

* * *

Busy as Jack Bowlen was through the years, one treas-
ured pastime he never neglected was reading. "I've lived
with books," he would say, "I've read seven or eight thousand; I've visited every country in the world through books;
I've met all the great people of history, have known all the
great minds through books." It was a rule with him to read
something good every night before going to sleep. So intent was he in that resolution that after getting settled in
a train berth at Edmonton one night, and realizing that he
had nothing good to read, he got up, dressed and walked
down Jasper avenue to buy a book.

And what would he do if he were starting over again?

"If I were starting again," he said, speaking from the heart, "nothing would attract me as much as a ranch and being a free man on it. You know, Grant, life on the land brings out the best in people. The finest men and women I ever encountered were those of the pioneer farm and ranch communities. I hope the spirit of those people lives forever."

CHAPTER XLVI

"GATLING GUN" SANDISON

IN almost every pioneer district there was a farmer with extragavant ideas; one who would attempt operations on a grand and dangerous scale. Only a few of those ambitious performers succeeded; the majority survived for a short time on borrowed capital and then failed when a year or two of frost damage cut their returns. J. W. Sandison, equally well known as "King" Sandison or "Gatling Gun" Sandison, was one of the spectacular examples and was, for a number of years, Brandon's biggest spender and best source of entertainment.

To discourage smoking and thus reduce the danger of fire around the farm, Sandison supplied free chewing tobacco for his hired help. And because he was critical of the Manitoba technique in washing soiled shirts and other clothing, he sent his laundry back to Scotland to be done properly. He was one of those frontier individualists about whom the Manitoba pioneers talked much and wrote practically nothing.

Neighbors in that community on Brandon's north side remembered the man as half hero and half scoundrel. In his heyday he was the biggest farm operator in western Manitoba and one of the two most publicized in all of the West. To the promoter, he was held aloft as an example of what could be achieved when an enterprising man seized the opportunities offered by Manitoba's virgin soil.

But as on other big farming projects, mistakes were on the same grand scale as the triumphs, and when the turn came in Sandison's farming fortunes, neighborhood admiration turned quickly to ridicule. Still, the fact remains that J. W. Sandison was a leading character in one of the colorful chapters in western development and even his mistakes —public demonstrations not likely to be repeated by those who witnessed them—had value. The scores of smoke smudges set out on his land on August nights failed to spare the crops from early frost but they served a purpose inasmuch as homesteaders thereabout were spared from pursuing the same futile technique. Of greater value was the demonstration that bigness in operations would not compensate for inefficiency and that big farms were more risky and vulnerable to failure than the family-sized units.

*   *   *

Sandison was a Scot who came to Manitoba in 1884, worked a short time at Carberry and then, with the help of a well-to-do father-in-law, bought his first land a few miles north-west of Brandon in the autumn of 1886. At first he was just another settler in a community of shifting population. Like the majority of people around him, he lived in a one-room shack. But in personality, Sandison was different, possessing the instincts of a gambler and the dynamics of a fire-cracker. He had big ideas with lots of nerve and he dreamed about being the biggest farm operator in the world. At one stage in his Manitoba career, it seemed the dream was being fulfilled.

In his first year on the Brandon land, Sandison had 400 acres of crop. Even that was regarded as a substantial acreage in 1887 but it was only the beginning. In the plant-

309

ing of that year's crop, he merely scattered the seed by hand on the stubble land and plowed it in. Growing conditions were favorable and the wheat responded better than the rough cultural methods merited. The Sandison ambition knew no restraint.

More land was broken annually until he was acknowledged to be Manitoba's biggest grain producer west of Carberry. In 1890 he had 1500 acres planted to wheat, 300 to oats, 200 of summerfallow and 800 acres of new land broken during the summer and backset by the use of 10 walking plows. This particular expanse of fresh breaking was just north of Brandon's experimental farm and so spectacular were Sandison's operations that work on the government farm suffered by comparison. The total of cultivated land was now up to 2800 acres and plans were being made for more.

The Brandon Sun, of Jan. 7, 1892, carried an item of news, telling that just before leaving on a trip to Glasgow, Scotland, "the wheat king of Brandon district ordered 13 new binders from the Massey-Harris firm and also paid the land commissioner of the Canadian Pacific, $22,000 for land which he proposes to add to his extensive farm." At the same time, the newspaper was proud to point at the admirable success of this leading citizen, reminding readers that, "eight years ago Mr. Sandison came to Manitoba as a farm laborer."

But the man's financing left much to be desired, even though, in most other respects his management was progressive. He was ardent in weed control and even at that early period he recognized a soil erosion hazard and sought cultivation methods to keep stubble on the surface as an aid in retarding soil drifting. Not as sound, of course, was his view that smudging by burning damp straw would aid in preventing frost damage to crops. August frosts were the most common source of loss. In a single night, flourishing stands of grain were damaged or ruined and settlers had every right to look for safeguards. Sandison chose to believe that smoke would shield his grain and to insure sufficient fuel for smudges, all straw piles were carried over for use

310

in the following autumn. But in spite of smudges, Sandison had frosted wheat as often as anybody else.

He kept good horses and had a few cattle, but it was in farm machinery that he was most progressive. Styles in equipment were changing rapidly at that time and every new implement had an irresistible appeal. In the spring of 1891 he was seeding 1600 acres of wheat with a "gatling gun," a broadcast seeding tool capable of spreading the grain with a great flourish. The name was stolen from a quick-firing weapon of war used for the first time in the fighting against Louis Riel's followers in 1885. That original gatling gun, predecessor of the more modern machine gun, was operated by a crank and bullets were fed from a hopper. The gatling gun broadcast seeder, mounted on the back end of a wagon and driven from a wagon wheel, was likewise fed from a hopper. Seed grain supplies were carried in the wagon box and a team of horses and two men could scatter grain on 75 acres a day without difficulty. Harrows following the broadcaster covered the grain, or at least some of it.

Binders were Sandison's constant weakness. He had dozens of them and at his dispersion sale, no fewer than 30 binders were offered by auction. Ten McCormick binders were acquired in 1890 and John Grant who farmed nearby recalled the day in 1892 when Sandison started 17 new Massey-Harris binders in one field. It wasn't efficient to have so many units working together because every time one stopped, others in the field suffered delay. But Sandison was a showman of the first order and enjoyed the numerous visitors attracted by his display. When he took delivery of a big order of binders, the parade from city warehouse to farm was conducted with all the order of a military unit and headed by the proprietor in person, well mounted on a prancing Hackney or Thoroughbred.

When the master tried to buy a certain repair for one of his binders and discovered it wasn't in stock, he was annoyed, bought two extra binders and had his men dismantle them so the pieces could be kept for repair parts. Most of the parts from the dismantled binders would never be required as replacements and the method was obviously an expensive way of buying repairs but it satisfied his sense of vanity and for a short time at least, there was no binder repair that his own workshop could not supply.

Stack threshing was common practice in those years, but it entailed extra handling of the crop and Sandison was the first in the Brandon district to adopt the more economical stook threshing. Herein was one experiment giving positive results.

To recover the crop on his land in good years, it required two complete threshing outfits, with a big and hungry crew of workers following each. As the two threshers operated simultaneously, the boss spent most of his time riding back and forth trying to supervise the divided operations and be at two places at once.

* * *

Every now and then, Sandison would trip away to Scotland and England. Neighbors said he went to pay his laundry bills. There were other reasons however. He was interested in immigration and may have had some government authorization to secure settlers. In some respects he was like a one-man board of trade but neither a board nor government would have condoned all his methods and actions—standing on a street corner in Glasgow or London, for example, holding jewel-laden hands aloft and shouting, "If you want to wear diamond rings on all your fingers, you must farm in Manitoba."

Evidently, that Old Country appeal for settlers was not wasted and quite a few followed him to the west. The Brandon Sun (April 14, 1892) reported: "Mr. Sandison, the bonanza farmer of Brandon, who returned from England, brought over with him 21 experienced farmers. He will set them to work on his newly acquired farm in the Souris district."

But Sandison's diamond ring prosperity was brief. Early in 1892, he started the construction of a big stone house. It was to be the most elegant in western Manitoba, a reflection of the Sandison personality. Every stone for the walls was selected with care and faced with skill. During an absence of two weeks in the summer, Sandison's supervision was sorely missed; when he returned, it was to find that stone masons had completed the walls but, there was an odd stone in one wall—out of character because of its texture or color. The master looked at it without emotion, said it did not match and could not remain. The workers explained that to replace the stone, much of the wall would have to be torn down. "All right," Sandison replied, "Tear it down." Tear it down, they did, and the offending stone was replaced.

But, sad to tell, Sandison never lived in the new house. Returning from the Old Country in the spring of 1893, seeding operations began about as usual at mid-April, but otherwise things were not as usual. Creditors were more numerous and more insistent than ever and before the spring work was completed, the celebrated farmer disappeared. Brandon people never saw him again.

For a while, the Sandison performance was the talk of the town and people began to understand. The best summary of the state of his affairs appeared in the Brandon Mail of May 18, 1893: "On arrival here a few weeks ago, he came face to face with creditors whose claims aggregated some $50,000, about $30,000 of which is to a bank very well stocked with chattel mortgages—the remainder to sundry persons, much of it to employees. At a meeting of creditors, he appeared, however, to have lots of cash to put in his large crop, most of the ground being ready, and the creditors all said: 'give the boy a chance.' A few days ago a rustle was heard among the leaves and Sandison has been scarce around here ever since. A Scotland Yard detective appeared on the scene, and it leaks out that while in the Old Country, Sandison, well stocked with copies of chattel mortgages, other securities, letters of credit, etc., bought right and left on credit, as high as $35,000 worth of diamonds at one shop. The diamonds and some other valuables he subsequently pawned off and raised probably $20,000 to $30,000 in ready cash. This money he flourished at the meeting of the creditors . . . Nearly all his effects here are in a state of bombardment, and Sandison is hunting for a climate fit for a white man to live in—the detective is hunting for the same climate."

"As nearly as we can get at it, he owes the bank about $30,000 . . . he owes sundry local people, including employees, $15,000, and from $50,000 to $75,000 to outside people, including English and Scottish houses. It is said that like all enterprising men while in the Old Country, he was well fortified with wives and in his late flight has forgotten to take Number One with him."

After Sandison's flight to parts unknown, creditors acted quickly. An auction sale announced for June was the biggest the country had witnessed. The horses were not sold until later when spring seeding was finished but without them there was so much stock and equipment that the auction sale continued for two full days. Later in the month, J. D. McGregor bought the horses.

* * *

It was a big show while it lasted but it couldn't last long; the leading actor was not really big enough for his part. Editors who had held the man up as a shining example of enterprise and virtue were now among the critics, emphasizing the lessons to be learned about prairie farming, among them that "big farming cannot be a success in this country any more than elsewhere." Sarcastic was the comment of the Brandon Mail (May 18, 1893): "The farmer of Manitoba must do a portion of the work himself; he cannot succeed by wearing 'red leggings', diamonds, kilts and any other of the garbs of farmer Sandison."

The really important lesson about the Sandison show, however, was too obvious to rate editorial or philosophical treatment—that spending more money than one makes is a sure way to ruin.

The big stone house remained a landmark but apart from a few stories lingering in the memories of the older residents who witnessed the Sandison spectacle, the name is all but forgotten.

"CRABAPPLE" STEVENSON

IF, as some people wanted to think, being a Scot, a Grit and a Presbyterian, would ensure unobstructed passage through the portals of heaven, Alexander P. Stevenson would experience no delays; and if more were required, it could be said that the midwest of Canada was a better place because of his work with trees.

Settlers were slow to recognize the importance of trees and, especially, in believing that apples and other fruits could be made to grow on western soil. For years Stevenson's was "a voice crying in the wilderness." To some of his fellow-farmers he was "plum potty" and "cherry crazy" and they utterly refused to believe they'd see standard apples growing on his homestead as he promised.

Even today, visitors who know something of the story, find pleasure in standing beneath the big trees on that south half of section 2-4-6-W, where Stevenson did unbelievable things with fruit. There on the homestead, when the nearest grocery store was 75 miles away and the nearest post office, 50 miles, he made his first plantings and initiated experimental work that was to mean much to the west.

315

Half a mile away and partly on Stevenson's land, the town of Nelson emerged around Nelson's grist mill, flourished and died. At its zenith, the town had a school, hotel, doctor, land office, a weekly newspaper called the Manitoba Mountaineer, an annual fair conducted by the North Dufferin agricultural society, and a population of one thousand.

"Best, largest and most prosperous town in Southern Manitoba," was the way the historian Robert Hill described it. It was incorporated in 1882 and everybody was sure the railroad would be built to it. A great future was assured. But the Canadian Pacific Railway bought the Manitoba Colonization Railway and building plans were revised. Nelson was bypassed. The town wilted; the Mountaineer ceased to publish in October, 1884 and one by one the buildings were torn down or moved southeast to a point where a box car set down for a station marked the beginning of the town of Morden.

The glory of Nelson departed quickly and completely. Today, nothing remains which would even suggest a townsite, but the work of Stevenson was more enduring. The farm still grows fruit and almost as though they were conscious of monumental responsibilities, the towering evergreens planted some time before the last spike was driven to complete the first trans-continental railway, stand as dignified sentinels.

*　*　*

Stevenson was an eight-pound Valentine, arriving February 14, 1854. Birthplace was beside historic Bannockburn but most of his early years were spent on the braes of Killiecrankie in Perthshire. He was the first-born of a big family and with many mouths to feed, it was customary for the oldest boy to get out and make his own way as soon as he was able.

Canada was the youth's choice and after sailing from Glasgow, he arrived at Toronto with remaining wealth of 60 cents. For two years he worked outside of that Ontario city, "ditching and farming," and early in 1874, with all his possessions packed in one accordian-type grip, he made his round-about way to western Canada—train to Colling-wood, boat to Duluth, train to Moorhead in North Dakota and, finally, river-boat to Winnipeg.

Manitoba maples were just breaking into leaf and Winnipeg's best beaten paths seemed to lead to the Dominion land office. Following one of those paths Stevenson inquired about homesteads. He was told that the country close to Pembina hills offered shelter, scenery and good soil. That was the combination he wanted, even though it were necessary to go far back from existing settlement in order to get it. After a few days of preparation, he and some friends started over strange trails in the general direction of Pembina hills. Their trip coincided exactly in point of time with the famous westward march of the North West Mounted Police. The police trek into Blackfoot Indian country was longer but perhaps no more difficult and trying.

This is the way Stevenson told it (Farmers' Advocate, Jan. 4, 1911): "In the spring of 1874, in company with five others, with ox and cart to carry provisions, I started for Pembina Mountains to look for land . . . The old Missouri trail was followed between Headingly and La Salle river, near Starbuck. Nearly two-thirds of the way was through swamps, with water two to three feet deep. The ox and cart were mired three or four times, and what a delightful time we greenhorns had, up to the waist in water, with millions of mosquitoes adding their cheerful notes to the proceedings."

"It was a hungry, tired crowd that camped late that night on the dry banks of the high smelling La Salle, trying to dry socks, etc. Our clothing had early in the day been made up into a bundle and tied high and dry on our backs during the passage of the swamps. The following morning we found our ox had broken loose and taken the road to the Boyne river. So we had to start on foot for the same place. The distance was 30 miles, a dead level plain, without a tree, shrub or twig, no house of any description, nor a drop of water to drink . . . Years have passed since then but the memory never fades of sufferings endured for

317

the want of water on that 30-mile stretch, walking on blistered feet on a hot day in the month of June."

Although Stevenson didn't know it, the stray ox was like a guiding star showing him the way to opportunity and happiness. The disgruntled travellers found their ox fraternizing with milk cows belonging to homesteaders Jim and Peter Campbell, close to where the town of Carman now stands. The Campbells were good people and Jim Campbell's attractive little daughter, Catherine Emily, made it easy for Stevenson to forget his blistered feet. When he left to continue his journey, he promised to come again. He did stop again, and again, never ceased to be grateful for the course his stray ox had followed, and five years later he married Catherine Emily and took her to his new log house on the homestead.

The Campbells were in a good position to offer advice about the land Stevenson wanted. "You'll find it about 20 miles to the southwest," they said. Leaving the ox at Campbell's so he'd have a good excuse for returning, Stevenson set out on foot and at the end of one day of travel he recognized the place he had seen in his dreams—black soil, hills behind, Tobacco creek cutting past the place he chose for a cabin, hardwood trees a few miles away and native fruits like plums and cherries in abundance. The nearest house was 20 miles away but that did not discourage him and promptly he began the long walk to Dufferin to make a formal homestead entry, saying as he walked, "It's great to own a farm."

* * *

Off and on for the next few years it was necessary to work for wages in order to support the homestead. He was working near Winnipeg when the grasshopper plague of 1874-1875 struck and consumed the crops. "The hoppers," wrote Stevenson, "settled down like a pall over the country, and nearly everybody who could go, left thoroughly convinced that the country was only good for the production of furs."

But in Stevenson's mind there was no thought of quitting. In 1875 he was gathering logs for a house, 12 feet

318

by 14. Then he thatched the roof, bought a supply of groceries and moved in. In the spring he bought a plow, a yoke of oxen, a Red river cart and planted his first field, "four feet square." That field was his garden, worked up with a spade.

There is a story about how a Nelson man got into poultry and the evidence points to Stevenson as the person concerned. He carried a setting of eggs from the Boyne settlement, 20 miles away, but having no hen under which to set them, some other arrangement had to be made. Finding the nest of a wild duck, he carefully removed the duck eggs and replaced them with 12 hen eggs. In three weeks time, the duck had hatched out 10 chickens for him and taking these, he placed another setting of domestic eggs with the wild duck and invited her to repeat. According to story, the amazing duck co-operated again.

After a year, Stevenson had neighbors, including A. Nelson for whom the town was named, and S. A. Bedford who, years later, became a superintendent of the Brandon Experimental Farm.

* * *

From the very beginning of farming operations, Stevenson was experimenting with fruits. He transplanted native plums and cherries and gooseberries. He wrote to Ottawa requesting fruit trees for experimental plantings but the people there were unenthusiastic. Better help came from the northern states and the crabapples and other sorts obtained there liked the Nelson soil and climate. In 1881, Stevenson obtained strawberries from Crookston and the result astonished everybody except the homesteader himself. About this time, William Saunders, first director of the experimental farms, heard about Stevenson's efforts and placed some hardy strains of standard apples at his disposal. The challenge grew ever greater. The man planted, transplanted and grafted—developed all the horticultural skills. Of course there were disappointments; for every tree or bush that measured up to hopes, hundreds were winter killed or rooted up and burned on the brush pile.

Transcendent crabs represented one of the first successes but by 1900, Stevenson was testing close to 100 varieties of apples, mostly of Russian origin. The old varieties like Duchess and Wealthy were doing well enough but the ones coming to the fore were new kinds like Hibernal, Blushed Calville, Charlamoff, Antonovka and Simbrisk. Two of Stevenson's seedlings named Pine Grove Red and Winnifred did well, also the plum seedling, Mammoth. The triumph of 1898 was a barrel of standard apples, no doubt the first barrelful to be produced between Ontario and British Columbia.

In 1901 the Western Horticultural Society sponsored a display of Manitoba-grown fruit in a dry goods store in Winnipeg and Stevenson was the main contributor, showing 22 varieties of standard apples, several hybrids and half a dozen kinds of crabs. It was the most convincing public demonstration the west had witnessed and Stevenson's Wealthy, Hibernal and Paton's Gem apples made many Winnipeg people halt from surprise.

Curiosity and hope inspired the earliest plantings but in time they began to pay some tangible dividends. In 1909, he sold $500 worth of apples alone and was actively in the nursery business. In one year he had 300 barrels of apples and people travelled miles to see for themselves and be convinced.

* * *

But Stevenson's first interest was public service. He was in demand to address meetings and for years he drove horse and buggy up and down the western countryside, doing inspection work for the Dominion forestry branch and giving advice about shelter belts, landscaping, fruits and all the aspects of farming. He had time for everybody who asked his advice. In the earliest years his advice to beginners was: "Use oxen for three years; keep out of debt; don't buy what you need but only what you can't do without."

He wasn't always that cautious, however, nor that serious. Attending a horticiultural convention on the United States side, he listened to some big stories and when a question about winter rabbit control in orchards came before the meeting, Sandy Stevenson took the floor and offered his solution; nothing to it, just place lighted lanterns beside the apple trees on a winter night. The light will attract the rabbits and they'll sit gazing into it until tears trickle down and icicles from their eyes freeze them to the ground. Then with the rabbits made secure, all the farmer or orchardist has to do in the morning is kick them over and take them for stew.

Stevenson was an authority on fruits but he believed in diversification. He added to his farm, bred Shorthorn cattle and Berkshire pigs, gave his crop land a rest now and then by seeding grass, planted shelter belts and ornamentals like lilies and roses, and ultimately had 25 acres growing fruit. Many of the things he planted have disappeared but the noble Scotch pines, white spruce and Colorado blue stand with majestic bearing as fitting monuments to his vision and purpose.

The farm with nursery was turned over to sons, Robert and Ernest, and in 1913, the pioneer moved to Winnipeg but not to retire in the usual sense. He was busy as he was enthusiastic until his death in California on Dec. 22, 1922.

* * *

While he lived, A. P. Stevenson was honored by success and honored by friends but more honors came after his death. In 1923, the Carter Gold Medal, presented by the Canadian Horticultural Council, was awarded posthumously "For Advancement of Horticulture in Canada." Also after his death, the Manitoba Horticultural Association, wishing to perpetuate his memory, struck a gold medal to be awarded from time to time by the A. P. Stevenson Memorial Board. It is the Stevenson Memorial Gold Medal, to recognize distinguished work in prairie horticulture, with emphasis upon variety improvement.

Of him it could be said: "If you seek this man's monument, look around."

CHAPTER XLVIII

FIRST FARMER ON PORTAGE PLAINS

WHEN the river boat International steamed down stream on its maiden voyage to dock at Fort Garry on May 26, 1862, it was making history and carried among its passengers a governor, a bishop, a judge, a contingent of the "Overlanders" whose eyes were fixed upon far-away Cariboo gold fields and the man who was to break a trail for thousands of farmers, Sodbuster John McLean, with wife and five children.

No doubt the skipper of the International was glad to see his assorted passengers go ashore because their British sentiment proved embarrassing to him. It was this way: The 24th of May fell while the boat was still south of the Manitoba boundary and the predominantly Scottish and English guests suggested that the good ship should celebrate by sailing under the Union Jack. The Minnesota ship captain would have none of it but he misjudged the spirits of some men aboard and ere long he discovered to his horror that the flag at the top of the ship's mast was nothing other than the cook's dirty towel.

He stormed as only a ship's captain has a right to do and ordered the rag taken down. But McLean and some miners gathered around the flagstaff, ready to forcibly prevent the order being carried out until they had an undertaking that the Union Jack would be hoisted. The captain capitulated and the Union Jack floated over United States territory on that birthday of "Good Queen Vic."

McLean was like that. If he thought the dish-towel should remain on the pole, it would take a better man to remove it. His years on the Portage la Prairie frontier proved to Indians and whites alike that there weren't many better men, in a physical sense at least. There were bigger men and ultimately there were bigger farm operators on Portage Plains but it was John McLean who led the parade of settlers to that part and it was to John McLean that homesteaders went instinctively for advice.

* * *

McLean was no youngster when he set out for Manitoba. He was born at Glenalmond in Perthshire in 1815. At the age of 22 he came to Ontario and farmed at Puslinch. There he married and remained until that bold decision to go west.

Soon after arrival at Fort Garry, McLean saw his Overlander companions take Red River carts for their long journey by way of Fort Edmonton to inter-mountain country where they hoped to find fortune in gold. They wanted McLean to join them but he told them he intended finding his treasure in fresh soil not as far away. He examined farming opportunities along the Red river and then drove west, passed Headingly, passed White Horse Plains and on June 13, 1862, he was at Portage la Prairie where Archdeacon Cochrane, surrounded by a few families, was conducting a mission. There were some gardens but trapping and trading were the principal occupations. Nobody was farming but McLean dug into the soil and what he saw brought forth the announcement: "We go no farther."

But anybody coming there to farm would be most unpopular. Farming would spoil business for trappers and traders. It was revolutionary, even in 1862. From a French half-breed, however, McLean bought about 120 acres of land where Portage la Prairie stands today. The property had 30 rods of frontage on Crescent lake, then called "the slough," and it extended north about two miles. The price was $375 and McLean paid in gold. A little later he bought an additional 40 rods on the west side of his property and thus owned a large part of the townsite of later years. When town taxes became too high for a man farming the land, he sold most of it for $30,000, reserving his homesite and adjacent lots close to the lake.

Had he not been a determined man, McLean would not have remained in the face of so much opposition to his idea of farming. Not only did the trading company want to get rid of him and all his farming notions but the Indians tried to burn him out and then to frighten him out . . . More than once McLean found it necessary to shoot when red men made it clear they wanted his scalp. Portage old timers tell, however, that John McLean never became so nervous or frightened that he couldn't shoot straight.

* * *

Robert Hill, Portage la Prairie's early carriage-maker and historian (History of Manitoba), relates some of the McLean experiences. Some of them would have fitted well into Hollywood's western pictures. There was that Sunday afternoon, for example, when a Scotsman with a top hat routed two Indians in war-paint. It seems that Mrs. Peter Garrioch who lived close by, slipped into the McLean kitchen to give warning that two Indians were hiding in the bushes beside the slough, evidently with the intention of stealing the horses or shooting settlers. McLean, calm as always, retired to his bedroom, changed his clothes and emerged in full dress—Prince Albert coat and tall silk hat—looking more like a diplomat than a homesteader.

He looked like anybody except John McLean and thus he was able to leave the house without exciting the suspicions of hiding Indians. He made a big circle to the west and came upon the Indian place of concealment from the rear. Pouncing upon the bucks, he seized the gun of one and threw it in the slough; and drawing his revolver on the other, he ordered him to discharge his gun skyward or some Indian brains would be blown out. The instructions were dutifully carried out and two totally disarmed natives accepted the additional advice to start travelling westward. For the artist seeking pioneer subjects, here is a suggestion: a frontiersman in stove-pipe hat and Sunday coat, jumping feet first into a nest of Indians who were conspiring to rob or kill him.

There was another gun-battle in the spring of 1866 which resulted in the death of a dangerous half-breed and the necessity of a trial at Fort Garry. The quarrel started when the ruffian's frightened girl friend sought protection at John McLean's side. McLean wrested a drawn knife from the enraged man's hand, while at the same time the half-breed promised to return and shoot McLean. Keeping his promise, the fellow brought his quarrel back to the McLean kitchen door and began shooting. But John's son, Alex Mc-Lean came to the rescue and fired a bullet from which the attacker fell and died soon after.

Alex was summoned to trial and though the jury was weighted with half-breeds whose sympathies might well have been with the slain man, he was acquitted. The McLeans knew that justice was on Alex's side but in view of the jury's composition, they wanted to be prepared for the worst. They were. Alex's sister sat against the court-room door to keep it open; he had some well-armed friends in the room and a fast horse tied conveniently outside. If the judgment had gone against him, he'd have made a dash for freedom and south to the American boundary. As shown at the trial, it was customary for people at Portage to go about fully armed and any good citizen considered it his right to shoot in self defence.

*　*　*

For the McLeans it was one brush after another with the natives who chose to regard anybody who cultivated soil as their enemy. When horses were stolen from the McLean hay camp, Alex, with his father's instincts and courage,

325

traced them to an Indian hide-out many miles beyond Rat Creek. People said John McLean could "smell a horse-thief with the wind against him," and evidently son Alex could do the same. At the Indian encampment, the chief warned young McLean not to take his horses away because he'd lose his life in such an attempt. But Alex, being a replica of John McLean, was not to be intimidated. With one hand on a horse's halter and the other on his cocked pistol, he ordered the camp residents to get out of his way and, strangely enough, they did.

Of such was life on the Portage Plains. Another Indian who had been stealing horses in the settlement, killing them and selling the carcasses as moose meat, was caught by the the man most likely to do it, John McLean. Justice in this instance almost miscarried. After arrest, this misguided Indian was tried before a local jury and according to Robert Hill, was "sentenced to be hung on an oak tree that grew in front of Fred Bird's old place." But John McLean protested that even the crime of elevating stolen horses to salable "moose meat," did not call for such severity and the Indian was sent down to Fort Garry from where he made a successful escape.

* * *

One way or another, John McLean was connected with about everything that happened around Portage la Prairie for some 20 years. When Portage held its first fair in 1872, John McLean was an exhibitor. When the first bonanza farmer, Kenneth McKenzie, came to the country, it was McLean who guided him to the good land at Rat creek, about ten miles west of Portage. With the aid of a pocket compass in Alex McLean's hands, they marked the boundaries and with two yoke of McLean's oxen, they plowed a furrow around 1800 acres on which McKenzie squatted and farmed. If more were required to infuriate the already worried Indians it was this demonstration of intention to further spoil the hunting ground. Stray bullets whizzed uncomfortably close to McLean whiskers but the man was undaunted.

In 1864, John McLean began carrying the mail between Portage la Prairie and Fort Garry and in the face of heat, cold and blizzards, the Queen's Mail went through. He knew what it was to make a night camp in the snow and to meet disgruntled Indians on the trails. Coming face to face with Chief Standing Buffalo and a big party of Sioux who took up residence near Portage in 1864, presented the possibilities of trouble.

On that occasion, McLean was transporting a load of provisions which the Portage people could ill afford to lose. When the hungry Indians demanded food, McLean threw them a bag of bread and biscuits without stopping for conversation, and while the natives were devouring the morsels, he was extending the distance between Indians and his valuable load.

And, of course, in the overthrow of the ill-conceived Republic of Caledonia which had brought a spell of "home rule" to Portage la Prairie, John McLean was one of the heros. Archdeacon Cochrane founded a mission there and in so doing, founded Portage la Prairie. He instituted a home-spun type of justice with three Johns, John McLean, John Garrioch and John Norquay serving as judges. But the aged archdeacon died in 1865 and anything resembling local government and justice deteriorated.

Into the vacuum sprang Thomas Spence, a man with the will but not the skill to be an autocrat. He did set up a loose administration with the imposing name, Republic of Caledonia, and, of course, Spence made himself president of the Republic. It was a nice arrangement for the president but downfall came suddenly when he antagonized a Mac-Pherson and the McLean, and realized too late the fury of enraged clansmen. It is an intriguing segment of western story but one which commands its own chapter.

When trouble broke at Red River and Louis Riel seized control, McLean was one of the first to volunteer to march against the insurgents. Along with Thomas Scott and others, he was taken prisoner and he was one of the last to see Scott before that fellow was shot on Riel's orders.

And when the shooting started at Duck Lake in 1885, Alex McLean talked things over with his father and was on his way to assist in ending the struggle. As one would expect of a son of John McLean, a young fellow who stalked stolen horses, exchanged bullets with crazed Indians and came through after being lost in a storm for 36 hours, he gave a good account of himself at the scene of fighting. He was in charge of an ammunition wagon at the battle of Fish Creek and the Portage la Prairie newspaper of May 12, 1885, reported with local pride about his services.

* * *

As farmers, John McLean and son Alex continued to be leaders. They had one of the first binders in the district, the Tribune and Marquette Review of August 22, 1884, reporting the purchase of, "the fancy self-binder which was manufactured by Cochrane M'f'g. Co., for the Provincial Exhibition held last fall." That placed the McLeans in the position of having the "finest carriages and farm machinery in this section."

In John McLean's last years, eyesight failed but not his stout spirit. Story has it that, blindness notwithstanding, there was one Portage la Prairie nose that was punched unceremoniously in those last years because John McLean believed its owner deserved it. The redoubtable John, father of Portage la Prairie agriculture, died August 9, 1902. It was the death of a nation-builder.

For almost a hundred years, Portage la Prairie has had a John McLean. The John McLean born there in 1947, great-great-grandson of the pioneer, was the fifth generation John McLean on Portage soil. That too, is a record.

Chapter XLIX

THE PROPHET McDOUGALL

IF THE "Prophet McDougall" could return to visit to-day's bustling City of Edmonton, he might very well exclaim: "I told you so." When he first saw the spot, in 1862, he noted nature's lavish gifts of soil and said, "This place will some day be a great metropolis." Old Fort Edmonton was created by and for the fur trade but Rev. John McDougall caught a vision of something greater than furs, a thriving agriculture.

His judgment that the country's biggest treasure was in its soil represented a viewpoint not many people had considered. But in making a 56-day trail-trip from Fort Garry to Fort Edmonton, a man of vision would have time to study soil and speculate about the country's prospects. In making such a journey in the '60s, the only settlers John McDougall saw were along the Assiniboine, on the Fort Garry side of Portage la Prairie. They were on "the best wheat fields in the world,' he believed, and why they did not hunt less and cultivate more, he could not understand. Apparently, the time had not come for settlement but, "someday," he said, ". . . thousands of homesteads . . . verily homes for millions."

As a pioneer with cattle and one who understood the Indians, McDougall was an invaluable counsellor to gov-

329

ernments in his time. But his primary interest was in rounding up human souls and placing the Christian brand on them. His father, Rev. George McDougall, was in the same work and over their western range extending from Norway House clear to Rocky Mountain House, these theological trailblazers could tramp, camp, mush and shoot with the best of the frontiersmen. Perhaps they owned clerical collars but if so, they didn't appear very often. John McDougall knew what it was to tangle with a wounded buffalo, to be lost on the prairie, to eat meat without salt and to bed down on frozen ground with "a few spruce boughs beneath and the twinkling stars overhead." And when the food was exhausted, the gloom just seemed a little thicker, the cold a little sharper and the loneliness a bit greater than usual.

* * *

Owen Sound was John McDougall's place of birth and Dec. 27, 1842, was the date. At that time, his father's mission field extended westward as far as Fort William. John was a robust boy, athletic and a lover of the outdoors. His interests inclined toward missions; his brother David's didn't. The boy was sent to college at Cobourg but formal education was halted in 1860 when the family voted to follow husband and father to a mission post at Norway House, on the north end of Lake Winnipeg.

After a couple of years at Norway House, George McDougall decided upon a westward tour to inspect the missions over which he had charge. John, whose time was being occupied by teaching young Indians, volunteered to go along to guide the canoe. The journey would be as far as Fort Edmonton, at which point the Rev. B. T. Rundle, first missionary in that distant part, made headquarters.

The farther west father and son travelled, the more inviting it became and the McDougalls heard a call that sounded like, "Come over into buffalo country and help us." John's mind was made up; he'd stay in the far west and when he arrived at Fort Edmonton late in 1862, he arrived to remain.

John McDougall was now on his own. If he starved, it would be his own fault. He was a thousand miles from a doctor and had good reason to hope he'd never need one. He was a freshman in "God's University" and the initiation was a bit rough. It was cold and snow was deep; and worst of all, food supplies were low. Almost immediately the young missionary went on an enforced buffalo hunt. Hunting a hundred miles east of Fort Edmonton he met the mail carrier from Fort Garry and begged for his letters from home. But the Royal mail bag could not be opened short of its destination and John McDougall, on horseback, followed the mail carrier back to Edmonton to get the letters, then two months old, from his mother.

But in the very next year after arrival at Fort Edmonton, John McDougall saw his father, mother, sisters and brother moving to that remote point to make a home and further the work of the church. There were two Methodist missions in the region—one at Victoria, 90 miles northeast of Edmonton, where the McDougalls would reside.

In this land of "feast or famine," danger lurked everywhere. The newcomers would have no stockade behind which to hide, and they'd have neither soldiers nor police upon whom to call in time of trouble. With uncivilized natives on every side, John McDougall said "We put our trust in Providence but kept our powder dry." (In Saddle, Sled and Snowshoe.)

Frontier dangers took many forms. When Peter Erasmus, interpreter and helper at Victoria Mission, shot a bull buffalo, John McDougall approached believing the animal to be dead. Instead of dying in the time-honored manner, however, the enraged monster sprang to its feet and gave chase. Only the fact that John McDougall was a sprinter saved him; he ran so fast he put the bull to shame, then turned and shot the brute.

Then there was the matter of the tooth-ache. An aching tooth can be cruel at any time but with neither dentist nor dental forceps within a thousand miles, a defective molar in the ecclesiastical jaw became a sore affliction. It was tormenting the man. He tried kindness on it and he tried cruelty; he poulticed it and he applied a red-hot iron but still it throbbed torture. At last George Mc-

Dougall, with help from the carpenter, filed a pair of mechanic's pincers to remotely resemble forceps. The older Methodist made five valiant attempts and then the rebel tooth broke off at the gum, leaving the roots and centre of pain securely anchored in the jaw to ache more than ever. Nine years later when visiting in the East, McDougall took time to have a dentist dig out the roots.

* * *

With the spring of 1864, it was clear that somebody would have to travel overland to Fort Garry for supplies for the two missions and John McDougall, now a resourceful frontiersman, said he would direct the carts. Such a journey could be monotonous but there were compensations. It was springtime and new life was bursting forth on every hand and spirits were gay. As John McDougall and his helpers camped one night beside westbound strangers and listened to boasts about athletic skill, he concluded it to be a missionary's duty to take the conceit out of these fresh easterners. He issued a challenge and next morning there were contests beside the trail, perhaps where Battleford is now located. John McDougall and his men won the races, jumps, throwing the stone, and demonstrated that they were too good for the newcomers. It was, almost certainly, the first athletic contest in the Saskatchewan country.

At Fort Ellice there was a treat in store. Mrs. MacKay, wife of the trader at the post, invited McDougall to stop for supper and served pancakes and maple syrup. It was the first meal without buffalo meat in nearly two years and what a memorable experience it was. Many years later, McDougall wrote, "verily, the memory is still sweet."

At Fort Garry the missionary bought numerous articles for the missions, oxen at $35 each, four milk cows at $15 to $18, a young horse at $70 and, with the memory of the pancakes still fresh, 10 sacks of flour at $8 each.

The return journey was not uneventful. One night, after the travellers had bedded down, an Indian bent on stealing the horses, crept close to the camp but was surprised to meet the missionary who could creep through darkness with no less skill. There was an exchange of gun-fire and the Indian felt the sting of Methodist buckshot. The thief may have been wounded but not so badly that he couldn't run away.

Fifty-six travelling days from Fort Garry and two major river crossings brought John McDougall back to Victoria. The time taken for the round trip was long enough to allow those at the mission to both plant and harvest garden stuff and barley. The latter offered the best hope for home-grown flour; with no mill, it could be soaked, dried, pound-ed to loosen the hulls and then winnowed to provide a fibre-free grist. "But," adds McDougall, "so long as we can get buffalo within 300 miles, we would prefer buffalo steaks to barley meal."

Nobody was complaining about diets. When Christmas came, bounty and distinctiveness marked the festive board at the mission. "We had no roast beef," wrote John Mc-Dougall, "nor pumpkin pie, nor plates of tempting fruit, but we had buffalo boss and tongue, and beaver tail and moose nose and wild cat and prairie chicken and rabbit and pemmican."

Even in other respects that Christmas lacked but little. There was neither choir nor organ but there were vigorous voices and lots of Yuletide singing. And though the preacher on that Christmas morning had no robe, he was clothed with the solemnity of earnestness. Christmas afternoon, they went for a sleigh ride behind the dogs, played football in the snow, ran foot races and made that far-away section of the Northwest ring with the spirit of the day.

* * *

During the summer of 1864, George McDougall tripped southward to visit Stoney Indians in the foothills and re-solved to ask his board to authorize a mission there. The outcome was that in November, 1873, John McDougall and his wife went to Morley where Mrs. McDougall was the first white woman. They were joined by brother David and wife and together they built a church and a post. When baby Jean was born to Mr. and Mrs. David McDougall, the wee one was the first white baby in all that is now southern Alberta.

At first the Indians were vengeful and difficult but the combined effect of John's theology and David's trade goods softened the hardest of them. They were impressed, too, by the McDougall cattle, the first in that dangerous southwest. John and David took 12 head of cattle from Fort Edmonton to Morley in 1873 and in the next year drove a bigger herd from Montana to graze there in the foothills. Even then the buffalo were so numerous at certain seasons that John McDougall, when making a journey from Red Deer river to the Missouri river, was never out of sight of the native herds. John's cattle brand was "JM" and David's was "O". Although not recorded until 1883, these brands were in use from 1874 and must have been the earliest in the Chinook Belt.

* * *

Near the beginning of 1876, tragedy visited the McDougalls. The snow was deep and food supplies were dangerously low. Rev. George McDougall brought word that buffalo were within a day's travel. Plans were made to go at once for meat. John, his father, a young cousin from Ontario and two Indians made up the hunting party and Monday morning found them on the prairie, ready to strike. The tenderfoot cousin from the East was left at the tent while the others went after the buffalo. Footing was not good and John had a bad spill when his horse fell. But in spite of fall, he managed to get six buffalo. Skinning and quartering followed and when the meat was loaded on the sleighs, George McDougall announced that he would ride ahead and cook supper at the camp.

The night was clear and the hunters were cheerful. But when John arrived at the camp, there was no light. The Ontario cousin didn't care for either prairie darkness or prairie cold and had buried himself in buffalo robes. But George McDougall had not come in. Where could he be? Guns were fired in the hope of attracting him but there was no response. Early next morning they began a search but the day passed without a clue. Tuesday night the wind shifted to northwest and brought a storm with it. The search had to be halted. Thursday morning the hunters broke camp and started for home, supposing the elder missionary, after missing the camp, had ridden on to Morley.

But father was not at Morley. Nor was he at Calgary (Fort Brisebois at that time). The search was intensified and on Saturday afternoon, they found his horse. After more days George McDougall's frozen body was discovered, lying in the snow, his arms folded across his chest. Reverently, the searchers placed the stiffened body on a sleigh and sadly they started on the homeward journey. There at Morley, near what is now one of the busy highway streets of the world, they buried Rev. George McDougall.

* * *

Now there was about twice as much for John McDougall to do, but he was able. His heavily muscled body could match that of any voyageur and, as always, he insisted upon sharing the hardships of camp or trail. He was consulted about a pass through the mountains for the Canadian Pacific Railway; he was called to assist when Indian Treaty Number Seven was being written and he was sought to serve as guide for travelling parties because when John McDougall was known to be present, travellers were safe from Indian attack.

There was the trouble at Duck Lake and settlers shuddered to think about possible outcome. Young Indians everywhere were restless in their hostility. But Father Lacombe talked to Crowfoot of the Blackfeet and Rev. John McDougall visited Sweet Grass of the Crees and both chiefs accepted the wisdom of peace. The new west owed much to those two courageous and selfless "Sky Pilots." They were fellow bishops in the Cathedral of the Great Outdoors. Their sacraments were somewhat different, but they preached the same brand of good will; they served the same God, and they went away almost together. McDougall died on Jan. 15, 1917, less than five weeks after the passing of his old friend of the other faith.

CHAPTER L

"CALL ME ARCHIE"

PIONEER Archie McNab who became Saskatchewan's lieutenant-governor was not one to boast but in a moment of confidence he would confess that birth in Glengarry county was about the best possible beginning for life. And certainly, a subsequent introduction to the lovely Gaelic tongue should be an added advantage. Of course, life in that Scottish-Canadian community was not all Gaelic and oatcakes. Even the boys worked hard. There on the home farm where Archie was born on May 29, 1864, the lad's education included more of picking stones and hoeing turnips than reading and writing.

Circumstances made one point clear in his mind; when ready to farm for himself, he'd go where there were no stones to pick and turnips to hoe. At the age of 18, he and his twin brother arrived at Winnipeg. Their combined capital was $65—too much to carry around but not enough on which to start farming. Their first jobs consisted of cutting trees in Winnipeg's Fort Rouge district. The boys might be green about some things in the West but nobody in Manitoba could teach these sons of the Ottawa valley how to swing an axe. They were more at ease with an axe than with a pencil.

336

Having saved a few more dollars, the young McNabs filed on homesteads at Virden and set out to make farms of them. The transformation followed a usual pattern, building log cabin, breaking sod with oxen, and wondering all the while if batching on the frontier was really much better than picking stones in Ontario.

There were the commonplace homestead disappointments. The first crops were frozen and the McNabs had nothing to sell. When supplies ran low, Archie asked a neighbor going to Brandon to bring back a bag of flour. The neighbor would do that but Archie was obliged to plan an absence from home when the flour was delivered because he didn't have enough money with which to pay for it. But he secured work as a section hand on the Canadian Pacific Railway and was able to pay off his grocery debts.

Frost was not the only worry in those years; even in the 80s there was drifting soil and when Archie McNab's land began to blow, he knew he'd have to cover it with something, so he "covered it with a mortgage." He and his brother raised $300 on each quarter, raised it to buy equipment, but it wasn't long until they decided to let the mortgage company have the farms.

Twin brother, Neil, went to Peace River and Archie became a grain buyer for a milling company. Buying grain proved more profitable than growing it and in 1902, Archie McNab went to the new town of Rosthern where he had an interest in a grain elevator and mill. Four years later, he bought the Leslie and Wilson Flour Mill at Saskatoon, a plant he sold ultimately to the Quaker Oats Company. At this point Archie McNab really adopted Saskatoon and Saskatoon adopted McNab.

* * *

"Archie McNab in Politics" could be the title for a colorful chapter in a colorful career. It began in 1908 and after 18 years in the provincial legislature, McNab had a record of no defeats at the polls. And nobody could tell of early political frays better than the said McNab.

He and Donald McLean, later Judge McLean, were on

the opposite sides in politics but loyal friends, nevertheless. McNab won the Saskatoon seat in the legislature in 1908 and 1912 but, in the election of 1917, he contested Elrose, thus leaving Saskatoon to his pal, Donald McLean, leader of the Conservative Opposition in the House. But when the election of 1921 approached, it became apparent that McNab could not continue to sit for Elrose and must return to Saskatoon. He did not wish to run against his friend, Donald, and went to talk things over.

"What do you say, Donald," Archie enquired, "if we get legislation to give each of the three cities double representation? Then there'll be room for both of us." Donald thought well of it and agreed the Grits and the Tories should run only one man each in Saskatoon. Sure enough, legislation came through to give Saskatoon, Regina and Moose Jaw two legislative representatives each and it appeared for a time that Conservative Donald and Liberal Archie would get acclamations.

But to complicate what seemed like a fine and cosy arrangement, the Progressives sprang to life and Harris Turner accepted a nomination. Archie admitted that if only some government post or directorship might be found for Turner, he and Donald would have no problem but Turner was not one to waver; he was running regardless of how others felt about it. At this point, McLean received an offer of a judgeship. "What should I do?" he asked friend Archie; "should I refuse this thing and run against you, or should I quit politics?"

Archie weighed the question carefully and advised in favor of the judgeship. Donald McLean did as advised and was out of politics, but with half a dozen or more candidates still in the election race, Harris Turner topped the polls, with Archie McNab running second and they went as Saskatoon's representatives to sit in the Legislature.

* * *

In 1911, Archie McNab became Minister of Public Works and held that port-folio for 15 years. Saskatchewan was building its magnificent Legislative Building and McNab decided to give it his personal attention and super-

338

vision. His tent was erected on the ground and there he stayed through most of the period of construction. He knew every worker by name and he knew exactly how many bags of cement went into the building.

The provincial jails came under his department's authority and Jack Byers of Calgary could tell about being with Mr. McNab on an occasion when he had to call at the Regina jail. The visitor volunteered to go along for the ride and the company. Once inside the jail, the Minister seemed to know everybody, inmates and all, calling them by first names. He inquired tenderly for wives and children, the state of the meals and when each one would be out. After watching the felicitations for a while, Mr. Byers enquired "Archie, do you know all the criminals in this country?" The Honorable Archie McNab didn't appreciate that question, and said, "They're not criminals; they're just bootleggers," and with a twinkle returning to his eyes, he added, 'and every one will have a vote next election."

Indeed Saskatoon people gave Archie McNab most of the credit for bringing the University of Saskatchewan to their city. The Act to establish the University was passed on April 3, 1907, and in August of the next year, the new Board of Governors secured Dr. Walter C. Murray of Dalhousie, to be president. Then came the question of location for the institution, with Regina, Prince Albert, Battleford, Moose Jaw and Qu'Appelle, as well as Saskatoon, keen to win it. Each of the proposed centres was visited and finally the Board met in Regina to make its momentous decision. Upon McNab's advice, Saskatoon had strengthened its position by securing an option on a thousand acres of suitable land at a reasonable price. And McNab was holding a watching brief, literally as well as figuratively, and there was a story about a ladder against the window of the building in which the Board was closeted. Anyway, Archie McNab was the first to shout that "Saskatoon has it."

When Saskatoon's Board members, James Clinkskill and W. J. Bell, returned triumphantly after the meeting, the

Hub City went wild with hilarity. There were blowing of whistles and ringing of Bells; there were music and oratory and after two days of it, they concluded with a torchlight parade, with Archie McNab in the lead. While he had not been the visible spearhead in the campaign, he was the acknowledged hero.

* * *

Archie McNab became Lieutenant-Governor Archie McNab of Saskatchewan on September 16, 1936. Some over-cautious acquaintances were worried about how he would get along in that position demanding a lot of poise and dignity. One thing certain, the new Lieutenant-Governor had no thought of redesigning himself or trying to be anybody except Archie McNab; the result was that he brought to the high office a kindliness, a simplicity and a personality which made him loved by all the people of Saskatchewan and many beyond. Though speech and manner were unconventional, his human qualities did more for the high office than any amount of dignity could have done. He attended all the ball games and cheered lustily; no convention banquet in Regina or Saskatoon was complete without him; when they called on him for a speech, he usually said the wrong thing, and if there was a rummy game in progress, he wanted to be in it.

In the course of the Saskatchewan Live Stock Breeders' convention at Regina in January, 1941, the lieutenant-governor was to be the guest of honor at the banquet in the Saskatchewan Hotel. Hour for the banquet was 6.15 and 500 people stood waiting for the arrival of the King's representative. Fifteen minutes passed and then thirty, but there was no sign of His Honor. Forty minutes late, he arrived wearing that smile which would "close the mouth of a lion," and leg-weary delegates filed to the banquet tables after him. One of the head-table guests sitting next to His Honor's secretary ventured a question about the reason for Mr. McNab's delay, expecting to receive a report about car trouble or illness at home. Reluctantly, the good lady disclosed that "His Honor was occupied; he was in a rummy game and up $1.40."

340

In 1938 when the Saskatoon Girls' Pipe Band made a tour southward and into Mexico, Lieutenant-Governor McNab went along. He had a great time, made friends everywhere. Short and chunky, he wasn't cut out to be a dashing drum-major but that fact didn't prevent him from leading the various processions on the foreign soil.

During their occupation of Government House, the McNabs entertained Canada's Governor-General, Lord Tweedsmuir, and in 1939 they entertained the King and Queen. To Tweedsmuir, the lieutenant-governor said, "Call me Archie; I've been called damned near everything but that's the name I like best." And the Governor-General called him Archie and loved the great and kindly pioneer.

The King and Queen asked questions about the trees and shrubs growing about Regina, especially the caragana hedges which had survived years of drought so successfully. Host McNab was impressed by their interest and saw to it that they had a package of caragana seed to take back to England. And when Their Majesties were dining at Government House on the occasion of a formal reception, the King had the misfortune to drop a spoon. At once the solicitous lieutenant-governor reassured His Majesty: "Don't bother to pick it up; we've got lots of spoons."

Yes, Archie McNab was a new model in Lieutenant-Governors. He would rather drive in his little green coupe than ride in the government limousine with a chauffeur at the wheel. But when he rode in the big car, it didn't prevent him from picking up the folk who were on foot along the way, whether he knew them or not. Somehow, he could always pack one more person into either limousine or coupe. Driving his small car from Government House into Regina one day, he invited a woman carrying a basket to have a ride. It was shortly after he became Lieutenant-Governor and, not recognizing him, she asked where he lived.

"Down the road in the big house," he said. Her next question was, "Are you the caretaker?"

"No," he replied, "but I could do that job just as well as the old chap who is in there now. They're trying to teach me to be the butler."

Every boy for blocks around knew the lieutenant-governor before he was there very long, just as every young fellow back in Saskatoon knew him and loved his humility and the twinkle in his eye. He talked the boys' baseball language; he showed them how to make whistles out of green poplar and, when he saw some of "the kids" going snaring gophers beyond Government House, he announced that he was going too. The arrangement was that the last person to snare a gopher would buy the ice cream cones. The First Citizen of the province wasn't the last to catch a gopher but he bought the cones, just as he intended to do.

* * *

Proud of his family, he was indeed. He had two daughters and four sons. Two of the boys served in the First Great War and two in the Second. Group Captain Ernest McNab led Number One Canadian Fighter Squadron in the Battle of Britain in 1940 and '41 and was awarded the D.F.C.

Mr. and Mrs. McNab celebrated their golden wedding anniversary in 1942. On May 29, 1944, Mr. McNab had his 80th birthday and, like the pioneer that he was, he said he'd like nothing better than to go on a long hike with his twin brother. On Feb. 28, 1945, Archie McNab retired from the office of Lieutenant-Governor and, a few weeks later, on April 29, after a short illness, he was overtaken by death.

A thousand pioneers said, "It was great to have known Archie." He was one whose natural qualities were unchanged by responsibility and social rank. He was Archie McNab and therein lay his dignity.

GRANT MacEWAN

Author, environmentalist, educator, agricultural scientist, journalist, farmer and politician, **Grant MacEwan** is one of western Canada's most respected and prominent personalities.

From 1946 to 1951, Grant MacEwan was Dean of Agriculture at the University of Manitoba. After terms as a Calgary alderman and an Alberta MLA, he became mayor of Calgary in 1963 and in 1965 was appointed Lieutenant-Governor of Alberta, serving until 1974. He holds honorary degrees from the universities of Alberta, Calgary, Brandon, Guelph and Saskatchewan, and is an honorary chief of the Blood Reserve.

Grant MacEwan has a total of forty-eight titles to his name — an impressive tribute to the prairies and a heartfelt celebration of the land and the people that shaped it. He now resides in Calgary, close to the hills he cherishes.